D0881181

Successful Test Management

Iris Pinkster · Bob van de Burgt
Dennis Janssen · Erik van Veenendaal

Successful
Test Management

An Integral Approach

With 67 Figures and 44 Tables

 Springer

Iris Pinkster
Bob van de Burgt
Dennis Janssen

LogicaCMG Nederland B.V.
Laan van Kronenburg 14
P.O. Box 133
1180 AC Amstelveen
The Netherlands
iris.pinkster, bob.van.de.burgt, dennis.janssen@logicacmg.com

Erik van Veenendaal

Improve Quality Services B.V.
Waalreseweg 17
5554 HA Valkenswaard
The Netherlands
eve@improveqs.nl

Library of Congress Control Number: 2004114046

ACM Computing Classification (1998): D, D.2, D.2.9

ISBN 3-540-22822-5 Springer Berlin Heidelberg New York

Springer is a part of Springer Science+Business Media

springeronline.com

© 2004, LogicaCMG, The Netherlands
Printed in Germany

Cover design: KünkelLopka, Heidelberg
Typesetting and Production: LE-TeX Jelonek, Schmidt & Vöckler GbR, Leipzig
Printed on acid-free paper   45/3142/YL - 5 4 3 2 1 0

Foreword

We all know that ICT plays a very important role in our day-to-day lives. But at what costs? A lot of time and money is used to develop, test and maintain information systems.

In times in which the economy is less rosy, companies also look for ways to reduce IT costs and are looking for ways to optimize their IT investments. Every Euro or Dollar spent has to make a positive return on investment, and information is needed that shows that business cases for projects are viable.

This demands for new ways to build and maintaining systems. By choosing for example iterative development methods the development cycles can be accelerated and involvement of stakeholders can be guaranteed. This results in less time spent on "useless" modules and systems that are not used in the end.

For testing, companies can achieve cost savings by applying a method for structured testing. By doing so the tests are documented in a standard way and this makes it easier to maintain and re-use. In 2002 we published a book on our successful test method: "Integrated Test Design and Automation: using the TestFrame Method" by testing experts Hans Buwalda, Dennis Janssen en Iris Pinkster of LogicaCMG. This was only a first step.

We kept working on better ways to get grip on test projects by searching for best practices in test management. This resulted in an approach where the tests are based on risks and linked with the requirements. This allows companies to better prioritize their tests. They can start with testing the areas with the highest priority. So, whatever happens, the most important parts are tested. Besides this, it is easier to communicate with the various stakeholders. All speak the same language and the testers are better able to tell what time and money is needed to cover the most important risks. This book describes the integral test management approach: from setting the starting points of the project through progress management to handing the testware to maintenance.

This means that besides a way to describe how to measure quality we also have a way to keep track of the status of the quality.

I am sure that you will enjoy reading this book and will be able to use a lot of topics mentioned to improve your test management process!

Paul Schuyt
Chief Executive
LogicaCMG Netherlands
Amstelveen, August 2004

Preface

Structure of the Book

This book describes the activities of a test manager based on the Test Management Model developed by LogicaCMG. This model describes the activities that the test manager carries out to create the conditions for the test project, such as setting up a test strategy, estimating and planning. The activities of the execution phase of a test project are also discussed, such as progress management, issue management and reporting to the client and stakeholders. All of the activities in the Test Management Model are linked to each other and form an integrated approach.

Target Audience

What audience is this test management book aimed at?

- Project leaders or project managers who are planning to lead a test project.
- Whoever is, or will be, responsible for testing within a line organisation.
- Test managers.
- Test coordinators.
- Test team leaders.

Organisation and Features

Along with a description of the theory of an activity, each chapter provides as many hints and tips as possible, indicating what works well in practice and the issues a test manager has to guard against. The appendices contain checklists and templates that supplement the chapters, so that the reader is able to get to work straight away.

The book starts with a general introduction to testing and test management. The Test Management Model is introduced with an outline of the activities contained in the model. Chapter 2 describes the heart of the model: namely, risk- and requirement-based testing (RRBT). The RRBT approach underlies all the activities of the test manager. These first two chapters are excellently suited for project managers and project leaders who seek an approach to test management. The basics of test management are described without going into too much detail.

After these introductory chapters, the test manager's activities are described in detail. These chapters are therefore suitable for readers who have, or are about to have, actual involvement in a test project.

- For the novice test manager, it is recommended that the book is read from front to back. All the activities and their correlations are dealt with. In this way, the reader is given practical information on everything that surrounds a test project.
- The more experienced test manager, or whoever is responsible within a line organisation for testing, can consult those chapters that relate to specific problems or on which more information is required. Where necessary, the chapters contain cross-references to other chapters. This provides readers who read the chapters separately with an indication of the correlation with other topics.

General Remarks

A few comments are in order at the outset:

- In this book, we use the term "information system" instead of software or application. We have done so deliberately, since an information system is more than just an application. An information system can consist of several applications with their interfaces and accompanying procedures. By opting for "information system", we wish to indicate that the test management approach in this book is widely applicable.
- In explaining the theory we often use test projects in our examples. We do not say that the theory can be used only in these projects; all theory, hints and tips given can also be used in maintenance situations.
- As we, the authors, are Dutch, we have used examples of test methods and their accompanying terminology often used in The Netherlands: namely, TMap and TestFrame. As the test management approach described is independent of the test method used, the reader can fill in his or her own methods.
- We consequently use the term "test manager" even though the target audience is broader than test managers alone. We have opted for one single term to avoid confusion and the need for continual reference to a list of titles from the target audience.

- Female readers should not feel left out because we refer to the test manager etc. as "he". Where this occurs, please also read "she".

Acknowledgements

Of course, we did not write this book alone. To write a book with practical advice, you have to have access to practical experience from many projects. To get this access, we created several "expert pools" for the various aspects of the Test Management Model. These expert pools consisted of people with various backgrounds. In this way, it was possible for us to look at test management from different viewpoints and collect a wide range of best practices, based on both theory as well as experience.

We would like to thank the people who helped us with ideas, documentation, experience and review comments. In alphabetical order we would like to thank: Bianca van Bilsen, Erik Brouwer, Ger van der Burgt, Dirk van Dael, Paul Fluitsma, Wouter Geurts, Erik Jansen, Hein Jurg, Sander Jongeleen, Erwin Kok, Marc Koper, Janos Löwinger, Rik Marselis, Richard Matthijssen, Martijn Meijer, Marcel Mersie, Diederik Nieuwenhuis, Mark Nijssen, Jan Paulusse, Jan Posthumus, Jos van Rooyen, Henk Sanders, Paul Scheffers, Chris Schotanus, Rini van Solingen, Jan Springintveld, Jon van der Strate, Eamon Trompert, Onno Verdonk, Bob Verhoeff, Eric van der Vliet, Jeroen Voorn, Rob Welten and Menno Wieringa.

If we have forgotten anyone who helped us out, we would like to apologise in advance.

The interviews with people in the expert pools provided the baseline of our book. This baseline consisted of the main content of the chapters and the relation with other chapters. The baseline was reviewed by some of our customers, who put a lot of time and effort into this exercise. For this, we would like to thank Jan van der Horst (Kadaster Apeldoorn), Henk van Merode (KLM), Eric Veracx (ABN AMRO Bank) and Ben Visser (ING Group).

Also, some well-known experts within the testing community helped us out with the writing of this book. They provided new insights and many useful comments. Thanks to Julie Gardiner, Paul Gerard and Lloyd Roden for all their efforts in this book!

Thanks also to our managers, who gave us the opportunity to write the book: René Albers, Bas van Gool, André Kok and Vincent Lucas. Their comments also led to some important improvements to the story we had to tell.

We owe special thanks to Elvira Beekman. In a very short time, she provided a lot of important input for many of the chapters. Working very quickly and yet maintaining a high standard of work is not easy, but Elvira did so without any problem. Thank you very much!

Amstelveen, 2004   *Bob van de Burgt and Iris Pinkster*

Contents

1

Testing and Test Management

Automated teller machines that issue the wrong banknotes, Space Shuttles that crash on landing, telephone networks that go down and websites that are vulnerable to hackers are all familiar examples of ICT systems that fail, and there are new examples almost every day.

Testing is attracting more interest now than ever before, and test management has an important role to play in realising the considerable added value that testing can bring in controlling ICT quality and risks. Professional test management is an essential condition for this, and this book describes the practical approach and model developed by LogicaCMG for setting up professional test management. The model forms the thread throughout the book. Before presenting an overview, this chapter will place test management in the perspective of developments in the testing profession.

1.1 The Concept of Test Management

Over recent decades, the consequences of faulty ICT systems have greatly increased, as a significant proportion of our activities, both at work and in our private lives, have become dependent on ICT. After money, people and equipment, information is now seen as the fourth business resource (Mors, 1994).

It is not surprising, therefore, that the failure of ICT systems has come to have a large financial impact. In addition to the sensational examples in space exploration, there are plenty of others nearer to home. Faults in electronic service provision, such as placing an order or banking through the Internet, easily lead to lost revenue, expensive complaints handling and corrective measures, to say nothing of the damage to the reputation of the organisation.

It is therefore logical that organisations put a lot of effort into getting the quality of their information systems up to the required level. Ensure that these systems will do what they have to do and not what they should not. The saying "prevention is better than cure" is particularly apt here. Testing is an information provider when delivering information systems because it is one way of measuring the quality of software. It is also a way of reducing risk of potential failures for an organisation. Some might even say that if there is no risk then there is no need to test. Testing consequently plays a crucial and essential role.

> Outside of ICT, too – among users and business managers, for example – the importance of testing is becoming recognised and is increasingly called upon.

Along with this, there has also been a natural increase in the importance of effective test project management. Many projects take too long and involve high costs, and even at the end of the project the information system still leaves something to be desired. On the other hand, intensive testing is carried out, even though it is unclear which risks are actually covered and it is difficult to say whether the information system actually will serve its intended purpose. It is all too common that a manager who is responsible for testing has no idea of how far he has progressed and is unable to indicate exactly how long his project will take to complete.

Bearing prime responsibility for testing, the test manager has a vital role to play in measuring quality. He does this by providing an insight into the risks involved in implementation and by supplying information at any point in time to senior management to facilitate informed decisions. Therefore, the test manager has to undertake close and regular monitoring. His sphere of influence goes beyond the scope of the test project itself.

The test manager directs the test project with a sharp focus on the interests of all the parties involved, starting with that of the client.

A professional level of test management means, among other things, the following:

- Test management has a clear and accepted position within the organisation and within improvement projects, including the corresponding responsibilities and competences.
- Test organisation complements the organisational set-up and takes account of all the available (central) testing facilities.
- The test manager communicates in a language that is understood by all parties involved. He provides management information to the client and other interested parties, clarifying what is being tested and to what extent. He consults with everyone concerned and indicates what the consequences of the choices made will be. System parts with high priority are tested as early as possible. Subsequently, with the aid of collected information, decisions can be made on the level of testing required for other parts, based on the defined minimum level of quality and required risk coverage.

- The test project is supported by a balanced budget and solid planning, enabling informed statements concerning the progress of the project.
- Test management facilitates the development and maintenance of metrics during the course of the project, in order to enhance the efficiency of testing (test process improvement).
- Targeted feedback from test management will help developers ensure that subsequent releases contain fewer design and program faults.

1.2 Evolution of Testing

It is useful to look at recent history and to consider the evolution of testing from that perspective. Testing came to maturity in many organisations under the influence of large projects, such as the millennium changeover and the preparations for introducing the euro. However, it is still only a short time ago that testing was left until the moment that system development was ready. There was no separate testing team, and testing was an activity that developers had to do in addition to their normal work. By several stages, testing has evolved into a profession in its own right. The following section describes some of the important phases of this development since the end of the 1970s.

1.2.1 "Intuitive" Testing

In the first phase, software developers are given plenty of time to write their programs, which they test themselves. When the system is ready, the project leaders invite a number of end users to test it over a few days, often at the weekend. If they report no critical issues and have a good feeling about it, the system goes into production on Monday morning. Far from testing being a separate phase in system development, it is almost a social event for a few end users. In the worst case, testing will show that the system completely fails to meet requirements. However, since it has been left to the end, there is no opportunity to make adjustments!

The question is, of course, what are the critical issues and what is the "good feeling" based upon? End users have their own expectations when they start the test. What one person considers extremely important may be of little interest to another. Their knowledge and experience may also vary widely. Do the end users involved have an overview of the full application, or has each individual only been involved in a part of it? Each one may give a different answer to the question of whether the quality of the application is good enough to go into production.

Testing, as described here, is still taking place in an unstructured manner. The project leader assumes that each end user knows what is important and will test accordingly. There is no test documentation, so at the end of the test period it is not clear which actions were carried out. Perhaps various end users have tested the same system functions? Worse, whole sections of the information system may not have been covered at all during the tests. That is difficult to determine in retrospect: nobody documented their tests.

Resolving the issues can also present difficulties.

While entering a new order for a customer, an end user sees a button that will take him to the customer's previous order. After clicking on this button, an overview appears of all the orders arranged by date. The screen shows a menu option of an alphabetical arrangement. Interesting ... so the end user performs the action. By clicking on an order, the invoice amount appears. The application can also flag up unpaid invoices. The end user has by now performed many actions, but only meant to enter a new order! When he tries to return to the order entry screen, something goes wrong and the application crashes.

In the absence of test documentation, replication of this issue is difficult. Does the end user remember the exact sequence of the steps he carried out? Perhaps he has forgotten, and is unable to replicate the issue. However, developers need this information to locate the problem. It is the only way they can get to a solution and improve the information system. Also, the degree of importance of an issue depends on the end user. If he works regularly with the tested functions, he will indicate that the issue is important, but he will find it of less importance if it is outside his field of operation. Nevertheless, these issues too might very well lead to big problems for the organisation as a whole.

Often, the clients decision is based on tests, while being unaware of how extensive they were, and the test findings provide insufficient insight into the quality of the system. Fortunately, this manner of testing is rare nowadays.

1.2.2 Testing with Design Documents

The next phase in the evolution of testing sees the use of design documents as a basis of testing. The testers begin by collecting documentation, usually functional and technical designs. Responsibility for the accuracy of the designs lies with the development team. The testers judge the design documents mainly on their suitability as a basis for testing. Often, testers start at the beginning of the design documents. For each function the testers come across, they design the required tests and carry on until they have dealt with all the functions, or, more likely, until the available time runs out.

The design of the functionality of an information system usually follows a logical sequence, which provides no indication of the testing priority. Neither are the connections within a design always clear. This means that there is only a small chance that the most important aspects have been tested by the end of the test cycle.

There is also a positive side. The use of design documents makes it easier for the testers to create test documentation. It gives them more to go on than the "intuitive" testing method, and at the end of the test they are better able to indicate what they have tested. The issues are resolved easier by the developers, since the testers document the steps taken. The outstanding issues are easier to place, since it is known which tests brought them to light.

This method of testing therefore provides the test manager with more material on which to base his recommendations, in comparison with the "intuitive" testing method. Even so, this advice, too, contains a random element. For if the test cases have not all been carried out, who is to say that the most important ones have been? And how does one know that the issues still outstanding will not create the biggest problems?

1.2.3 Requirement-Based Testing

A subsequent improvement in the quality of testing is possible if requirements are taken as the basis for testing. Requirements are the most important specifications that are defined for the project, both for the business and for ICT. This provides the testers with better indications for preparing the tests than design documents. Requirements give more insight into the priorities of the client and other involved parties, and the testers can take particular account of these.

However, there is a hidden danger here, too. The testers follow the list of requirements. For each requirement, they search for the corresponding descriptions in the design documents and prepare the tests with these. At the end, test cases are set up for all the requirements and the test execution can start. Naturally, as always, time is limited. Starting test preparations from the top of the list of requirements can mean, for all kinds of reasons, that not all of the requirements have been worked out when the allotted time is up.

At the end of the test execution, the testers can indicate more accurately what the quality of the system is, as they know to what extent each individual requirement has been met. However, they do not know which requirements are wrong or have been forgotten – they are guided by the list of requirements, and a wrong interpretation of the requirements on their part leads to incorrect conclusions.

This type of requirement-based testing is still very much focused on the question: does the product meet the specifications?

Reviews or inspections can improve the quality of the requirements, but it is very difficult to make a complete list of requirements. Other measures are necessary to cover this problem. Risk & Requirement Based Testing is such a solution.

In many projects, the requirements are not fully available at the start of the test project. Such projects tend to be characterised by a multitude of change requests: after all, the end users are discovering more and more what the application means to them. A professional change management procedure is therefore essential!

Torpedoes were developed for a submarine with a launch installation. The following requirement was defined: after launching, the torpedo had to seek a heat-emitting object. With this requirement in mind, the testers set to work. It was decided to test under safe conditions, i.e. in the middle of the sea and with an unmanned submarine. This turned out to be a good choice. Out at sea, the torpedo could not find a target other than the submarine that launched it, because the submarine radiated heat. The torpedo turned around and headed for the submarine. The requirement was met; the test was a success. The developers had built exactly to specifications, but it was hardly the desired result! This incorrectly formulated requirement was only revealed during the test.

In this specific case, the requirement concerned was modified after the first test: if the torpedo were to turn 180 degrees, it would explode. The testers quickly carried out this version, only to meet with disaster again: the torpedo jammed in the launcher. The submarine had to turn around to get to harbour...

Fortunately, the third version succeeded.

By making use of the requirements, the test results come closer to fulfilling the needs and wishes of the stakeholders. This enables the test manager to report better on the status of testing. He provides the test results per requirement, and can also indicate what has not been tested. The testers can link the issues with the requirements, and outstanding issues give the client an idea of the quality per requirement. Should a requirement have too many outstanding issues, then the stakeholders can decide to carry on with testing until every requirement has been met to an acceptable level of quality.

Testing is even better when the stakeholders assign priorities to the requirements. The testers can then focus on the requirements with the highest priority, and issues are given the same priority as the requirement that is related to the test case with which the issue was found. In this way, the developers can see which issues they need to resolve first. At the end of the test project, the client is better able to determine the quality of the application. He can at least assess whether the requirements with the highest priority have had all their issues resolved. For requirements with a low priority, he is able to see the nature of the outstanding issues. Based on this information, he can take a decision on either to go into production or to continue with testing.

1.3 The Challenge for Test Management

In the previous paragraphs, we looked at the phases in the evolution of testing in the recent past. This mainly focused on testing itself, rather than on controlling a test project. The first part features significantly in the literature on testing. Emphasis is on the different phases of the test project, on the techniques to be employed, while the management of the test project is dismissed with a few sentences. That is a missed opportunity.

In a transport company, a standard budget is allocated per project to testing, i.e. 30% of the development budget. This is based on past figures in the traditional COBOL environment. A project is now being started with the aid of Visual Basic. In this environment, development is faster, and less time is allowed for testing. However, the amount of functionality that has to be tested is the same as in the COBOL projects, meaning that a proportionately higher test budget is required. Since this was not planned for, the test manager runs into difficulties. The expectations do not match the means available to him.

A bank has decided to introduce automated testing. It is a good idea, since many regression tests will take place in future releases. The test manager takes proper account of this in his plans. However, owing to limited experience in this area, there is a delay in the development of automated test scripts, which holds up test execution. With testing on the critical path it eventually forms a bottleneck in the project. The implementation date is not achieved. How could the test manager have prevented this situation from occuring?

The test manager has the job of realising the test project on time and within budget. He wants to be able to show at any point how far testing has progressed as well as the level of quality the information system has reached. In this way, if the risk appears to rise above an acceptable level, he can take timely measures. The test manager is expected to be of considerable assistance to the client when it comes to deciding whether or not to put the system into production. By showing which risks have been covered and which ones are outstanding, he can assist the client to make better decisions. He provides an insight into the quality of the information system. The test team has tested the most important aspects at every point by starting with those that represent the highest risk.

Test management has its own assignment and its own responsibilities besides project management. This means that a test manager must be proactive and self-assured, and should not accept without question that the planning and budget for the test project are set by the project manager.

This is part of the remit of the test manager, though naturally in consultation with the project manager, so that the best possible conditions exist for the project.

The answer to this challenge for test management lies in the following two concepts:

1. Testing based on Risk & Reqirement Based Testing, whereby product risks are leading and linked to the requirements.
2. The professionalisation of test management within the organisation.

These concepts are an integral part of the test management approach of LogicaCMG. The model is the thread through the rest of this book. The following section describes the model and gives an overview of all the activities carried out by a test manager within a test project. The core is Risk & Reqirement Based Testing, which places risk management at the centre of testing. The next chapter expands on this. Test management can also be seen as the shell surrounding the test process. The set-up of the test project has no effect on the test management approach described. It is a general approach that can be used in combination with different test methods. This can be compared with the project management approach PRINCE2.[1] With this, it does not matter whether a system development project is phased with, for example, the systems development method (SDM) or the rational unified process (RUP). In that sense, comparison can be be made between PRINCE2 and the Test Management Model. This comparison is included in Appendix A.

1.4 The Test Management Model

LogicaCMG's Test Management Model is characterised by the following points (see Figure 1.1):

- The model is an integral unit of coordinated activities. It is an approach that offers support from the beginning of a test project up to the moment of implementation and transfer.
- The model is made up of modular units. While the integration of the management activities delivers considerable added value, it is also possible to introduce a part of the activities into an organisation. Introduction of the approach can therefore be tailored to every organisation.
- The model is dynamic and iterative. This means that during the course of a project, it is possible to go back to earlier phases; for example, to adjust the test strategy in the event of altered product risks. This allows experience to be directly applied to the project.

---

[1] PRINCE2 is a worldwide standard for project management.

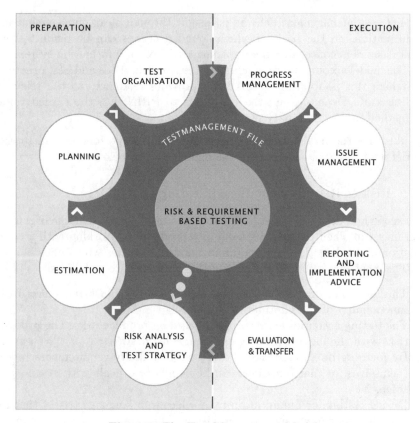

Fig. 1.1. The Test Management Model

- There is a division between the test project preparation activities of the test manager (i.e. planning, choice of strategy and the development of management instruments) and the test project execution activities of the test manager (the actual managing and communication of the status of the test project). Test management execution includes managing all the operational project activities, such as the development of test cases and automated test scripts, as well as managing test execution.
- There is a central role for risk management, and Risk & Requirement Based Testing is the approach to this. It is also the core of the Test Management Model. It is carried over to all the test management activities: the strategy is established based on the risks; progress management is based on the number of risks covered; reporting shows the outstanding risks and which requirements have already been covered.
- The model is aimed at the quick delivery of added value to the organisation. No lengthy preparations, but fast delivery of products that the organisation can immediately put to use. The most important product

that test management delivers is insight through clear management information, on the basis of which sound decisions can be made by the stakeholders concerning the implementation of an information system.

- The model accommodates a number of existing methods and best practice. Where this is applicable, this book provides references to the relevant literature. Examples are the references to PRINCE2, the earned value method and evolutionary planning.

To illustrate the model, and as an introduction to the following chapters, a brief description of each part of the model is given below.

1.4.1 Risk & Requirement Based Testing (RRBT)

The scope and depth of a test are determined by the risks that the organisation may run when putting a system into production. Working with a combination of product risks and requirements demonstrates where gaps lie.

The most important advantages of this approach are as follows:

- The focus lies on risks to the business instead of just the (described) functionality of the information system.
- The testing activities are prioritised based on product risks. The product risks with the highest priority can be tackled first.
- By focusing on product risks, overlooked or faulty requirements reveal themselves, so that omissions can be caught and dealt with at an early stage.
- During testing, communication takes place in a language (risks) that all stakeholders understand. The provision of high-value management information to the client and other stakeholders is a core task of the test manager. Most organisations already think in terms of (product) risks. Since reporting will be fit in with this, involvement in testing is greater than when a mere list of issues is communicated.

Risk & Requirement Based Testing (RRBT) is described in Chapter 2.

1.4.2 Test Management File

All documentation used and produced by the test manager and the test team is archived in the test management file. This is a directory structure to which all project members have access with different authorities. It is therefore possible at all times to check on which decisions were made based on what information. The test management file, which is described in Chapter 4, makes a test project easily transferable.

The left side of the model (**PREPARATION**) shows all the activities related to the preparation of the test project. During preparation, the scope and depth of the tests are first determined, followed by estimating, planning and test organisation. This is in fact where the test project is defined.

1.4.3 Risk Analysis and Test Strategy

Within a test project, both the project risks and the product risks play an important role. Project risks are those that have a bearing on the execution of the project, and product risks are those that the organisation will face if the system does not function successfully. To define and manage these risks, the test manager has to carry out an analysis of both types. He incorporates the identified project risks together with their risk countermeasures into the test plan. The product risks are the basis of the test strategy. They are linked with the stakeholders of the project or the system. The test strategy also establishes which risks are covered by which tests. The test manager can use the strategy if the time available is less than planned. In this case, he can provide a documented indication of the effects that implementation of the system will have and which product risks cannot be assessed. He can also indicate which of the quantitative acceptance criteria contained in the strategy have been met. Based on that information, an informed decision can be made on whether to put the information system into production or to supplement the budget. Risk analysis and test strategy are detailed in Chapter 5.

1.4.4 Estimation

Many test managers wrestle with the problem of budget allocation for a test project. Since the scope of the test project is described in the test strategy, it can be used by the test manager as a basis for budget allocation. The allocation itself can take place in several ways. Chapter 6 describes various methods, with their advantages and disadvantages. This helps with finding a suitable approach to a certain situation, for each situation is unique. Chapter 6 introduces a pragmatic model, the test effort estimation model (TEEM), specially developed for test budgeting based on historical metrics (see Section 6.2.7).

1.4.5 Planning

The number of hours required for the test project is determined and laid down in the budget, allowing the test manager to plot the testing effort within the given time. He then establishes the necessary resources and plans first for the highest risk areas, so that if unforeseen circumstances lead to time pressure, the most important tests have been carried out.

A detailed plan of a complete project offers the illusion of accuracy, as the execution of a test project is subject to many influential factors. For that reason, evolutionary planning is the method of choice: the first phase of the project is surveyed in detail and a global plan is issued for the subsequent phases.

The planning, just as with PRINCE2, is product focused, so that added value is delivered to the organisation as quickly as possible. Instead of extensive preparation followed by execution of the tests, small units are developed including preparation and execution. This immediately demonstrates the status of particular parts of an information system. The planning for test projects is detailed in Chapter 7.

1.4.6 Test Organisation

In a test project, there is always a need for a good mix of technical, testing and business expertise to be available at the right time. Some organisations have central support for testing, such as a test competence centre or a test centre. The test manager has to take account of these facilities when organising the test.

The organisation of the test project is detailed in Chapter 8.

The right side of the model (**EXECUTION**) shows all the test manager's activities that are concerned with the execution of the test project. This includes managing test preparations and test execution and all the surrounding factors that require attention, such as issue management, reporting, advice, evaluation and transfer.

1.4.7 Progress Management

Three "business" controls are available to the test manager for managing progress: time, money and quality. He needs to have continuous insight into the status of the test project: progress (time), budget exhaustion (money) and the outstanding and covered risks (quality). Chapter 10 discusses the earned value method (EVM), which is used to obtain and keep control of the test project. This method helps to monitor the business controls of time and money. With regard to reporting on quality, the results of the test execution are registered with the test cases. These test cases are related to the product risks that have to be covered. Managing based on the variables of time, money and quality is supported by the test control matrix (TCM), which is described in some detail in Chapter 10.

1.4.8 Issue Management

During test execution, the test team will encounter various issues. It is important that these are recorded accurately and that their status is actively monitored. The test manager requires this information for reporting on the quality of the information system. In setting up the test, a relationship is established between the test cases and the product risks. The priority of the product risks determines, via the test case, the priority of the issue. This gives the client insight into the risks that are still outstanding in the system because of (as yet) unsolved issues.

Well-organised issue management also provides the developers with a means of investigating where and under what circumstances the issues manifest themselves. By also recording in the issue administration the particular phase of system development in which the issues should have been found or prevented, a basis is laid for process improvement – not only of the testing process, but also of the development process. Issue management is detailed in Chapter 11.

1.4.9 Reporting and Advice

During execution of the test project, it is important that the test manager keeps the client and all other stakeholders informed. At the end of the test project, or during the transfer from one test level to the next, he should provide a report with advice on the quality of the information system. Considering that quality is also discussed in the periodic progress reports, his conclusions should not come as a surprise. Information on the covered and outstanding product risks forms the core of the report. This delivers management information on which the organisation can base its decisions. Of course, project risks are also part of the reports. These often explain deviations between planning and realisation. Reporting and advice are detailed in Chapter 12.

1.4.10 Evaluation and Transfer

Evaluation takes place during and at the end of the test project. Interim evaluations are important for improving aspects of the current test project. The final evaluation provides an indication of the extent to which the formulated test assignments have been met. The final evaluation also provides insight into the possibilities for improvement in future projects. Such improvements may involve the development process as well as the testing process. During the test project, metrics can be maintained based on the goal–question–metric (GQM) method for the purposes of process improvement (see Appendix F).

When the test project is completed, the test manager will hand over the products in the test management file to a maintenance organisation. Before doing so, he will update the documentation to reflect the status of the project. Because changes in insight and requirements during the project have an impact on the test strategy, it is important for the next release of the information system that these details are incorporated into the test strategy. Not all products of the test project will be maintained in the maintenance organisation; those that are not to be maintained are archived.

Evaluation and transfer are detailed in Chapter 13.

1.5 Conclusion

The test management activities described in the model form the baseline of this book. With each of the topics, reference is made to the core of the Test Management Model: namely, risks and requirements. By using this model, the test manager is constantly aware of these important aspects of the tests and can take them into account. He has a model to hand that will assist him to take the right steps and make the right decisions.

The following chapter first expands on the core of the model, i.e. Risk & Requirement Based Testing.

2

Risk & Reqirement Based Testing

Risk management plays an important role in management practice. In test projects, two types of risk are involved: project risks and product risks. Test project risks are related to problems that may endanger the test activities in a project. At the same time, insight into the product risks is important if decisions have to be made on whether to put an information system into production. In consultation with the parties directly involved, the stakeholders, the test manager surveys these risks and their impact.

The tests that cover the highest risks are given preferential treatment. This approach is known as risk-based testing.

In addition to an overview of the product risks, the test manager also needs an inventory of the requirements: the needs and expectations of the organisation. He links these requirements to the appropriate product risks. Based on this information, the test team creates tests that cover those risks. This approach is called Risk & Reqirement Based Testing (RRBT). Based on this approach the stakeholders are able to make informed management decisions on both the project and the information system.

Many management activities are concerned with identifying and controlling risks. Risk management, scenario projections and contingency planning have been considered a part of life in government, politics and industry for a long time.

Risks can have both external and internal causes. A few examples of external risk-bearing factors are fraud, infrastructure, legislation, competition, terrorism, political and social developments. There are of course also risks that arise from changes that are brought about by the organisation itself, such as mergers, the introduction of a new product or a new production method. There is also finance-focused risk management, specifically practised by financial institutions.

Dictionaries define "risk" as a danger of damage or loss. Sometimes the probability of the danger is added. These definitions contain words that should ring alarm bells with test managers and all other project members:

danger, *damage* and *loss*. Even the word *probability* does not make it any easier: it is not even certain that the danger will materialise. Which parts of an information system harbour the greatest probability of damage or loss? And how significant might this damage or this loss be? One thing is certain: test managers need to provide a clear insight into risks and minimise them. Risk management is therefore essential.

The type of risk management described here aims at identifying risks connected with the development and implementation of an information system. The risk is the probability that development and implementation will cause measurable economic damage to the company, and perhaps other, less measurable damage. Damage could be that the results of a project are less favourable than expected, or that the organisation will suffer direct or indirect loss. It therefore goes beyond the ICT domain and also concerns business risks. Examples of damage that may occur are:

- Loss of market share.
- Compensation claims.
- Damage to image and reputation, e.g. through corrective measures.
- Increase in aftercare and higher maintenance costs.
- Costs of internal provisions that are higher than planned.
- Extra staffing needs.

Implementation of risk management within the Test Management Model takes place based on Risk & Reqirement Based Testing (RRBT). RRBT is a testing approach in which structurally mapped risks and accompanying requirements form the basis for formulating and directing the testing activities.

RRBT has various advantages. It provides an unambiguous framework within which to prioritise tests, distribute the testing effort and direct the project. If there is pressure on the time or resources available to the test project, the test manager is able to indicate which risks the testers can no longer cover. The client can then take a decision on which risks the organisation can afford to take or decide to allow for extra time and money to address the outstanding risk. Identifying these risks is done in agreement with the client and the stakeholders, who indicate which risks are of the greatest significance to them, thus optimising the involvement of the stakeholders in the test project. With RRBT, therefore, "value for money" is paramount, because at whatever point the project is halted, the testers will have completed tests that concern the highest product risk.

It is also possible, with the aid of RRBT, to report to the stakeholders in terms of risks. The advantage of this is that everyone is communicating at the same level. Whereas previously the client was confronted with a report on the executed tests and the outstanding issues (which meant little or nothing to him!), he now receives a report in his own language: risks to his business. Armed with this management information, he is now able to make an informed decision.

In this chapter, several types of risk will be described. Subsequently, RRBT will be explained, in terms of both the advantages of the approach and the way in which it gives form to risk management. Finally, it will be shown how the results of RRBT contribute to the management of test projects.

2.1 Distinction Between Project Risks and Product Risks

All of the risks involved in a test project are divided into two categories:[1]

- project risks.
- product risks.

This distinction is important, as it concerns two entirely different types of risks, each requiring a different approach to control them.

Project Risks

Project risks relate to managing the testing process. In this, a distinction can be made between ICT project risks and business project risks. The latter relate to the time and budget allocated to the project. The ICT project risks are linked with the conditions required for testing the information system: the availability of enough people with the right expertise, a stable test environment and familiarity with the testing method used.

For this type of risk, as in project management, the test manager will describe risk countermeasures. The project risks and these risk reduction measures are included in the test plan, which forms part of the test management file.[2] The test manager will monitor these project risks continuously throughout the course of the project and can act upon them.

The earlier the test manager is involved in the project, therefore, the better he is able to anticipate these risks.

Product Risks

Testers focus mainly on this second category. They look at the requirements, or absence of them, at the stability and complexity of the information system,

---

[1] Within PRINCE2 a distinction is made between project risks and business risks, the latter term corresponding to product risk in test management. The term business risk can be confusing. It is easy to think that this refers only to the risks originating in business, but product risks with an ICT aspect are also of importance here. For this reason, we deviate slightly from the PRINCE2 terminology.

[2] The test management file is the subject of Chapter 4.

the quality of the documentation, the quality of the coding and the non-functional requirements. The test project can cover all of these product risks with appropriate tests.

The business is directly affected by the consequences of product risks that relate to the functionality or the usability of the system. But the ICT department is also concerned when product risks materialise. It has to maintain the information system and will experience problems if the system does not have a transparent architecture, making maintainability more difficult and more expensive.

We can now set out the project risks and the product risks against the ICT and the business domain. The matrix in Figure 2.1 provides an overview with examples of possible risks and their origins.

	Product risks	Project risks
Business	Unsatisfactory quality Incorrect functionality Not user-friendly	Project overrun in: time money
ICT	Difficult to maintain Low efficiency Difficult to install	Bad test environment Insufficient resources Unfamiliarity with the testing method

Fig. 2.1. Examples of project and product risks categorised by business and ICT

In summary, the test manager is confronted with project risks and product risks, and must manage both types. He must be aware that risks can have their origin in the business domain as well as in ICT. Furthermore, he must deal with the two types of risk in different ways: he can document the project risks with their risk countermeasures in the test plan, and he can include the product risks in the test strategy. The test plan and the test strategy both form part of the test management file (see Figure 2.2).

At the beginning of the test project, the test manager focuses mainly on the project risks. Which risks threaten the delivery date? Which risks put pressure on the budget? As the project progresses, attention will shift to the product risks, since it is necessary to prove that the information system meets the agreed level of quality expressed in covered product risks. However, the test manager must never ignore the project risks. He must continually ensure that the list of project risks and their risk countermeasures are up to date. The management of test project risks is detailed in Chapter 5.

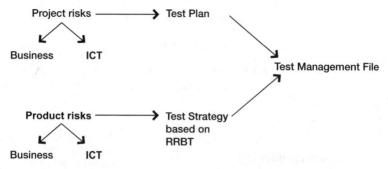

Fig. 2.2. Position of the projects risks and the product risks

2.2 Steps Within Risk Management

The test manager uses risk management to deal with risks in a structured way.

Risk management consists of the following steps (see Figure 2.3):

- Identify risks.
- Classify and assess risks.
- Allocate and select risks.
- Monitor risks.

The earlier a picture of the risks is obtained, the better. With this information the test manager might increase the awareness of the client and other stakeholders of the perceived risks the organisation might face with the application of the information system. It is also advisable to carry out these steps at predefined moments during the project, such as at the start of an important new phase in the project, or after major changes.

2.2.1 Risk Management and Risk & Requirement-Based Testing

With testing based on RRBT, specific attention is paid to situations where the system may function incorrectly. This might cause damage to the organisation or has an effect on the feasibility of the business case. The business case describes the reason behind the project proposal and this is translated into the aims of the project. Testing establishes whether an issue, which represents a risk to the product, exists or not: the risk is thus "covered". Naturally, priority is given to the most significant risks in terms of the scale of the potential damage and its impact on the business case.

Testing based on RRBT therefore provides information about the quality of the end product, i.e. the information system to be implemented.

The client's concerns about the quality aspects of the end product become the focus of the tester's attention and there is an essential shift in testing focus: the intention is not just to find faults, but also to provide all the

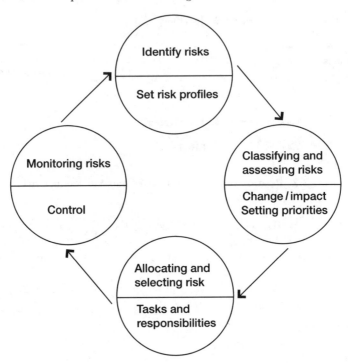

Fig. 2.3. Risk management process

interested parties with insight into the quality of the information system. This helps them to gain confidence in the system.

RRBT focuses on the following matters:

- *Risk analysis*: concentrating on the quality aspects of the system, in a structured and systematic manner.
- *Requirements*: combining them with product risks and examining their relationships.

The basis of RRBT is therefore a thorough risk analysis carried out in consultation with those directly involved. Where no systematic business and ICT risk management exists, RRBT can help to increase awareness of its importance.

The test manager estimates his budget requirement based on the product risks to be covered. If this does not fit within the client's available budget, the test manager and the client can negotiate based on these risks. At every stage, the test manager is able to indicate which product risks he will not be able to cover on a reduced budget. The client and stakeholders are better able to determine the level of risk that is acceptable to them. This means that the test manager must plan in terms of risk, and must also report in terms of risk.

The RRBT approach has the following advantages:

- With limited time, money and qualified resources, testing concentrates on the most important matters first. It begins by testing the product risks with the highest priority, thus delivering the most optimal test.
- RRBT is an effective way of involving the client and stakeholders in the project. Communication takes place in terms of risk, a language understood by everyone; it offers a framework for structuring input, with a learning curve for future projects; and it facilitates a systematic weighing of investment in testing against potential damage.
- It offers a negotiating instrument to client and test manager alike when available means are limited.
- Linking the product risks from the risk analysis to the requirements identifies gaps.

With this approach, RRBT substantially complements the requirement-based testing described in the previous chapter.

The steps involved in risk management apply to the identification of both product risks and project risks. We have seen that for RRBT, the product risks are important. Therefore, in the remainder of this chapter we will concentrate on risk management of these product risks.

2.2.2 Identify Risks

To obtain a picture of the product risks as complete as possible, the test manager must involve those stakeholders who have a direct interest in the information system. That means involving people from various departments and with various backgrounds: for example, the client, customers, experts, the project team, the project leader, users, the maintenance department, a marketing manager and the developers. The stakeholders should represent both the business and ICT. This is the only way that a product risk analysis can deliver as complete an inventory of all the risks as possible that has a bearing on the quality of the information system.

The risks can be identified in a number of ways: by using past experience, checklists of recurrent risks, and also by holding workshops. The combination of these methods often delivers the best results. Whichever method the test manager selects to identify the product risks, the important thing is to get a complete picture. The more complete this picture, the better the test project can be set up and managed.

Past Experience

It is useful to establish where in the past the most problems arose. There will probably be evaluations or other records to hand. These can provide good indications for the current test project.

Risk Checklists

Checklists can also be used for product risks that are often associated with this type of information system or project. For the novice test manager, a standard list like this can be a good starting point. He is more in danger of missing product risks or of not knowing where to begin than an experienced manager, and a checklist can help here. He can also use the checklist to assist the stakeholders in identifying the risks. If such a list does not exist, consider starting one.

Appendix B provides a sample checklist of product risks.

Workshops

Workshops can be held, preferably with variable composition so that not all the representatives are together in a single session. Circumstances will of course dictate the choice.

As many relevant documents as possible can be used in the workshops, especially when the requirements are not yet complete. These can perhaps refer to the business case or be a description of the business processes.

For this way of working, practical experience in leading such sessions is necessary. Branch knowledge is also essential for the test manager. If necessary, the session should be facilitated by an independent and experienced moderator, including minute taking.

In order to give the various steps within risk management more form and substance, an example is worked out in the remainder of this chapter. After the description of each step, the example is used for purposes of clarification.

A bank uses a system that allows customers to withdraw cash from an automated teller machine (ATM). A crucial function is the interface with the customer, checking the account balance and the withdrawal of funds. No matter what option the customer selects, a connection is set up with the bank's server. It makes no difference whether the ATM belongs to the customers home bank or to another bank. All the customer details are stored on this server. When a balance is requested, the system looks up the account number and shows the balance. When a withdrawal is requested, the system checks whether the amount is available in the account. If so, the system issues the cash and prints a receipt. If there are insufficient funds available in the account, the system issues a message to that effect. At the same time, the customer is informed of the amount he is able to withdraw. He can then choose to proceed or to stop. The developers are working on a new release of this system.

Within one of the bank's departments, the test manager organised a workshop to identify the product risks. Those present, apart from the

---

test manager, were: the client, an information analyst, a developer and an end user.

This workshop resulted in the list of product risks given in Table 2.1.

Table 2.1. Sample list of product risk for the ATM

Product risk
Customer cannot perform a transaction
Customer receives no cash from the cash drawer at the end of the transaction
Customer is not issued with a receipt at the end of the transaction
The wrong message is displayed to the customer
The system is unavailable to the customer for longer than 15 minutes
It takes longer than 2 hours for the system to be restored after a fault
On first use, the customer does not understand the procedure to be followed

The list contains both business product risks (i.e. the system is unavailable to the customer for longer than 15 minutes) and ICT product risks (i.e. it takes longer than 2 hours for the system to be restored after a fault).

2.2.3 Classify and Assess Risks

The previous step has resulted in a list of product risks as complete as possible. The risks are analysed in this next step, which achieves the fastest results if the stakeholders who participated in the first step also take part in this one. The participants do not require explanation, are familiar with the list of risks and can set to work immediately.

The Classification of the Risks

It is hard work for the test manager to recite continually the list of product risks when he is communicating the status and progress of the test project. Everyone concerned might easily lose track of the multitude of product risks. For the sake of order, it is useful to link the product risks to the quality attributes as laid down in ISO9126.[3] For this, the test manager takes the list of product risks and consults with the stakeholder who has indicated a specific product risk. He does this for every product

---

[3] The quality attributes are: functionality, reliability, usability, efficiency, maintainability and portability. These can be further subdivided into subattributes. Appendix D provides an overview of all the quality attributes and their subattributes.

risk. In this way, each product risk is linked to a quality attribute. Linking product risks and quality attributes also has the advantage of finding "missing" product risks. The list of products risks will become more complete this way and this will improve the the quality and coverage of the test.

The quality attributes of ISO9126 contain a standard list of attributes that may be of importance to an information system. This list can therefore also be used as a checklist. Are product risks identified for every quality attribute? Is the quality attribute for which no risk has been indicated not important to this test project?

The ISO9126 list can prompt the stakeholders to think of risks which they had not identified earlier in their brainstorming session or by using a checklist.

Linking the product risks to the quality attributes in the example with the ATM results in Table 2.2.

Table 2.2. Example of linking product risks to quality attributes for the ATM

Product risk	Quality attribute
Customer cannot perform a transaction	Functionality
Customer receives no cash from the cash drawer at the end of the transaction	Functionality
Customer is not issued with a receipt at the end of the transaction	Functionality
The wrong message is displayed to the customer	Functionality
The system is unavailable to the customer for longer than 15 minutes	Reliability
It takes longer than 2 hours for the system to be restored after a fault	Maintainability
On the first use, the customer does not understand the procedure to be followed	Usability

---

The test manager will communicate with the stakeholders about the four mentioned quality attributes: functionality, reliability, maintainability and usability.

No product risks were mentioned relating to the two other quality attributes, efficiency and portability. The test manager asks whether they are not important to the current test project. The stakeholders indicate that, indeed, portability is not an option. A product risk does arise relating to efficiency, i.e. that if the cash drawer does not open within 30 seconds, the customer possibly walks away. The test manager adds this product risk to the list.

Table 2.2 can quickly lead us to the first arrangement of tests to be developed. In the example, the test manager and the test team need to develop tests for five quality attributes. They can perhaps combine the development of the four tests relating to functionality. The decision of whether to do this depends among other things on the priority assigned to the various product risks: they must be assessed accordingly.

Assess the Risks

The priority assigned to a particular risk determines the amount of time the test team will spend on minimising this risk. Therefore, the test manager has to ensure that priorities are assigned to the product risks. There are various ways of doing this:

- the relative priority;
- the systematic priority;
- the MoSCoW priority.

The relative and the MoSCoW priorities are qualitative methods: the risks are prioritised relative to each other. The systematic priority is a quantative method: the risks are ordered based on the outcome of a specific formula.

Relative Priority

The priority of a product risk is determined by the probability of a problem materialising and the impact that problem would have if it materialised. The probability and the impact can be set against each other as in Figure 2.4. This results in four quadrants (Veenendaal, 2002). The test manager decides together with the client and the stakeholders into which quadrant the various risks are placed. The priorities that the test manager and the stakeholders assign can be high (H), medium (M) or low (L).

Quadrant I signifies a problem which has a low probability of occurring, but which would have a high impact in the event that it did occur. The test

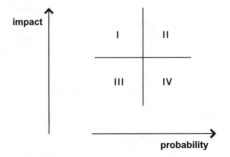

Fig. 2.4. Relative priority

manager and stakeholders decide on the priority of these product risks, i.e. the level of risk that is acceptable to the organisation. At first sight, this will result in a medium priority, but may change to high or low priority, depending on the organisation's assessment.

Quadrant II signifies problems which will probably occur, and which will have a high impact if they do. These problems are therefore immediately designated as high priority, and the test manager will definitely test the product risks in this category.

The problems in quadrant III are of low priority. They are unlikely to occur and would have a low impact.

Lastly, the problems in quadrant IV are those having a low impact, but a high probability of occurring. Again, the test manager together with the stakeholders determines the priority, depending on the level of risk acceptable to the organisation. Here, too, the priority rating will initially be medium, but may change to high or low.

Systematic Priority

Another way of defining the priority of the product risks is to use mathematics. In this, the same variables are used as with relative priority, but with an attempt at quantifying them.

$$\text{Risk} = \text{probability} \times \text{impact}$$

It is a much quoted formula, but the data for a calculation like this are very difficult to define. Risk is the result of uncertainty. It is therefore practically impossible to define a probability and an impact!

A formula gives a feeling of certainty, and therefore extra caution is necessary. "There is only a 5% risk that I won't be able to process a customer's bank account, so there's no problem." That is the logical reaction of a desk clerk on hearing this percentage. He is actually saying that the relation between the bank account and the customer within the information system needs no further attention. The test manager must be alert to such a result. How sure can we be of the chances of failure and the potential impact? We are dealing here with a false sense of security. Imagine that heart-monitoring equipment is tested. A 5% chance of failure suddenly sounds much higher, even more so if you yourself depend on such equipment. Being guided by a simple percentage can therefore be dangerous.

MoSCoW Priority

Another method of defining the priority of product risks is the MoSCoW prioritising model.[4] With this, the test manager can make use of an example chart as shown in Figure 2.5. For a product risk that materialises, a distinction is made between financial and non-financial consequences. A further distinction is made between consequences for the customers and for the department. The test manager then looks at the effects: that is, whether all customers are affected or just one; whether there is a workaround or no alternative solution at all to the problem. This combination then determines the priority.

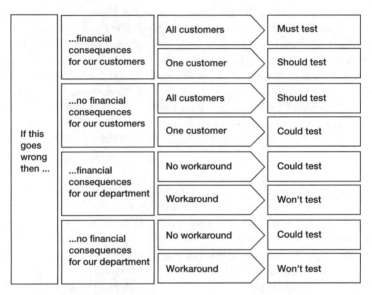

Fig. 2.5. Example of MoSCoW priority chart

The test manager follows the flow chart for every product risk.

If a fault in the information system makes it impossible to buy and sell shares (reliability), this will lead to financial consequences for all customers of the stock exchange. Imagine a bear market, where customers are anxious to sell their shares to protect their profit, or a bull market, where they are keen to buy shares in the hope of future profit. According to the flow chart, this is a "Must test" problem: therefore a high priority rating.

---

[4] MoSCoW here stands for "Must test", Should test', "Could test" and "Won't test", with "Must test" signifying the highest priority and "Won't test" the lowest. This is similar to the priority rating for requirements, where it becomes "Must have", "Should have", "Could have" and "Won't have".

Imagine that it is not possible to register complaints about the stock exchange (functionality). This would have no financial consequences for the department: the operation of the stock exchange is unaffected. The department decides to register the complaints manually as a temporary measure and process them into the system later. Since this workaround is available, the result is a "Won't test" situation.

A test manager may be able to copy this flow chart exactly as it stands, but he would need to take care that the questions are indeed the right ones. For example, the chart assumes that there are various customers. If an organisation only has one customer, the test manager will need to make the necessary adjustments. He will also have to examine the priorities and whether the appropriate level of importance is reflected. For example, events can lead to organisations suffering damage to their reputation, such as a bank that loses its AAA status through delay in reporting to the nation's central bank. At first sight, this may appear to be of non-financial consequences for the department, and the model suggests that such problems are always given a low priority rating: "Could test" or "Won't test". However, it is possible that an organisation's reputation is of such importance that it results in a "Must test" situation. The model therefore must be adapted to the organisation's situation.

The client indicates that it would be a high-priority product risk for his bank if customers were unable to withdraw cash from the ATMs. The customers will, on the first few occasions, go and use the facilities of another bank. However, if they repeatedly have problems withdrawing cash from their bank, they will naturally close their accounts and go to another bank. This would cost the bank a significant loss of revenue.

The test manager knows, therefore, that it is very important to the bank that this application functions correctly. What are the priorities of the various product risks? To find out, the test manager follows the MoSCoW model in consultation with the stakeholders. This results in Table 2.3. For the sake of clarity, the "Quality attributes" column is omitted here. A complete template including all the columns is provided in Appendix C.

The possibility of combining the four risks relating to functionality was mentioned above. This would provide the test manager with the first grouping for testing the information system. However, the importance of the product risks within the quality attribute functionality is not consistent. There are two product risks with a "Must test" priority and two with "Should test". During the rest of the project, the test manager will use these priorities to report on the progress of the development and execution of the tests.

Table 2.3. Combination of product risk and MoSCoW priority

Product risk	Interim flow chart result	MoSCoW
Customer cannot perform a transaction	Financial, all customers	Must test
Customer receives no cash from the cash drawer at the end of the transaction	Financial, all customers	Must test
Customer is not issued with a receipt at the end of the transaction	Non-financial, all customers	Should test
Wrong message displayed to customer	Non-financial, all customers	Should test
The system is unavailable to the customer for longer than 15 minutes	Non-financial, all customers	Should test
It takes longer than 2 hours for the system to be restored after a fault	Financial, no workaround	Could test
On the first use, the customer does not understand the procedure to be followed	Non-financial, one customer	Could test
The cash drawer does not open within 30 seconds	Non-financial, all customers	Should test

For the sake of communication, it is useful to base the first grouping on the same quality attribute, putting similar tests together. The tests developed within a quality attribute "inherit" its priority. Maintaining varying priorities within a quality attribute has a distorting effect on this step, and for this reason it is better to split the quality attribute. In this example, this would mean that the test manager would make one grouping for the functionality attribute with "Must test" priority, and another for the same quality attribute with "Should test" priority. Whichever choices the test manager makes, he records them in his test strategy.

The MoSCoW model gives in our opinion the best means of determining the priorities of the product risks. It is less subjective than relative priority and the test manager avoids the false certainty of a mathematical formula.

2.2.4 Allocate and Select Risks

Analysing and prioritising risks is of little use unless something is done with them. After identification, classification and assessment, someone has to take responsibility for the risks. The test manager can assist with this.

In the earlier steps, there was contact with the stakeholders having a direct interest in the information system. In most cases, they will also be the ones bearing the responsibility for a succesfull implementation. The test manager agrees with these stakeholders which risks are within scope and which tasks belong to active risk management. Being responsible for a risk also means being pro-active: take, for example, a change in the requirements. This has an impact on development as well as on testing. The test manager has the responsibility to make the consequences of the changes clear. What are the consequences for testing? Is the list of product risks still complete or must more be added, changed or removed? Is it still possible to test all product risks?

The test manager can make clear what the consequences would be if the risks were not covered by testing. This raises the stakeholders' awareness of the product risks and their importance.

When all the product risks have been allocated, the test manager can decide together with the stakeholders on how they are to be dealt with.

The test manager indicates his budget requirements, based on the agreements about which product risks will be tested. If this does not fit within the client's total project budget plan, the client and the test manager can negotiate on the basis of the risks and the test manager can indicate which risks he is unable to cover with a reduced budget[5]. It is easier for the client and the stakeholders to determine the level of risk that is acceptable to them. This means that the test manager must plan in terms of risk, and must set up the progress reports based on risks.

A number of other rules apply to the testing of product risks. In many projects, time and money are limiting factors, which makes it impossible to test everything. A simple example shows this, see Figure 2.6 (Graham, 1999). Therefore, the test manager and the stakeholders must make choices based on a cost–benefit analysis (Gilb, 1999). If the expense of eliminating the risks is going to be greater than the resulting benefit, the responsible manager abandons the idea. The object is to achieve the aims of the test project within the conditions of time and money.

A system has 20 screens, with an average of 10 fields per screen. The fields can be populated in two ways, e.g. 3-1 and 3 Jan. In these fields, there are 100 possible values to be entered: upper case letters, lower case letters, numbers, etc. Therefore, for a complete test we are dealing with:

$$20 \times 4 \times 3 \times 10 \times 2 \times 100 = 480{,}000 \text{ tests}$$

If a test takes 1 second (excluding problems, faults and retesting), this test will take 8,000 minutes = 133 hours = 16.7 days (of 8 hours). A more realistic time per test would perhaps be 10 minutes. We are then speaking about 4,800,000 minutes = 80,000 hours = 10,000 days (of 8 hours) = 27 years.

---

[5] A covered risk is a risk for which one or more test cases are executed. So the client and the stakeholders know whether the risk materialises or not.

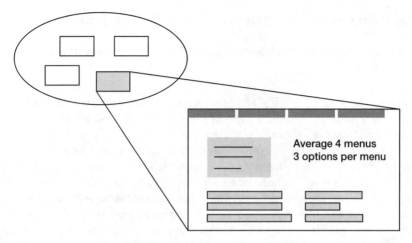

Fig. 2.6. Example of a need for limitation

The test manager and the stakeholders therefore have to make choices, and so the priorities assigned to the product risks in the previous step now come into play. Which product risks will be covered depends on the time available. Those with the highest priority – "Must test" – are covered first. It is then examined whether there is sufficient time to cover everything with "Should test" priority, and so on.

If product risks are not covered within a test project, this of course does not mean the responsible parties need do nothing. The risks have been identified and analysed, and will have to be covered by other means. Contingency measures must be created, just as for the project risks.

2.2.5 Monitor Risks

Risk management is not a one-off activity. Every substantial change may have consequences for the list of product risks. Risks may disappear or change, and new ones may arise. Those delegated the responsibility in the previous step must continue to monitor and review the risks.

Continuous monitoring and reviewing of the product risks means that the test manager and everyone else involved in the project always have an up-to-date list to hand. Risk management does not mean eliminating all the risks. By following the above steps, the managers gain an overview of the risks and their priorities, which helps them to decide on which risks to focus more in the next phase of the test project and which ones require less attention.

2.3 Using Risk Priority Within the Test Project

Agreement must be established on action to be undertaken if a product risk materialises.

During the execution of a test, there are unforeseen problems with the test environment. The end date of the project cannot be changed and the client decides to carry out fewer tests. The materialisation of this project risk results in an impact on testing the product risks. If the test manager agrees in advance what is to be done in these circumstances, no one is taken by surprise. The stakeholders know whether their risks still fall within the test project, and no time need be wasted on meetings about what is and is not now eligible for testing. Because the risks with the highest priority were tackled first, the testing has been most optimal, considering the circumstances!

To be prepared for these situations, it must be clear which tests can be abandoned. The choice is made based on the priorities assigned to the product risks by the MoSCoW method, beginning with those that have the lowest priority rating.

The client and stakeholders try to make decisions on this before testing starts. Much stress and delay during the crucial operational phase of testing is avoided by taking these decisions in advance.

The client and stakeholders consult with the test manager and the decisions are put into the test strategy.

If it proves necessary to abandon certain tests, this continues until the tests to be carried out fit within the time frame that is left, or until the point where the client and stakeholders find the level of outstanding product risk unacceptable. This method is known as the strategic test slicing method

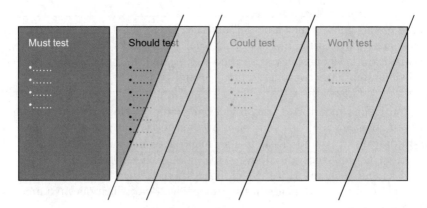

Fig. 2.7. The strategic test slicing method (STSM)

(STSM), see Figure 2.7. If the level of risk is unacceptable, the client and stakeholders must take a decision on the test project: whether it can be extended, for example, or wether more testers will be added to the project so that the total number of tests can still be performed up to the acceptable risk level.

2.4 The Combination of Product Risks and Requirements

Product risks alone are an insufficient basis for test cases. Requirements are also necessary, whether for a completely new information system or a new release of an existing system. Product risks point to what can go wrong, while requirements and the background documentation describe the specifications and expectations and how they have been worked out. By linking the requirements to the product risks, better insight can be gained into the functioning of the information system and the effects of its non-functioning. The testers work out this information in test cases via design documents and test conditions.

The test strategy determines the sequence in which the product risks are tested, with the MoSCoW priorities as a guide (Figure 2.8).

At the start of a test project, not all of the requirements may be known. As stated earlier, by linking requirements to product risks, the test manager can establish whether requirements are lacking for certain product risks, or whether they conflict. Further, the list of product risks might improve. This relation between product risks and requirements is explained in Figure 2.9.

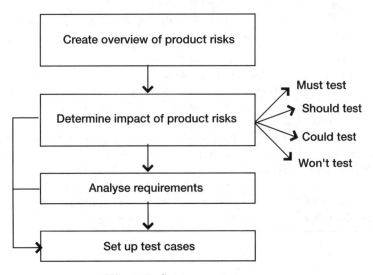

Fig. 2.8. Setting up test cases

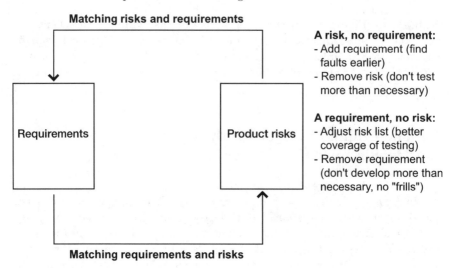

Fig. 2.9. Matching product risks and requirements

The deficiencies and ambiguities must be communicated to the client, who alone can provide clarification, e.g. by asking the relevant department to expand on or explain the requirements. This is even more necessary where product risks with the highest priority are concerned! A test manager can thus report the problem with the requirements, but it is not up to him to solve it. As it is not part of the test project, the test manager would therefore need to redefine his task, if asked to do so.

In projects with an iterative way of development, these steps will be taken several times.

Table 2.4 shows the result of the first linking of product risks and requirements for the ATM in our example.

It is clear that requirements are missing for five product risks. The test manager also notes that the requirements are incomplete: the customer sees not only a message stating that the funds are insufficient, but also a message telling him how much he can withdraw. In addition, the test manager cannot find requirements for people wishing to make withdrawals who are not customers of this bank. He also notes a vague requirement: the cash drawer must open within a set time. Within what time?

The test manager shows this table to his client, who can undertake subsequent action. When all the requirements are complete and linked to the product risks, the setting up of the tests can begin.

Table 2.4. Linking product risks, priorities and requirements relating to ATM

Product risk	MoSCoW	Requirement
Customer cannot perform a transaction	Must test	Customer can perform transaction via own bank
		Customer can perform transaction via other bank
		Customer can choose from set amounts
		Customer can select amount/choice of banknotes
Customer receives no cash from the cash drawer at the end of the transaction	Must test	
Customer not issued with a receipt at the end of the transaction	Should test	
Wrong message displayed to customer	Should test	Insufficient funds message displayed
The system is unavailable to the customer for longer than 15 minutes	Should test	
It takes longer than 2 hours for the system to be restored after a fault	Could test	
On the first use, the customer does not understand the procedure to be followed	Could test	
The cash drawer does not open within 30 seconds	Should test	The cash drawer must open within a set time

Priorities Within Risky Projects

Priorities as so far described are assigned to the highest level of the test grouping: the so-called clusters.[6] All the lower levels of the test are automatically given the priority of the cluster. For risky projects, this way of prioritising is perhaps too simple. In such cases there is often a need for better, more specific product risk priorities, so that the client and stakeholders can make better informed and more accurate decisions.

---

[6] The test grouping results from using a testing method. How the first breakdown into clusters is achieved is described in Chapter 5.

We take it a step further in that case. Within the first division into clusters, the testers will define what is to be tested: the test conditions.[7] These test conditions are given their own priority rating: high (H), medium (M) or low (L).

Such a priority reflects the relative priority within the cluster, and so a high-risk test condition within a "Must test" cluster cannot directly be compared with a high-risk test condition within a "Could test" cluster.

Assigning priorities at the level of the test conditions enables the test manager to give exact advice. He can use the strategic Test slicing method (STSM) for this, too. Instead of abandoning tests at the level of, say, "Could test" and "Won't test", the priorities of the test conditions are now used as well.

A development project is running out of time and the client does not want to change the delivery date. The system must therefore be tested in a shorter time than was originally planned. The client, together with the test manager, consult the MoSCoW scheme and decides to leave aside the "Could test" and "Won't test" clusters. The other two fit within the test project frame. It is established in the test strategy that in the event of unforeseen circumstances, only the H and M test conditions should be elaborated for the "Should test" cluster and for the "Must test" cluster, the H, M and L test conditions must be elaborated.

Since this further expansion on prioritising involves extra administration and more decision making, it is advisable only to use this method with complex, risky projects.

2.5 Conclusion

The choice of Risk & Requirement-Based Testing (RRBT) as an approach influences the entire test project, as the Test Management Model has already shown. The consistent application of the RRBT principle delivers the advantages described earlier.

In carrying out his test management tasks, the test manager must bear in mind the principles and approach of RRBT at all times. The risks play a part in every activity:

---

[7] The terms cluster, test condition and test case are used within LogicaCMG's TestFrame method. Other methods use different terms for structuring their test sets such as: logical test case, physical test case, test script, etc. These methods can be used here as well.

- The test strategy is set up based on the product risks.
- In budget allocation, extra resources are planned for the high-risk areas.
- In planning, it is assumed that extra time will be given to areas of high risk, and that they will be planned at the beginning of the test project.
- In defining the communication and reporting structure, the test manager proposes to report in terms of the product risks. The same applies to the evaluation at the end of the test project.
- The issues are documented with the accompanying product risk.

Outstanding issues say something about the risk an organisation still runs when putting an information system into production. At the final transfer and evaluation, the test manager can check whether he has satisfied the original assignment. In being guided by risks in the manner described, a sound and manageable test project is created.

The first step the test manager takes at the start of a new test project is to perform a quick scan. In doing this, he gains a first impression of the feasibility and practicability of the test project. This is the subject of the next chapter.

3

The Quick Scan

It is advisable for the test manager to first carry out a brief feasibility study of the test project. In this "quick scan" phase, the test manager establishes the status of all the important aspects of the test. To do this he employs various components of the Test Management Model. Among other things there are the presence and usability of standards, organisational and budgetary instruments, management involvement and availability of resources. This inventory process should not be too lengthy. Its duration depends on the scale and complexity of the project, but should be no longer than 5 days. The test manager can use the information to start the necessary preparations at an early stage. The results of the study are discussed with the client and other stakeholders and are used to finalise the assignment of the test manager. The quick scan is only used to make an inventory and is not part of the test project preparation.

3.1 Basic Information

Immediate Cause and Stakeholders' Involvement

First, the test manager focuses on the motivation behind the project. Why was the project started, and who initiated it? It is wise also to establish what benefit and purpose the information system will give to the business. Is the project a follow-up to an earlier project? What agreements were already made before the test manager became involved? The business case is an indispensable source of information here[1] because it contains the reasoning behind the

---

[1] See PRINCE2. Within PRINCE2, the business case is the determining factor. There must first be a business case, to be able to start a project. It primarily sets out the *reasoning* behind the proposal, translated into the goals of the project, establishing a relationship with the business priorities and relevant policy principles. Also, a concretisation in terms of results is obtained, based on

project and the expected benefits to the organisation. This essential information must be immediately established and analysed. Absence of the business case will lead to critical questioning. If a business case is described, it should be examined for the available information required to set up and manage the test project.

Subsequently, with the aid of the business case, the test manager identifies the stakeholders in the project. They are the interested parties who can define the risks from both a business and an ICT perspective. In practice, the list of product risks will steadily increase during the course of the study. Those who have an interest in a successful result are important decision-makers as well as a valuable source of information. They will also want to be kept informed on the status and progress of the project.

Assignment

The assignment should provide a basis on which to set up the test project. If the client has not provided an assignment, the test manager must formulate one himself, with the business case as a starting point. Naturally, the assignment should be discussed thoroughly with the client.

The assignment consists of two parts: a definition of the problem and a definition of the goals. The first describes the actual problem, and the second must clearly explain what the client wishes to achieve in the future. The test project is set up within these conditions.

To create as much clarity as possible for all parties, the assignment must be as unambiguous and explicit as possible; in other words, it should be described along the lines of the SMART principle. The assignment must therefore be: Specific, Measurable, Achievable, Realistic and Timely. If not, it must be revised.

A stock broking firm wishes to improve testing by setting up a regression test. The assignment states: the development of an automated regression test set for the system relating to the functions of entering, consulting, amending and removing orders. The regression test is only concerned with testing the "good" situations (use of the system in accordance with the user's manual and functionality design); negative tests are excluded. The development of the test set must be realised within the period of 1 January 2003 to 30 April 2003 by the test team, supported by subject

---

the objectives (by means of performance indicators and an investment analysis). Finally, the most important conditions, and consequences, of the proposal are described. A business case therefore provides insight into the return on investment (ROI) of a project. Whenever a phase is completed, the connection between the project and the business case is examined and this forms the input for a go/no-go decision for the next phase.

knowledge from the users' department of "Order Administration", since the regression tests have to be executed on 1 May 2003. The time available to realise this is effectively 30 workdays. The test manager has agreed that the project can be realised within these conditions.

Specific. The product to be delivered is specifically and clearly defined.

Measurable. Tests should only provide positive coverage of the functionality concerned; this can be indicated quantitatively.

Achievable. Client and contractor agree that the project can be realised within the set time and budget.

Realistic. The project duration is 4 months, while the actual work will take 30 workdays.

Timely. The project must be completed by 1 May 2003, otherwise the product loses its added value to the organisation.

Context of the Project

We are concerned here with the organisational environment of the test project. What information is available on the project or programme of which the test project is a part? Which products have a bearing on the test project? Which departments and other projects are involved?

Apart from the client, the programme or project manager of the coordinating project is an important partner who can provide much information.

Furthermore, these questions make it clear to the test manager with whom coordination is required outside of the project, who should be informed on the progress of the testing later, and what types of information are needed by the stakeholders to make their decisions. This might be external suppliers, or customers and purchasers. What are their requirements, and what dependencies do they create. Details on information systems that are related to the system under test are also relevant, as they can expose additional risks.

Standards, Procedures and Facilities

It is advisable during the quick scan to examine which standards and procedures are available in the organisation, and whether they are mandatory. The application of these can save a lot of work, since the test manager then does not have to concern himself with, for example, the selection of a tool for recording the issues, or a project management tool for managing the progress of the test project. This is important information!

3.2 Specific Information According to the Test Management Model

So far, we have been concerned with the collection of general information about the test project. We now look at information that is tied more closely to testing and the test project itself. The steps contained in the Test Management Model form a practical checklist for the test manager here, and ensure that no relevant issues are overlooked.

The Test Approach

The first step according to the Test Management Model is the choice of approach to testing. As discussed, this book gives preference to the Risk &Reqirement Based Testing (RRBT) method.

It is possible, however, that the organisation uses a different approach. In that case, it is important to find out why this particular approach has been selected and to bear these arguments in mind as much as possible. In view of the great advantages of a risk-based approach, the test manager should try to incorporate it into the existing approach. At any rate, time should be allocated to the introduction of the test management approach and conveying the most important principles and advantages of it.

Risk Analysis and Test Strategy

The test manager now examines what has been established in the past concerning the most important project and product risks. Information is also required for the initial set-up of the test strategy. Apart from information concerning the interested parties, this includes quality attributes, test levels and acceptance criteria, among other things.

The test manager first draws up an inventory of the known project and product risks, and tries to categorise them by domain (business or ICT). In this phase, with newly built systems, there are often more known project than product risks, since the solution for the development is not yet complete. In the case of a new release of an existing information system, assessed product risks of prior releases might be available.

During the quick scan, the test manager also tries to establish what risks have materialised in the past. This is an effective approach, especially if it concerns testing a new release of a system for which various tests have already been carried out. Also, the inventory of risks from similar projects and evaluations of other test projects can alert the test manager to potential problems.

If the organisation already has an available test strategy used for prior releases of the information system, that will be a good starting point. The organisation has obviously progressed as far as to consider the testing set-up.

The test strategy will perhaps later require adjustment when more is known and the test approach has been selected.

If there is no test strategy as such, the test manager must first create it during the risk analysis and test strategy phase detailed in Chapter 5.

With the information that can be collected at this stage, the test manager is able to form an idea of the scope of the test project.

Initial Budget and Planning

The test project forms a part of another project or programme; therefore to obtain information on the initial timetable and planning of the test project, the test manager must be aware of the budget and planning relating to the total project. He must also have a description of the project result: what is obtained when it is completed (Kor, 1999; Wijnen & Kor, 1997)? By what standard is the success or failure of the project measured? This may involve, for example, acceptance criteria and physical products, but may also involve final reports.

On the basis of the test strategy of prior releases of the information system and the results to be delivered, a foundation can be laid for the initial budget and planning. If sufficient time is allotted to testing, an initial plan can already be set up, e.g. a first categorisation of the various test levels that are required, and when they may be started and finished. If, on the other hand, it becomes clear that insufficient time has been reserved for this, the impact must now be discussed with the client.

If members of the test team are already present in the organisation, they can of course assist in setting up the initial budget and planning, and can help to provide a rough first estimate. After all, they are the ones with experience of the information system and its quality level. In this way, the estimate is more reliable and provides a better idea of feasibility. It also promotes involvement of the testers.

The Test Organisation

To get a good idea of the (test) project, there must also be information on the test organisation. How does the organisation handle a test project?

Perhaps the organisation has a central test department. By having a centralised test team it is easier to establish dedicated career paths and specialised training can be given to the testers in that organisation because it is seen as a discipline in its own right.

The organisation may have a test competence centre, with extensive testing facilities. The test manager will be able to obtain advice there on the procedures and standards, among other things.

Another possibility is that testing has to be arranged independently within the test project. If an organisation works in this way, there is a good chance that each test project has more or less developed its own standards and procedures. The test manager can then choose those that have demonstrated their success in previous projects and that best suit the new test project. He can supplement them with his own insights and experiences.

Progress Management

In progress management too, ways must be found of connecting with the method used in the organisation. It must be examined whether the test manager can report on the business controls of time, money and quality in accordance with this method.

Issue Management, Reporting and Advising, Evaluation and Transfer

Also in regard to issue management, reporting and advising, and evaluation and transfer, the standards and procedures used within the organisation can be employed. The same goes for the tools available for these activities. The information obtained is then used as a starting point in determining the action required to complete the set of procedures for the test project when necessary.

Issue management must in any case be set up in such a way that not only the issue itself but also the associated product risk and its priority are established. This gives an insight into the significance of the outstanding issues and an impression of the quality of the information system.

Reporting takes place on the business controls of time, money and quality. Quality relates to the covered and outstanding product risks – it is possible that an existing reporting standard may be applied. The quick scan should also show which persons and departments are to be reported to and with what frequency.

A test manager has to establish at which points evaluation is advisable or required: at the end of the test project, or intermittently, or after each phase? This can have implications for the existing standard or procedure. On transfer, it should be clear which part of the organisation carries out the maintenance of the testware and the test environment.

3.3 Availability of Documentation

What documentation is available? And what is the status of this documentation? This concerns, among other things:

- a requirements document;
- a functional design;
- a technical design.

The documentation must of course be as complete as possible, and relate to the latest version of the information system. If this is not the case, input will be required from the domain experts. The product risk analysis can be used to indicate the shortcomings in the requirements and as the basis for the test. The test manager may find out that reviews are executed on the documentation. This tells him whether input from the test team is also required for carrying out these reviews, and whether the organisation takes a responsible approach to the matter of documentation.

3.4 Availability of Testware

During the quick scan, a survey is carried out of the available testware. If testware is present, it must be examined whether it can be reused. This is particularly important in the case of testing subsequent releases of an information system. It saves a lot of time, since the testers are not obliged to work out the tests from the beginning. They can focus more on creating testware for the additional or changed functionality. Furthermore, the knowledge in the testware can be put to use. It saves the testers from unravelling all the documentation or collecting information from the domain experts. Reuse is made easier by using a structured test method.

3.5 Availability of Supporting Procedures

The presence of the following procedures will help to make the testing process go as smoothly as possible (Koppens & Meyberg, 2000):

- Configuration management ensures that the test manager has the correct version of the information system, the test environment and the relevant documentation.
- Issue management provides the appropriate procedure for managing issues. The aim is to safeguard information on issues and always to have a good overview of reported issues. Which issues have been solved and come back to the test team? For which issues is a temporary solution (workaround) available? There are issues which can be solved immediately, but also ones which require a lengthier and careful search for their underlying cause.
- Problem management ensures that the real problem is tackled, and not the symptoms alone. Issues can be seen as symptoms of a problem.
- Change management means that there is insight into the changes the test team will need to introduce into the testware.
- Release management makes it clear to everyone which changes have been made in a particular release, which problems there may still be (known errors), how the new release should be installed and what the release

planning is. Change and release management therefore ensure that the test manager and test team can anticipate the changes and adjust the test execution schedule accordingly.

3.6 Reporting and Coordination

The test manager naturally ensures the structured registration of the results of the quick scan. It will often happen that not all the information is available, or that it is still subject to change. In that case, the test manager makes assumptions that he will have to verify later. These assumptions have to be documented.

The test manager subsequently discusses the conclusions resulting from the quick scan, supplemented with the known issues, bottlenecks and ambiguities, with the client and other involved parties. The moment when the test manager discovers problems that are obstructing a reliable test is the time to bring it up for discussion and to seek a solution. Later in the project, possible solutions become scarcer, and the negotiating position of the test manager is thus weaker.

Naturally, the test manager adds the results of the discussion to the report.

3.7 Conclusion

The quick scan forms the initial basis of the test project. Subsequent phases of test management will build on this.

The report and the many documents that follow it must be well managed. For this purpose, the test manager opens a test management file. This will be detailed in the following chapter.

4

The Test Management File

In order to maintain a good overview of the test project, the test manager must establish and manage all information relating to it. This means not only the documents created by the test manager himself but also, for example, the testware developed by the testers and all other information of importance to the test project. Having a clear structure helps the test manager to provide information to the stakeholders in a clear and efficient manner giving them a better insight into the project. The test management file discussed here equips the test manager with a model for distributing information.

A quick scan has been carried out, and with that the first step in the test project has been taken: the test manager has the first overview of the test project. The results of the quick scan provide a good impression of the feasibility of the test project. This important information is the starting point for the test plan, which in turn provides the basis for the subsequent steps. The test plan lays the foundation not only for the test project, but also for its filing. It provides the reference framework for each important step in the project; each subsequent step will have to comply with the agreements, assumptions and preconditions established earlier. The test plan will be detailed further later in this chapter.

The advantages of administering and structuring the project information in a test management file are:

- The information provides an effective tool for project management, and particularly for prompt intervention. The test manager is able to refer at all times to the original instruction and the benefits that the information system is ultimately expected to deliver.
- The impact of proposed changes can be assessed quicker and more accurately. With the information contained in the test management file, it is possible, for example, to indicate accurately the consequences of changing functional requirements or time lines.
- All the documents created by the testers during the project are structured and filed with cross-referencing, so that they are easily accessible to

everyone involved. In this way, no costly time is lost in searching, for example, for testware and associated information such as requirements and functional designs. Also, the relation between the various components of the testware is quickly apparent.

- The availability of the information in the file on the testing itself and the testing process makes communication with the parties involved much easier because of the standardised structure.
- At the end of a test project, the test manager can immediately transfer all the information to the organisation. Also, the completed test projects can be compared more easily.

It is advisable to document all the essential decisions and their arguments so that the project history can be reconstructed and justified. Thus, the test manager can demonstrate at any given moment why a particular decision was made and what the input for this decision was.

The test manager keeps all the information that is important to the test project in the test management file. The outcome of the quick scan (as discussed in Chapter 3) will be the first document to be filed in the test management file. This chapter will discuss the set-up of the test management file. The following chapters will discuss the activities of the test manager according to the Test Management Model. The documents that will derive from these activities will subsequently be added to the test management file.

4.1 Layout of the Test Management File

Figure 4.1 shows how the test management file can be structured.

The labelling in this directory structure corresponds to that of the Test Management Model. All the project members – such as the testers, developers and other stakeholders – are given access to the test management file. The activities they may carry out depend on the authorisation the test manager has allocated to them. Testers may read and write to all of the directories, while the developers, for example, are given a view-only authorisation.

The documentation standard of the organisation can influence the structure of the file. Depending on the scope and complexity of a test project, all of the directories, or only a number of them, are filled. However, the file should at the very least contain the following documents:

- The documents that describe the set-up of the test project, such as the test strategy, the test organisation and the test plan.
- The products of the test analysis. These are required for executing the tests.
- The issues found during execution of the tests.

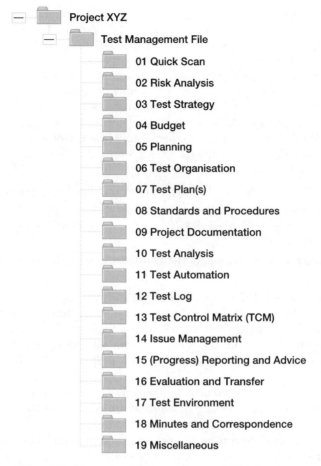

Fig. 4.1. Example of test management file structure

Test analysis, test execution and issue management are necessary for the test manager to be able to set up the reporting. These reports contain information that the client will use in making an informed decision at the end of the test project regarding the implementation of the information system.

The documents relating to the Test Management Model are discussed in depth in the relevant chapters of this book. This chapter describes the contents of the other directories, namely: test plan, standards and procedures, project documentation, test analysis, test automation, test log, test environment, minutes and correspondence, and "miscellaneous".

4.2 Test Plan

The test plan is a vital document in every test project. In this plan the results of the test project preparations are explained and documented. This is supplemented with subjects such as the assumptions and preconditions specific to the project. The test plan therefore is an important management and communication tool for the test manager and the testers. It is very suitable for use in communication with the client and the stakeholders, and also for communication within the test team (Black, 1999).

The IEEE 829-1998 standard for software test documentation defines a test plan as follows:

A document describing the scope, approach, resources, and schedule of intended testing activities. It identifies test items, the features to be tested, the testing tasks, who will do each task, and any risks requiring contingency planning.

This definition also clearly shows the relationship with the Test Management Model:

- The scope of what does and does not fall within the test project is determined in the test strategy and is based on the defined product risks and associated priorities.
- The approach describes the basis of testing within an organisation; in the test management approach, this is Risk & Requirement Based Testing (RRBT).
- The resources and equipment required for the test project are specified in the budget and planning of the test project and in the choices made during the setting up of the test organisation.
- The risk analysis results in project and product risks. The test manager and the stakeholders use the product risks and their priorities to determine what falls within the test and what does not.

The test plan must fit within the total project plan, which provides a description of all the parts of the project, from writing the business case via system developing and testing to the moment when the information system goes live.

Although all of the activities are important in themselves, the main aim is the final product, e.g. the test strategy or the budget. The reasoning behind the development of these final products is not included in the test plan, but in the activity-specific folders of the test management file. Only the final results are included in the test plan.

> Within a bank it is usual to use three kinds of budgeting techniques for setting up the budget of an extensive test project. One of these is the standard (a model based on metrics), and two other methods are a form of checking. The total budget formulation covers over 10 pages, including all the assumptions. The formulation of the budget is not of interest to readers

of the test plan, who are more concerned with the result and its influence on the total test project. Furthermore, a comprehensive description only distorts the picture of the test plan for the reader (the client, for example). Adjustment would be required in two places in the event of change (if, for example, some functionalities require more extensive testing when the risks are assigned a higher priority than was first estimated): in the budget itself and in the test plan. This not only is a duplication of work, but also means that the chance of inconsistencies arising is great. At worst, it is even possible that the management of the project is negatively influenced by faulty information.

4.2.1 Project Test Plan and Detailed Test Plans

As test manager, you set up test plans on one or more levels, depending on the scope of the test project. The highest level is the project test plan. If a test project consists of several test levels, the project test plan describes the total test project with all the various test levels. The detailed test plans are derived from this, each one providing an elaboration of one test level. Figure 4.2 shows the relationship between the project plan, the project test plan and the detailed test plans.

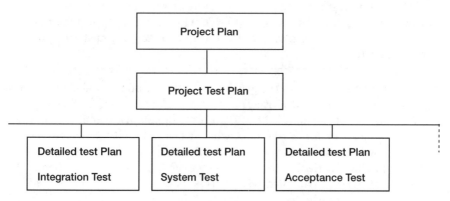

Fig. 4.2. Relationships between project plan, project test plan and detailed test plans

If a distinction is made between a project test plan and a detailed test plan, the test manager must of course first decide on the content of both plans. In outline, the subjects within the plans will correspond, but the level of detail will vary. The test manager can choose to include information on the test project along general lines and the reasonably stable information in the project test plan. All the information expected to be specific to the test levels can be included in the detailed test plans.

Within a chemical corporation, one fixed procedure is selected for issue management in projects involving software supplied by third parties, partly owing to the specified method of communication with the external supplier. This procedure is established in a project test plan, because it applies to every test level. A reference to this procedure may suffice, because it is embedded and standard in all projects.

The project test plan will also describe how the transfer between test levels must be arranged. This concerns both the logical and the physical transfer. The logical transfer is given form by creating entry criteria and exit criteria per test level (when may a test level be started and what must be done to confirm that a test level is completed?). The physical form describes how an information system should be released and distributed between environments (Janssen, 2002).

The primary function of the department of sales and customer service within a credit card company involves selling credit cards and processing complaints. The specific aim of the system test within this organisation is to demonstrate accurate functionality in the information system. Since sales (and sales administration) support is completely automated and complaints administration is partly processed manually, the exit criteria set for the system test state that all the test cases relating to risks in the area of sales must be met to the agreed level, while complaints administration does not have to work perfectly for the system to be transferred to the subsequent test level.

It must be made clear in the project test plan for all the stakeholders how the test levels relate to each other.

The purpose of the detailed test plan is to communicate detailed information on a single test level: who does what, when, and with which resources? This plan will therefore mainly be consulted and approved by the people working on that particular test level to see what is expected of them. The test manager uses the detailed test plans to be able to direct test levels.

When setting up the test plans, the template supplied in Appendix E can be used. To comply with the IEEE 829 standard at least all headings have to appear in the test plan even if they are not used. The latter has to be explained. The test manager can also add items to the test plan if need be.

4.3 Standards and Procedures

During the quick scan, the test manager makes an inventory of the standards the organisation uses, if any. The standards that are relevant to the test project should be included in the test management file, or there should be a reference to the location of the procedures concerned. Everyone involved in the test project is then able to read the content of a standard or find a template. Standards, procedures and templates developed in the test project also belong in the file. The test manager can of course choose to include the standards and procedures in the relevant directories as well. For example, the guideline on analysis may be included in the test analysis directory.

4.4 Project Documentation

In setting up the test project and tests, the test manager and the testers will use documentation that has been created by others.

The project test plan, for example, must cohere with the plan of the developers. The test manager will include their plan in the test management file, or a reference to where this document can be found.

In setting up the tests, the testers make use of functional and technical designs and user manuals. They will appreciate these being included in the test management file.

The same goes for Service Level Agreements (SLAs) concluded with suppliers, as well as the conditions that, for example, the support and maintenance department applies to the tests.

4.5 Test Analysis and Test Automation

The test management file also contains products that the testers deliver for test analysis and test automation, both products of the operational testing process, e.g. test cases and test scenarios. The test analysis directory contains the products of the various tests described in the test strategy. Subdirectories can be included within this directory – for the various test levels, for example.

It is also advisable to apply standards to the test analysis, so that all testers set up and document the analysis in the same manner. Which standards have to be used depends on the testing method used. This standard must be set up in such a way that the testers can give a clear indication of which tests cover which risks.

The test automation directory will contain the scripts produced by the test automation developers.

4.6 Test Log

In the course of a test project, all kinds of situations can arise which influence the test project. A couple of simple examples are as follows:

- A tester has been allocated 8 hours per week of support from a domain expert. The expert is going to help him set up the correct test cases. However, the expert keeps getting other tasks with higher priority. The tester is unable to verify whether he is on the right track, resulting in a delay to the test project;
- The testers require a new version of an information system. However, they are unable to install it themselves, and require the help of the technical support department. Because of problems in the production environment, the installation is postponed. Again, the test project is delayed.

The test manager most definitely needs this information for his reporting on the test project. Both he and the testers can indicate in a log situations that result in deviations from the original plan. An example of a test log is given in Table 4.1.

Table 4.1. Example of a test log

No.	Date/time	Name	Description
1	10 Dec. 2002 13:52	Iris	Training of junior testers postponed owing to budget freeze. Around 8 more hours per week lost on on-the-job training and reviews to guarantee quality
2	12 Dec. 2002 08:10	Bob	Issue tool still not installed after 3 weeks. Busy 6 hours per week with checking status of the various issues, ensuring that no duplicated issues are reported and examining whether all the relevant information is included with an issue as agreed with the developers

The logged information must be as specific as possible. When it becomes clear that the problem of the domain expert's unavailability has resulted in a delay of 20 hours, say, it must be entered immediately in the log. The test manager uses the information in the test log in creating his reports. If a situation has a significant effect on the test project, he writes an exception report (see Chapter 8, Section 8.2).

Table 4.1 provides an example of the minimum amount of information that the test manager wants to see in a test log. He knows when the comment was made and who made it. If any explanation is required, he can immediately ask what the actual cause of the problem was.

4.7 Test Environment

The test plan must contain a general description of the test environment. In the test environment directory of the test management file, the test manager can include documents that provide a detailed description of the test environment and the reasons for selecting it.

Possibly the test manager prefers to test all the test levels in a production-like environment. For considerations of cost, he may propose, for example, to the client that only the users acceptance test should be tested in a production-like environment, since setting up such an environment is expensive. The other tests are carried out in a laboratory environment. It is important to make such a choice explicit, since it can have unexpected effects and incur additional risks.

A bank decided to set up a test environment for a web application without including the firewall that was in production. The reason for this was the time it would take to set up and install the firewall. Also, it was assumed that the firewall would have no influence on the functionality of the application, and that the firewall would have a negligible effect on the performance of the application.

In the test environment, the application operated according to expectations: the functionality was accurate and the performance was just within the set requirements. However, when the application was put into production, the performance was dramatically poorer than in the test environment. The influence of the firewall appeared to have been grossly underestimated. The results were drastic: only half of the required daily transactions could be processed, resulting in an immediate drop in turnover, overloading of the call centres and customers using other channels that had not been reckoned with. With the implementation of the following release, a firewall was placed in the test environment.

There is also room in this directory for supplementary information on the various test environments – for example, SLAs on maintenance of the test environment and installation procedures relating to a particular version of the software. Release notes, too, can be included in this directory. To be able to retrieve all this information easily, the directory will have to be further subdivided into test environments and, within those, versions.

4.8 Minutes and Correspondence

Decisions are made during meetings of the test team, measures are set in motion and activities declared completed. All this information is laid down in minutes in the usual way. If these minutes are immediately stored in the directory, all the parties who have access to it are able to stay abreast of outstanding points, decisions, etc.

Minutes of meetings attended by the test manager also belong here: for example, those in which agreements with the developers are made, or consultations with the client on progress. This information is also important to the testers, giving them a general perspective on where the test project stands.

Even e-mails and other correspondence containing important information to the test project qualify for inclusion in this directory.

4.9 Miscellaneous

The test manager can use this category to store all other information relating to the test project. For example, memos on the organisation within which the project takes place, and the holiday plans of project members.

4.10 Management of Documents in the Test Management File

Unfortunately, it happens all too often that a test plan is created at the beginning of a test project, and never adjusted thereafter to take into account changed circumstances. The test strategy, too, often meets the same fate. In those cases, neither the test plan nor the test strategy is of any help to the test manager in managing the test project. It also happens that, when changes have to be made, testers carry them out directly with the existing testware. As a consequence, questions concerning a previous version of the testware can no longer be answered. If the project unexpectedly has to go back to an earlier version of an information system, the relevant testware is no longer available.

Configuration management and version control are thus very important. The test manager should realise that a test project has three "categories" of products and documents, each requiring a different form of management:

- The first category can be summarised under "Standards & Procedures" and "Project Documentation". The test manager must ensure that he always has access to the latest version of these documents, but does not have to manage them himself. Other departments create these documents and are responsible for version control and configuration management. Naturally, the test manager will need to apply version control to the documents his own test project adds to these directories, such as a developed template.
- There are also products and documents that are created within the test project and which must conform to the version of the information system under test. For example, the testware developed by the testers. In this way, it is always clear which testware is used to test a particular version of an information system.
- The third and final category covers the products and documents which are developed within the test project and which are subject to version

control and configuration management, but do not have to conform to versions of other products or documents. Examples of these are the test plan and the test strategy.

Obviously, no management is required by the test manager for the documents in the first category. But it is important that the test manager ensures that he participates in the team responsible for assessing the changes, so that he is aware of them at an early stage and can immediately indicate the consequences from the testing perspective.

In setting up version control and configuration management for products and documents developed within the test project, the steps defined for software configuration management (SCM) (Bersoff, 1984) may be followed, which are:

- identifying the components;
- setting up a management procedure;
- carrying out an audit;
- status accounting.

In the following subsections, we will look closer at these steps and the use of tools in the management of the test management file.

4.10.1 Identifying the Components

First of all, the test manager establishes which products and documents will come under version control and configuration management. These products and documents should also be labelled. It must be clear to everyone which version of the products and documents is concerned and whether there is a relationship with any other products or documents, and, if so, which one. A second version of a detailed test plan for a system test of information system XYZ would be given the following label, for example: "System test plan XYZ 1.1.2". This indicates that this version of the detailed test plan follows on from version 1.1 of the project test plan and that it concerns version 2 of the detailed test plan.

4.10.2 Setting Up a Management Procedure

If the testware has to be changed, this must be done in accordance with a fixed procedure. It must be clear at any given moment which tester has which product on hand. Only with the help of a sound procedure can the test manager and the testers maintain an overview of the status of the various components.

The administrative procedure for the components that have to conform to an information system must constitute a part of the procedure that the developers use for software management. The versions will therefore keep pace with each other. As for the other components, the rule is applied that the person who is about to introduce a change does so in accordance with the fixed procedure that has been agreed within the test team. Of course, the procedure itself is also established in the test management file in the standards and procedures directory.

4.10.3 Carrying Out an Audit

Certainly in the case of long-running test projects, an audit will take place regularly, so that it is clear whether version control and configuration management are proceeding according to the rules. This audit can be carried out by an outside party, or by a group within the organisation.

The audit consists of two parts: verification and validation. With verification, the auditor examines whether changes have been implemented as agreed. Validation should show that the correct documents are in use. Are these the documents that the test manager needs for his reports? Are all the documents present that the testers need in developing the testware?

4.10.4 Status Accounting

To maintain a good overview of the status of the various components, agreement is necessary on the status information and the way in which a component is transferred from one phase to another.

If a product or a document needs to be changed, the following details must be available:

- The date on which a document is handled.
- The date on which the change is ready according to the planning.
- Who has taken responsibility for implementing the change.
- Which changes are required.
- Which changes in the release concerned have actually been implemented.
- The status of the document.
- The actual date on which the changes were implemented.

This creates a good overview of the status of all the products and documents. If changes have been in process for a very long time, it is known whom to approach concerning progress.

An auditor can use this information to see whether changes have been implemented as agreed.

4.10.5 Use of Tools in Managing the Test Management File

In a large project involving a considerable number of documents, managing all this information manually can become a time-consuming affair. There are many tools available on the market that are well suited for automating document management. With the aid of these tools, documents can be secured against simultaneous updates. Version numbers are automatically generated, and it is recorded who has processed the document and who is currently processing it.

The test manager can also seek congruence with the tools that the developers use for version control and configuration management of the software components and the system documentation. This saves a lot of time: the test manager does not have to set up version control and configuration management himself and the organisation is familiar with usage of the tool.

4.11 Conclusion

To keep a test project manageable, good document management is absolutely essential. The test management file plays a central role in this. The test plan within this is a collection of end products of other activities that are carried out during the preparation phase of the test project. The test plan also contains a description of how the test execution phase of the test project is set up. The first activity in the preparation phase is the subject of the following chapter, and that is risk analysis and the development of a test strategy.

5

Risk Analysis and Test Strategy

"It isn't possible to test everything!" This is something that must be understood by all the stakeholders. But how do you decide what has to be tested? A good test strategy is necessary because, otherwise, time and effort will not be focused in the best possible way and it will be hard to communicate the status of the covered product risks. In the test strategy, the test manager indicates what is to be tested, but also what is not to be tested. This is decided on the basis of the product risks and the priority assigned to them, assessed by the product risk analysis. To implement the test strategy, allowance has to be made within the test project for the project risks: which elements might obstruct the progress of the test project?

A test strategy sets out the steps that the test manager will take to allow optimum use of the testing capacity and control or cover the product risks within the time available and with the resources available, before the system goes into production. It is a document that is *not* project documentation but more like system documentation, because it can be reused in following projects concerning the information system to be tested. This is why we advocate a separate test strategy and test plan (which is part of the project documentation and will be discarded after completion of the project). Both items are part of the test management file.

The focus of the test strategy is not only the identification of the product risks, but also the assignment of priorities for those product risks. Once priorities are set, the test effort can be focused on those parts of the information system that present the biggest product risks to the organisation. Since the test strategy clearly defines what exactly is to be tested and to what extent, and furthermore contains the acceptance criteria, it forms the basis of the budget and planning of the test project.

The test strategy must not only be developed and approved, but also executed, and therefore a number of preconditions must be met. This is not always the case in practice. Every test manager is occasionally faced with a test environment that is not set up in time, or specifications that are not available or only partly so. Such issues form risks that can influence the execution of the test project. It is therefore important that these project risks are recognised, and measures designed to limit and manage them.

5.1 The Test Project Risk Analysis

In Chapter 2, Section 2.1, it was indicated that there is a distinction between project risks and product risks. In this chapter, the project risks are discussed first, and the product risks are examined during the explanation of the test strategy.

There are many factors that can affect the success of the test project. For example, the test environment can present problems in the course of the project, so that a part of the test has to be carried out anew. Or the documentation may be incomplete, leading to incorrect predictions of test results. Every disturbance of the project can have an influence on the available time, the budget or the quality of the information system.

In order to avoid such disturbances as much as possible, the test plan must also contain various preconditions that must be complied with if the test is to progress according to the agreed plan. For example:

- The development team should deliver the information system the day before the planned start of the test execution, so that the test team can perform an intake of the test object (the so-called "intake test", see Section 7.4).
- A user manual should accompany the delivery of the information system.
- The technical support department should be available throughout the duration of the test project when the test data have to be stored in the database.

To restrict influence on the available time, budget and desired quality, it must be known prior to commencement of the test project which project risks may affect the project. It must also be clear which measures will limit or remove those risks.

Risk management is indispensable, if the risks are to be kept under control. In Chapter 2, Section 2.2, there was a general description of the steps within risk management. In this Section, we will go deeper into these steps in relation to a test project.

Risk management concerning the project risks consists of the following steps:

1. Identifying the project risks.
2. Classifying and assessing the project risks.
3. Allocating the project risks.
4. Monitoring the project risks and the action to be undertaken.

Steps 1 to 3 are expanded on in this chapter. Step 4 is a continuous activity on the part of the test manager during the execution of the test project.

5.1.1 Identifying the Project Risks

In identifying the project risks, the aim is to discover what the risks are and where they are to be found. To do this, the project and the environment must first be analysed. It is possible to employ the methods already mentioned for identifying product risks: past experience, a checklist and a workshop (see also Chapter 2, Section 2.2.2). In this Section, one more method is added: interviewing the experts and asking them what they see as the biggest project risks.

Appendix G contains a checklist to aid in identifying project risks.

The project risks can be both internal (within the test team) and external (in the test project environment). As a test manager, you can manage internal project risks; the external risks produce dependencies and are more difficult to control. The external risks must be monitored, meaning that measures must be defined and set out for the management of risks, approaches made to persons responsible and escalation procedures initiated. The test manager also needs to work with the project manager to try and establish contingency plans for the project risks.

In Table 5.1, a number of examples are given of internal and external project risks that regularly arise in test exercises.

Table 5.1. Examples of internal and external project risks

Internal project risks	External project risks
Resources	Availability of requirements
Availability of (test) knowledge and skills	Changes to the requirements
Available training	Has the previous test level been carried out according to plan?
Use of test techniques	Fixed, tight, delivery date
Availability of test environment	Planning by the developers
Existence of back-up/restore facilities	Quality awareness within
Use of test tools	the organisation

The internal and external project risks mentioned can have their origins in the ICT domain or the business side of the organisation.

5.1.2 Classifying and Assessing the Project Risks

In classifying and assessing the project risks, the aim is to define the weight of a risk: the degree of influence the particular risk has on the test project.

So far, little attention has been paid to the set-up of requirement management. Furthermore, the risk of many changes being made to the requirements is known to be high. Without requirement management, it is difficult to stay abreast of the changes and the impact of those changes on the test. This is therefore a high-priority risk that must be managed.

One of the stakeholders also mentioned the risk of the relative inexperience of the test team. However, this project risk is of less importance as there is a comprehensive training plan and the testers can quickly be brought up to the required level.

It is advisable to use the method of relative priority for the project risks. In consultation with project management, the importance of the various project risks is decided: high, medium or low (see Chapter 2, Section 2.2.3).

Thereafter, the "trigger" must be found: how does the tester know that a specific project risk really is materialising? A risk usually creeps in slowly and unannounced!

During this step the test manager can begin to think ahead to measures that can be taken to prevent or minimise the impact of project risks. Things to bear in mind are:

- *Prevention.* The measure must ensure that the project risk does not materialise. This type of measure is often chosen if the importance of the project risk is very high.
- *Reduction.* If the project risk materialises, contingency measures ensure that it has a minimum impact. Here, too, the focus is on the most important project risks.
- *Correction.* A measure of this type ensures that the planned activities commence as soon as the risk actually materialises. The chance of the risk materialising is small and the solution can be realised quickly.
- *Acceptance.* No action required. With this, the project team assumes that the chance of the risk materialising is so small and the required preventive measures so expensive that the project risk and its consequences are accepted as they are.
- *Transfer.* The risk is passed to a third party (by means of a guarantee or penalty clause, for example). This type of measure makes sense if the chance of the risk materialising is high, while internal measures would not be sufficiently effective.

5.1.3 Allocating the Project Risks

The established risks form a way of communication with the client, project management and the test team. Identifying the risks alone is not sufficient. The measures that the test manager has established should be entrusted to a person or group, who must ensure that the defined measures are carried out within a previously defined time, in the event of the project risk materialising. However, the test manager remains responsible for monitoring the risks. He will therefore have to check regularly whether the measures have been carried out, whether any risks can be written off, and whether additional project risks are presented, perhaps as a result of changed circumstances.

The test manager specifies here the escalation paths that are available to him if those responsible fail to take the correct measures, or fail to take them in time, or if the risk materialises despite the preventive measures that have been taken.

The test manager can summarise the information relating to this step and the previous steps within the project risk management in a risk log table (see Table 5.2). This provides a good overview and a clear means of communicating with the client and stakeholders.

Table 5.2. Overview of project risks

No.	Project risk	Impact	Trigger	Owner	Counter-measure	Status
1	Availability of test environment	High	Intake test unsuccessful	Technical mainte-nance	Establish agreements in an SLA	Under supervision

The risk log table contains a short summary of the project risk (what can happen), what the impact on the project is when the risk materialises, what triggers the occurrence of the risk and which countermeasures can be taken to assure the risk does not materialise or, if it does, how to minimise the impact. It also states who is the owner of the risk (who supervises if the risk actually materialises) and what the current status of the risk and the countermeasures is.

The test manager refers to this table during the project discussions. He should not attempt to discuss all of the project risks, as this can be quite a list! He should restrict himself to the project risks of the highest importance. The risk log, of course, is not frozen during the project: the test manager evaluates the project risks frequently. This means that project risks may become obsolete and will be removed from the risk log, while other project risks may appear which have to be managed at a later stage of the project.

Appendix G contains a checklist for project risks, which are divided into the following categories:

1. The organisation within which the test project and test team are found.
2. The test project.
3. The test team.
4. The selected testing method.
5. The information system.
6. The test environment(s) necessary for carrying out the various tests.
7. Specific risks that accompany automatic testing.

The test manager includes the list of relevant project risks in the test plan, as described in Chapter 4, Section 4.2.

He will also be concerned with product risks, which are a part of the test strategy and which we will now discuss.

5.2 Developing the Test Strategy

The test strategy is the basis of communication with the client, the stakeholders and the test team. It details which product risks are to be covered by testing and the extent to which this will be done. It also indicates what does not form part of the test project, which requires input from the stakeholders. Eventually, the test strategy forms the starting point for the test team for the set-up and execution of the test. In developing a test strategy, the test manager goes through seven steps. Briefly, these are:

Step 1: *Identify the stakeholders* – Who are the parties concerned with the test project, and who is responsible for accepting the various tests and should therefore be involved in the test project?

Step 2: *Carry out the test product risk analysis* – What are the risks that are directly related to the information system to be tested? What should be tested in order to meet the requirements and wishes of the stakeholders?

Step 3: *Link the relevant product risks to the quality attributes* – Which product risks can be linked to which quality attributes?

Step 4: *Determine the test levels* – What are the best ways of testing the various product risks and quality attributes?

Step 5: *Determine the acceptance criteria* – At which point do the client and stakeholders find the quality of an information system acceptable? What acceptance criteria do they apply?

Step 6: *Set up the cluster matrix* – Group the tests so that logical clusters are created within which exactly one stakeholder is taking responsibility.

Step 7: *Set up the cluster cards* – A cluster card contains all the information that is of importance to the testers in setting up the tests for a specific cluster. The test strategy is clearly set out in the cards, showing all the parties involved. The cluster cards form the end of the test strategy and the beginning of the test analysis.

We will describe the steps in detail below.

5.2.1 Step 1: Identify the Stakeholders

Stakeholders are employees or departments that have a direct interest in the correct operation of an information system. When identifying the stakeholders, bear in mind not only the "real" end users (those making use of the information system), but also the developers who appreciate maintainable software, the marketing department that wants to have a marketable product, or the internal security department that does not wish information to be accessible to outsiders. In having an interest, they also have a responsibility. It is to the stakeholders for whom the test project is being carried out.

In identifying the stakeholders, the test manager may overlook departments, as their interest is not always immediately obvious. During initial discussions with the client, the most visible stakeholders will be identified. The organisation chart included in the quick scan (see Chapter 3), for example, can serve as a basis. In order to trace the missing stakeholders, the test manager asks himself the following question: who (which department) has a (direct) interest in (parts of) the information system?

> On Monday morning, the postman delivers a box containing a new suit, which the recipient had wanted to wear the previous Saturday evening. He complains to the postman and makes him take the suit back. The cause of the late delivery lies with the clothing company that sent the package too late. Although the postman gets the blame, the stakeholder is the clothing company. Only the clothing company has a direct interest.

Amongst others, the stakeholders are to be found in one of the following categories:

- *End users.* The employees who will have to work with the information system, such as the accounts receivable assistant who is presented with a new invoicing system, or the worker on a conveyor belt in an automobile factory that has a new paint installation. One information system can simultaneously involve end users from various departments. A stock control system involves, for example, end users in both the warehouse and the purchasing department. The end users can also have group representation, e.g. in the testing of a web application. Various types of end users can access this application: a business user or a private individual, with one wanting to perform a transaction and the other merely seeking information. A number of people from all of these groups may then be asked to participate in a group that represents the whole.
- *Marketing departments.* The marketing department must be able to sell the company's products; for example, with the aid of an information system with set parameters that enable the marketing department to offer a new product quickly to customers. This often happens in banks and insurance companies. Think of the many forms of mortgages. If a new product can be offered before the competition does so, it can deliver a large market share in a short time.
- *Support departments.* The helpdesk, which has to provide support to the users of the information system, for example.

- *System Develpement departments.* Without the software development department, there is no information system and without the infrastructure department there is no platform on which to run it. The maintenance department guarantees the future quality of the information system.
- *Internal security.* Every information system must be secure. Access via the network must be controlled and in the case of many (business-critical) applications, a comprehensive audit trail and detailed record of everything that happens in the application is required. In some organisations, this department also monitors the use of standards and procedures.

For the record, stakeholders are not limited to these categories; it is important to perform a broad stakeholder analysis at the start of the project.

An overview of these possible stakeholders is provided in Figure 5.1.

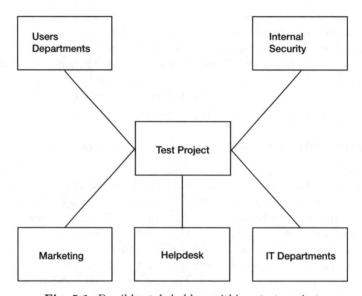

Fig. 5.1. Possible stakeholders within a test project

5.2.2 Step 2: Carry Out the Test Product Risk Analysis

How does the test manager, together with the stakeholders, determine which product risks are important?

An insurance company does a lot of business through brokers. It is therefore important that the software that the company supplies to the brokers works correctly, otherwise offers will be put together that do no comply with the terms and conditions of the insurance company. For example, the premiums may be calculated as too high or too low, whereby "too high" often means that the broker will recommend another insurance company to his customer, and "too low" means a reduction in the insurance company's turnover and profits. Many product risks in this example therefore relate to the accuracy of the calculations in the information system.

The steps within risk management are the same for product risks as for project risks: identification, analysis, allocation and monitoring.

In Section 2.2.2 and in Section 5.1.1, a number of methods are mentioned for identifying risks. The test manager can also employ these methods to identify the product risks.

In parallel with the checklist of project risks, Appendix B includes a sample checklist of product risks, which the test manager can use as a basis. The checklist is divided into categories of possible stakeholders, making it easier for the test manager to communicate with the stakeholders.

There is another method the test manager can use: posing "what if" questions, based on process descriptions. In this way, it is possible to reveal a product risk that has a bearing on the functioning of the information system, and the place it has in the operation of the organisation. "What if" questions can also work very effectively if they are not based on a process description. For example, questions such as "What if the loading time of the pages on our website is longer than 7 seconds?" reflecting on efficiency, or, "What if amendments to the information system for the introduction of new products cannot be carried out and tested within 3 days?" reflecting on maintainability.

The test manager gets the best result with this method if it is presented in the form of a structured walkthrough. The advantage of a structured walkthrough is that the writer expands on his document and the listeners can put questions to him. There is an opportunity for discussion during the session, and this provides everyone with a clear picture of the product risks that an organisation runs. Each time the writer has explained a process description, or part of one, the listeners pose "what if" questions.

The test manager will have to think hard about whom he invites to the structured walkthrough. A group that consists solely of people with a lot of background knowledge of the process will mainly ask "what if" questions of a routine nature, based on their past experience of the process. For that reason, it is good to include people who have little or no experience of the process, for they will look at it from a completely open perspective and can come up with surprising questions.

The sales department of a kitchen supplier contacts a customer wishing to purchase a product, indicates the types of products available, orders the materials and resources required to put the product together, and a transport company subsequently delivers the product to the customer. Finally, the customer receives an invoice.

"What if" questions could be:

- What if the wrong product is delivered to a customer?
- What if the product is delivered to the wrong address?
- What if an order is cancelled and the company is left with the ordered materials and resources?

It is possible that during a structured walkthrough, certain potential product risks will fall away, as the participants are satisfied with the answer. Other questions remain unanswered or inadequately answered, leading to actual product risks. If the test manager has also used a checklist, the product risks arising from the structured walkthrough are added to it. Obviously, general product risks can be replaced by specific product risks, and in this way the checklist is increasingly tailored.

The product risks are also given priorities. These are determined in accordance with the MoSCoW rules, as described in Chapter 2, Section 2.2.3.

5.2.3 Step 3: Link the Relevant Product Risks to the Quality Attributes

The product risks found are now linked to the quality attributes. In this way, it is easier to communicate concerning the risks with the client and the stakeholders.

The test manager is advised here to use a standard list of quality attributes, supplied in the form of the ISO9126 standard (ISO, 2001) and consisting of the following attributes and subattributes as shown in Figure 5.2.

These quality attributes are further explained in Appendix D.

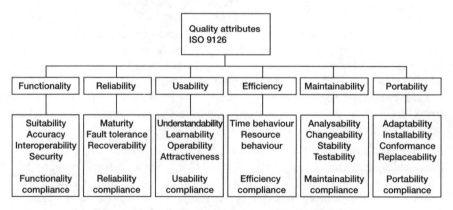

Fig. 5.2. Quality attributes according to ISO9126

The test manager, together with the stakeholders, may choose to link the product risks to the quality attributes alone, or to use the subattributes for this as well.

A travel agency uses the BookSafe flight reservation system. When a customer enquires at the desk, the information system first shows various possibilities, enabling the customer to seek the most suitable flight. A few of the BookSafe possibilities are as follows: the customer can choose between, for example, a direct flight or one with one or more stopovers. The system also offers another possibility: a search for the fastest route from A to B, or for the cheapest route. Naturally, the customer may also indicate which class he prefers, and this will influence the final price. Before the booking is confirmed, the assistant can print out a complete overview for verification. The actual reservation can then be made.

The test manager has agreed with the stakeholders that product risks will be established and linked only to the highest level of attributes from ISO9126.

Below are a few examples of the product risks the stakeholders have identified:

I   In calculating the fastest route, the system does not use the correct times. This could lead to a customer missing his connecting flight.

II   In calculating the price, no allowance is made for the requested class. This leads to the customer being over- or undercharged.

III   It takes too long before a full overview appears on the screen before printing. Someone else may have booked the flight in the meantime.

IV   The system is in use all day by all of the travel agencies in the company. If BookSafe goes down, none of the offices is able to book flights.

V   Changes are made regularly to the system. There is no time to provide additional training to every sales assistant in every agency following each change.

VI   The wrong flight numbers are used, with the result that the customer is booked onto the wrong flights.

Together with the stakeholders, the test manager links these product risks to the quality attributes, giving the overviews as shown in Tables 5.3 and 5.4.

Table 5.3. Risks/quality attributes grouped according to quality attribute

Risk	Quality attribute
I	Functionality
II	Functionality
III	Efficiency
IV	Reliability
V	Usability
VI	Functionality

Table 5.4. Risks/quality attributes grouped according to quality attribute

Quality attribute	Risks
Functionality	I, II, VI
Reliability	IV
Usability	V
Efficiency	III
Maintainability	No risks defined
Portability	No risks defined

An overview of this kind can also help the test manager and the stakeholders to identify new product risks. The test manager sees that a product risk has not been identified for every quality attribute: portability and maintainability do not appear on the overview. He can now check again with the stakeholders whether this is correct, or whether there will be other product risks to come. After discussion, the stakeholders indicate that maintainability is not their concern. Portability, however, has got them thinking. Not all of the travel agencies work from the same platform, and it is therefore very important that BookSafe works on various platforms. This product risk and quality attribute are subsequently added.

In this way, the instruments for identifying the product risks and the quality attributes complement each other very well. The stakeholders are provided with as comprehensive an overview as possible of the total number of product risks (see Figure 5.3).

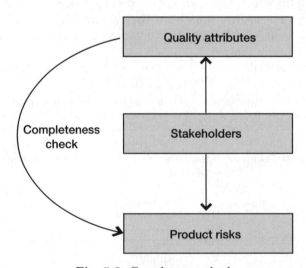

Fig. 5.3. Completeness check

The test manager can now allocate the various quality attributes to the stakeholders identified in Step 1. These stakeholders all have an interest in the information system, expressed in the quality attributes and the associated product risks (see Figure 5.4).

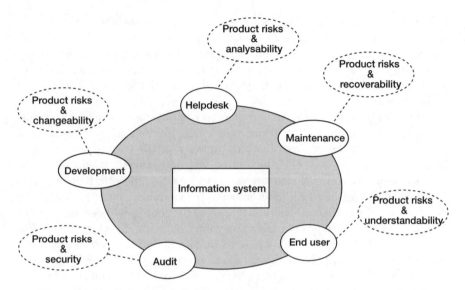

Fig. 5.4. Example of stakeholders and their associated quality attributes

Following Step 3, the test manager has an overview of product risks grouped by quality attribute and knows which stakeholder is responsible for which attribute/product risk.

Occasionally, several stakeholders will feel responsible for the same quality attribute. Two captains on the same ship will seldom agree on the course to be followed, therefore distinction must be sought in their requirements so that in the end only one stakeholder is responsible per quality attribute or set of product risks. If only the highest level quality attributes are being used, a distinction can perhaps be made by using the sub-attributes. Of course, this still means that stakeholders will have to communicate with each other on what they will be testing, so that both sides know what aspects are covered. The test manager has an important role to play in this, making sure that all product risks are covered by the stakeholders and not too much overlap exists.

Another possibility is to investigate whether a distinction can be made in the acceptance criteria per quality attribute. If, for example, it concerns security, the requirements for setting up the firewall might fall under technical support, and requirements for restricting access by means of password/user ID under the department responsible for internal security. The test manager can assign the quality attribute "security" to both stakeholders, but with a clear indication of who is responsible for which acceptance criteria.

5.2.4 Step 4: Determine the Test Levels

It is useful to divide the total test project into various levels to enable testing of the requirements which cover the recognised product risks. Good coordination is also extremely important as regards who will test which part of the information system. A much used phasing method is the V model (Daich et al., 1994). With this, the various phases of testing integrate with the levels of development.

In Step 6, the product risks and quality attributes are arranged in a cluster matrix according to the various test levels. However, situations are also possible whereby the product risks and quality attributes are not arranged by test level but by test environment or test department. It can be established in consultation with the stakeholders which quality attribute the test team can best test in which environment. For example, accuracy – whereby it is examined whether all the mortgage calculations have been carried out correctly – can be tested in a laboratory environment. However, if a performance test is to be carried out, e.g. to examine whether the overview of items is displayed within 10 seconds, a complete production-like environment may be required. If such an environment cannot be found, this could then become a project risk.

It is also possible for different departments to be responsible for specific test levels. For example, the tests relating to installation of the information system can be carried out by the maintenance department and the system test by the development department. The product risks and quality attributes are then assigned to these departments.

In the following part of this chapter, we will assume a breakdown by test level.

5.2.5 Step 5: Determine the Acceptance Criteria

The stakeholders indicate which criteria the information system has to comply with for them to accept it. When the previously set criteria are complied with, the test team is finished with testing and the product risks have been reduced to a level acceptable to the stakeholders.

An acceptance criterion can be set up in many ways. It is important, however, that agreements on this are clear, specific and measurable.[1] An acceptance criterion indicating that a test is accepted when the test team has finished testing is neither specific nor measurable, for when is the test team finished with testing? Is it when all the lines of program code have

---

[1] When setting acceptance criteria, think along the lines of the SMART rules: Specific, Measurable, Achievable, Realistic and Timely.

received at least one hit; is it when the time has run out, or when all the previously defined tests have been carried out to completion?

The acceptance criteria can be divided into two groups:

- The amount of testing carried out.
- The quality of the information system.

Examples of acceptance criteria indicating how much testing has been carried out are:

- 98% of all the lines of code must have received at least one hit;
- the branch coverage must be 80%;
- 75% of all the "Must test" conditions must have been carried out.

As regards the acceptance of the quality of the system, the following are examples of criteria:

- The MTBF (Mean Time Between Failures) is two issues per day maximum.
- No further issues with the highest priority should be found for the course of one whole week.
- The MTTR (Mean Time to Repair) falls within the requirement set for maintainability.

Since, in Step 2 of setting up the test strategy, the product risks have been given a priority, the acceptance criteria for the quality of the information system can also be linked with these. All the product risks have a priority between "Must test" and "Won't test". On the basis of this, the stakeholders can now indicate what their "comfort level" is: with what percentage of executed and approved tests are they in agreement? In this way, it is possible to set specific and measurable acceptance criteria for the test project. The test manager can therefore decide objectively when the test project is finished. This puts a clear aim in sight, since the right amount of testing is being carried out – not too little and not too much (resulting in the optimum use of budget and time resources).

An insurance company has surveyed and prioritised all its product risks. In establishing the "comfort level" and as agreed between the stakeholders and the test team, the percentages as shown in Table 5.5 are to be maintained within the project.

Table 5.5. Stakeholders' "comfort level"

Priority category	Percentage of tests carried out and approved
Must test	100
Should test	80
Could test	30
Won't test	Rarely tested

These are the minimum percentages for acceptance of the information system and are, for course, linked to the product risks, so stakeholders will know which product risks are covered in the "Should test", "Could test", etc., and are traceable. The "Won't test" category is merely mentioned in the test set, but not processed in test cases. Since the insurance company considers the risks so low, no effort will be expended in testing this part.

Example Test Strategy

In setting up the test strategy, the test manager must chart the stakeholders, the product risks and the test levels. The following case describes the first steps in setting up a test strategy for replacing back office systems with the ERP systems of SAP.

This case describes an implementation project in which the support of a good test strategy is of great importance. The company in this example is one of the larger nationally operating cleaning companies, which we will call CLEAN. CLEAN has a head office and various branch offices, and the project consists of the replacement of the whole of the back office with SAP. The original back office is a collection of various systems. SAP will be used to support the whole of the primary business process. This will cover such things as employee timekeeping through to invoicing the hours worked. It will also include payroll calculations, expenses, stock control, sales, etc., processed via this system.

With the implementation of the new back office system, the following problem areas arise:

- There are many stakeholders, all with their own interests.
- The new SAP system has to be installed centrally, while most of the users' current work is decentralised.
- SAP is a completely new system for the organisation, and until now it has worked only with custom applications.
- The organisation is familiar with testing, but not with structured testing.

The implementation of a completely new back office system is of extreme importance. The company therefore decided that testing was the approach to make sure all risks would be covered. The first step taken towards this is developing a test strategy. In view of the strict deadline that has been set for the project, it is not possible to test everything, so choices have to be made, and these are set out in the test strategy. The development up of the test strategy is done by closely studying the available documentation (project plan, decisions, etc.), as well as by talking to the employees, project members, managers, developers, etc. In setting up the test strategy, the following points, among others, are important:

1. It must be established who the stakeholders are.
2. A product risk analysis must be carried out.
3. The product risks must be linked to the quality attributes.
4. It must be decided which tests are to be carried out.

1. Stakeholders. At CLEAN, various stakeholders are defined. With an eye on the time factor, it is decided to divide them into four main groups: users (both head office and regional), developers, the client and managers.

2. Product risk analysis. After the stakeholders have been identified, a product risk analysis is carried out. This produces the following risks, among others:

- The system will be installed centrally, but the biggest user group is decentralised.
- There are a number of very important interfaces present, which are of crucial importance to the system.
- The SAP module to be implemented has not yet been used much by other organisations, therefore standard SAP faults may still be present.

It must be indicated in the test strategy which product risks are to be covered and which not. This will depend on their priority, as assigned by the stakeholders. The test manager also states which stakeholder is responsible for a product risk. This results in Table 5.6.

Table 5.6. Relationships between product risks, priorities and stakeholders

Product risk	Priority	Stakeholder
System being installed centrally, but biggest user group is decentralised	Should test	Users
Number of very important interfaces that are of crucial importance to the system	Must test	Managers
SAP module being implemented not yet used much by other organisations; standard SAP faults possibly present	Must test	Users

3. Linking product risks to quality attributes. By means of interviews with stakeholders, the test manager has examined which quality attributes belong to the various product risks. This is demonstrated in Table 5.7.

The other quality attributes on the ISO9126 list do not concern CLEAN and therefore it is stated that they will not be tested in order to set expectations on what is going to be tested.

Table 5.7. Linking product risks to quality attributes

Product risk	Priority	Stakeholder	Quality attribute
System being installed centrally, but biggest user group is decentralised	Should test	Users	Resource utilisation
Number of very important interfaces that are of crucial importance to the system	Must test	Managers	Interoperability
SAP module being implemented not yet used much by other organisations; standard SAP faults possibly present	Must test	Users	Maturity

4. Test levels. The TDI (Time-Driven Implementation) method was developed by LogicaCMG for implementing SAP. From the model shown in Figure 5.5, it can be seen how testing within CLEAN relates to the SAP TDI phasing.

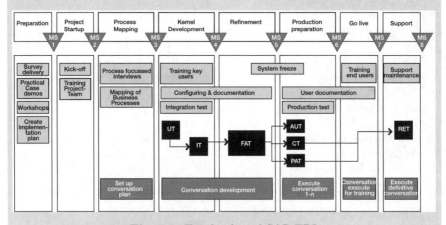

Fig. 5.5. Test levels and SAP TDI

The next steps within the CLEAN test project will be the setting up of the cluster matrix and the cluster cards.

CLEAN experiences the setting up of the test strategy positively. The stakeholders are involved, and clearly indicate what they consider to be important. CLEAN therefore expects that SAP will be implemented on time and that no significant flaws will surface afterwards.

5.2.6 Step 6: Set Up the Cluster Matrix

A cluster matrix is an overview in which the test manager brings together the stakeholders, the quality attributes or set of product risks and the test levels. He can then see at one glance who is responsible for which quality attributes and within which test level they are being tested.

In many cases, it is obvious which quality attribute can be linked to which test level. The quality attribute "usability" clearly forms part of a user acceptance test. For other quality attributes, the choice is not so restricted, making categorisation much more difficult. The quality attribute "suitability" can crop up in a system test, but also in an acceptance test. In a system test, more emphasis will be placed on the presence of certain functions, whereas in an acceptance test the "suitability" emphasis will be more on the clarity and accuracy of the functions in daily use.

Help texts are written for the customer administration system of a telecom operator. Various aspects of this are spread over a variety of test levels. For example, the system test will test whether the correct text is displayed (if an incorrect customer code is entered, the system should display the appropriate error message on the screen). In the user acceptance test, the help texts themselves will also be tested, for understandability of the text. For example, a developer will be satisfied when the message "E03" is displayed denoting an incorrect customer code, while the user will be better served with: "The customer code does not exist; please enter code A, B or C."

In order to determine which test level can best be used to test the quality attribute, the test manager can ask himself the following questions:

- Which quality attribute is best tested in which test level?
- Are there quality attributes that can simultaneously be tested within a particular test level?
- What preconditions apply in carrying out the test for each individual quality attribute?

"Understandability" can be tested in various test levels wherever there is a user interface, e.g. in the system test, and also during an acceptance test. If "understandability" is to be tested at the same time as "completeness of the information system as a whole", then a more or less complete system is already required at this stage. Testing within an acceptance test would appear to be advisable here. With a system test, it can happen that only parts of a system are offered for testing, as opposed to the whole information system.

The cost aspect can also play a big role in the allocation of quality attributes to test levels. The earlier a fault is located, the cheaper it is to correct. The test manager will therefore also have an eye on the earliest stage at which certain quality attribute aspects can be tested.

The test manager sets out the stakeholders, test levels and quality attributes against each other in a cluster matrix, as shown in Figure 5.6.

Quality attributes and the associated product risks are now linked to stakeholders and to test levels. The cluster matrix is an important aid in maintaining a clear overall view, and in grouping the quality attributes in a logical manner. It produces a preliminary division into logical clusters.

Stakeholder	End user	Marketing	Support departments	IT departments	Internal security
Unit test					
Integration test					
System test				Recoverability Analysability Changeability	Accuracy
User Acceptance test	Suitability Under-standability Learnability			Interoperability	
Production Acceptance test				Time behaviour	

Fig. 5.6. Example of a cluster matrix

5.2.7 Step 7: Set Up the Cluster Cards

The cluster matrix contains the first (main) clusters. This should provide an indication of the relative importance of the various quality attributes within this first division of clusters. The level of importance is determined by the number and severity of the product risks. If all the quality attributes in a single cell have the same level of importance, then one cell can constitute one cluster card. If the importance level of one of the quality attributes differs, the test manager adds more cluster cards. This is necessary because in arranging the tests, they will automatically take the same priority as the cluster. If, in the example of the cluster matrix in Figure 5.6, the importance level of the quality attributes "suitability", "understandability" and "learnability" is a "Must test", then one cluster card is sufficient. However, if "learnability" has an importance level of "Should test", the test manager makes separate cluster cards.

Bear in mind that these are not by definition the final clusters. It just provides a preliminary breakdown. During the test preparation, the test analysts can make a more detailed cluster breakdown. They will also develop the cluster card in such a way that it is traceable to the test conditions and test cases.

The information on a cluster card is divided into the following categories:

- key information;
- assignment;
- execution;
- result.

Figure 5.7 shows the breakdown of a cluster card.

The information in the cluster cards enables the test manager to monitor the test project. The testing effort is distributed over the various clusters, corresponding to the level of importance indicated by the stakeholders. The information in the cluster card guides the tester in his preparations for the relevant test.

At this stage of the test process, it is not a major problem if the test manager cannot yet fill in all the fields of the cluster card. While the blank spaces remain, they form project risks that must be monitored, or activities to be carried out.

The test strategy can now be seen in outline, but the cluster cards may still be subject to change. We know which quality attributes are important and which product risks and requirements are being covered by testing. It is also known which stakeholders are involved with which quality attribute and therefore (partly) who is responsible for further completion of the details in the cluster cards. The test strategy should now be approved by the stakeholders.

During the course of the test preparation and execution, the test manager will have to consult continually with the relevant stakeholders concerning the completion of details on the various cluster cards. Changes or additions to the cards are documented during the processing of the relevant cluster. In this way, the test manager is not obliged to supply a new test strategy each time.

The changes in the cluster cards do not always concern the blank fields, but can also be triggered by changes to the requirements and/or the product risks. These changes can of course have implications for the cluster cards, the tests to be carried out and, consequently, the planning. This means that the test manager must check regularly that the content of the cluster cards reflects the real situation.

The cluster cards provide the test manager with an overview, but also form a touchstone for coordination within the organisation. In order to get the stakeholders as involved as possible in the test project, it is advisable to have the cluster cards formally approved by them. In this way, the cluster cards constitute little "contracts" with the stakeholders for the tests being carried out on their behalf. The stakeholders can determine whether their interests are sufficiently covered by the content of the cluster cards. However, allowances should be made for what is usually done within the organisation. An organisation that wants nothing to do with strict contracts will not respond positively to signing a range of cluster cards. In such a case, the test strategy and the individual cluster cards should at least form a means of communication, so that all stakeholders are mindful of the tasks and responsibilities that the test manager expects of them.

KEY INFORMATION	
Cluster name	Logical cluster name
Information system	System name and version
Test level	Within which test level will this cluster be included?
Test department	Which department will test this cluster?
Stakeholder	Who has an interest in, and responsibility for, the correct working of this cluster?
ASSIGNMENT	
Product risk(s)	Which product risks could materialise if this cluster is not processed, or if faults appear in this part during production?
Requirement(s)	Which requirements are linked to the product risks covered in this cluster? Testing should prove that the requirements are met (proven added value to the organisation)
Priority	What is the importance of this cluster? The importance corresponds to the priority of the product risks, and influences the sequence in which the test manager will plan the clusters. Use the MoSCoW classification: "Must test", "Should test", "Could test" and "Won't test". By inferring the cluster importance from the product risks and their importance, we avoid having the stakeholders allocate the highest importance to all the clusters
Quality attribute	Which quality attributes underlie this cluster?
Source material	A reference should be included here to the requirements, the documentation and interview reports upon which the design of the test will be based

Fig. 5.7. A cluster card

EXECUTION	
Test approach	How will the test be executed? The test manager's choice depends on, among other things, the test level, the quality attribute to be tested, the available source material, the organisation and the circumstances A further breakdown is created into: • Static testing: auditing and reviewing • Dynamic testing: testing the application itself The test techniques which will be used: decision tables, entity life cycle, data flow analysis, etc. A choice is also made here between manual or automated test execution
Test environment	What test environment is required to be able to carry out the tests described? Both the technical environment and the necessary resources and time-dependent aspects should be mentioned here Which test data will be used?
RESULT	
Acceptance criteria	At which point will the stakeholder accept the cluster? Ensure that the acceptance criteria are set out explicitly. All the parties involved should know in advance when the test project will be complete

Fig. 5.7. (continued)

When the test manager transfers the test management file to the maintenance organisation, it should contain the latest version of the cluster cards. The maintenance department can then use these if a new release of the information system has to be tested (see Chapter 13).

Appendix H provides a test strategy template, containing all the steps described above and a cluster card.

5.3 Conclusion

The test strategy provides the test manager with information on the stakeholders, the product risks, the quality attributes and the test levels that are important to the test project. On the basis of this information, the test manager can estimate the budget. In the following chapters, we will show how that is done, and how this budget carries through into the planning stage.

6

Estimation

It is not easy to draw up an estimate at the very beginning of a test project, since only general information is available at that time. There is a choice of methods for estimating, suited to a variety of situations. A number of these methods are discussed in this chapter. The estimate can be refined by keeping metrics during test projects. This provides figures about the history that can be used in subsequent test projects. We will describe how these can be transferred into a model and produce more accurate estimates.

An estimate defines the boundaries in time and money within which the testing is allowed to operate. However, it is no simple matter to draw up a good estimate that is not too tight, but also not too liberal. An estimate that is too tight creates unrealistic expectations, while one that is too liberal leaves too much opportunity for carrying out extra, unplanned tasks.

The success of a test project estimation depends partly on variables that are almost impossible to influence. For example:

- the date on which the developers deliver the information system to the testers;
- the testability of the information system;
- the competence of the developers and any suppliers involved;
- the number of issues the testers will find;
- the time required by the developers to solve the issues;
- the availability of the test environment;
- the stability of the test environment.

The consequences of all these variables are not immediately apparent. It is therefore useful to split the estimate over three phases: test project preparation, test project execution and test project closure.

The *preparation* of the test project is less dependent on different parties. It is therefore reasonably easy to estimate the time required for this phase. It involves such matters as the execution and setting up of:

- a quick scan;
- a risk analysis and a test strategy;
- a budget and a plan;
- a test plan;
- a test organisation, including meeting and reporting structure.

Estimating the *execution* of the test project is much more difficult. The testers are set to work designing the tests, and executing them. They find issues that are related to the information system to be tested, but also to the developed testware. It is not possible to estimate in advance how many issues will be found, the significance of these, or how much time the developers require to bring the system up to the required level of quality. And issues can result in more test runs than were expected.

The degree to which the *closure* of the test project influences the estimate depends on what follows from the project: will a maintenance department take over the maintenance of the testware, or does testware maintenance form part of the test project? If maintenance has to be set up within the test project, this means extra work and therefore extra budget requirements.

When drawing up an estimate, three elements are important: the size of the information system to be tested, the test strategy and the productivity.

The size of the information system to be tested is determined by the number of functions within the system and their complexity. The number of interfaces has a bearing on the size. Are there various interfaces for a single functionality, or is there a single interface that coordinates various functionalities? Have the various functionalities been developed along the same lines? Which of these functions and which non-functional requirements (such as efficiency and maintainability) fall within the test project, and to what extent they are tested, has already been described in *the test strategy*. All of this information forms input for the estimate. To be able to estimate the number of hours required to design and execute all the tests in the test strategy, information is required on productivity. The *productivity* is made up of two factors. The first is the productivity of the testers; this depends on their knowledge and skills. The second factor is the productivity of the environment; for example, the availability of test tools and the quality of the information system to be tested.

At a petrochemical company, an assumption was made in drawing up an estimate that an "average" test analyst can design 50 test cases per week. The test set to be set up covers 200 test cases, and it is therefore assumed that the capacity requirement is 4 weeks. At an internal cost price of € 2,000 per week, the required budget is € 8,000. However, it turns out that the test analyst who has to carry out this activity is a junior who is less productive than the average tester and develops only 25 test cases per week. His internal cost price is somewhat lower, i.e. € 1,500 per week. On those grounds, the estimated effective time is 8 weeks with a budget of € 12,000.

All of this information forms the basis for drawing up the test estimate. Drawing up an estimate creates the possibility of indicating from a sound basis how much time and money are necessary for testing. So knowing this the test manager must not simply accept the budget that the client makes available.

To be able to continue using the estimate as a means of communication and management, the budget and how it is spent are monitored and maintained, and this takes time. In the event of an important change in the project or significant change in the conditions, the test manager must be able to see the impact of this on the original estimate.

The more information that becomes available during the test project, the more precise the estimate becomes, provided that the information is translated into consequences for the estimate. For example, if it becomes clear that certain functionalities are much more complex than was supposed, or that the quality of the information system under test does not comply with the conditions set.

One can also make use of data collected in the past. These data are the metrics. A metric is a quantified representation of a process or product attribute that characterises the product or process item to be measured. Metrics can help refine the original estimate.

In this chapter, we will first discuss how to draw up an estimate in general terms, and then describe seven methods of estimating. In Section 6.2.9, all the methods will be summarised with their advantages and disadvantages. Finally, in Section 6.3 we explain factors that can influence the estimate.

6.1 Estimating

The drawing up of an estimate is surrounded by uncertainty.[1] That is why it is practical to do it in a series of steps:

- Drawing up a draft version of the estimate.
- Reviewing and refining the draft version.
- Creating involvement.

6.1.1 Drawing Up a Draft Version of the Estimate

First of all, the purpose of the estimate will be defined. Why is the estimate being made? What decisions will the client make based on the estimate? How precise must the estimate be to give enough confidence? The answer to these

---

[1] PRINCE2 (20.7 Estimating (PL4)) provides an overview of the most important points of focus, hints and tips in drawing up estimates. Many of these are included in this chapter.

questions determines the effort the test manager must make in creating the estimate. It is wasteful, for example, to invest a lot of time and energy in creating an estimate which is only required to provide a general indication of the budget that is necessary for converting a manual test to an automated version. It is different if the client wants, for example, a very precise estimate for the execution of a performance test. In that case, as much detailed information as possible must be collected.

With this purpose in mind, the test manager must gauge the time required to draw up the estimate. At this point, he must decide on the method to use. There is a suitable method for every situation. Depending on the chosen method, it will take more or less time to draw up an estimate, for each method requires a different level of information. The length of time required to collect the information will also vary. To manage the uncertainty factor, it is recommended to use two methods side by side. Eventually it will be necessary to crosscheck the results of these two methods and, together with the stakeholders, arrive at one final estimate.

The next step is to draw up the actual estimate. To do this, the test manager needs to collect the information required. An important source of information is past experience, and there are probably evaluations of previous projects available within the organisation. Details can be obtained from these evaluations that will be an aid to drawing up the estimate for the current test project. Naturally, the test strategy is an indispensable source of input as well, for it establishes the extent to which testing must be carried out to cover the stated product risks. The test manager interprets the information: what is the quality of the information and how complete is it? Perhaps a number of assumptions have to be made and preconditions set for points on which there is insufficient or no information.

The test manager must record these assumptions and preconditions with the estimate. This applies as well to all the other information used in drawing up the estimate. He can then explain the estimate at any given moment. He can use the information to support the estimate, while the assumptions and preconditions can be used for later adjustments.

When drawing up the estimate, the test manager must always keep the stakeholders of the project informed of the chosen method for estimating, the assumptions and preconditions that are being used, as well as all the other information used and decisions made. The stakeholders can then react if, for example, questionable assumptions have been made.

6.1.2 Reviewing and Refining the Draft Version

To create support for the estimate, those directly involved, such as the client and the testers, must be invited to review and refine it. The aim is, of course, to arrive collectively at a single estimate that everyone considers feasible considering the risks to be addressed.

6.1.3 Creating Involvement

The estimate may now be further distributed to a wider group of interested parties, such as all of the stakeholders who were identified in the test strategy. Everyone is then aware of the estimate for the test project, the assumptions and the preconditions.

If the organisation has a formal structure, it will be necessary to have the estimate approved by the client (assuming that he is the one who pays for the project). In an informal organisation, verbal approval will be sufficient. If the estimate turns out to differ from the expectations of the client and the stakeholders, a discussion can be initiated concerning the scope and depth of the test.

6.2 Methods of Estimating

We will discuss the following methods:

- top-down estimating;
- bottom-up estimating;
- using percentages;
- estimation by analogy;
- expert judgement;
- fixed budget;
- the Test Effort Estimation Model (TEEM).

This is not an exhaustive list of estimating methods, but it contains those that can be used in most common situations. For a description of further methods, we refer the reader to Collard (2003) and Boehm (1981).

Following the explanation of each estimating method, in Section 6.2.9 we provide a summary of the methods discussed. This consists of a description of the situation in which a test manager can best use a particular method or combination of methods, and a summation of the strengths and weaknesses.

6.2.1 Top-Down Estimating

With top-down estimating, the test project is viewed from a high level (Figure 6.1). The scope and depth of the test are described in the test strategy. The test manager can compare this information with the scope and depth of a similar project. The information pertaining to the earlier project regarding duration, participants and equipment can be copied to the current project. In this way, the total costs of the project can be estimated in one go. These costs can later be distributed over the various phases and products which make up the test project. But regular checks must be made to see how closely the first project corresponds with the current project: for example, regarding complexity, the expected number of test cases and the number of

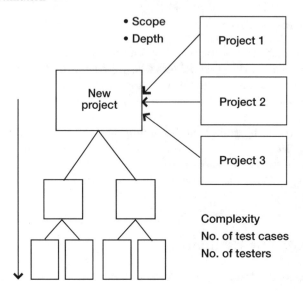

Fig. 6.1. Drawing up a top-down estimate

testers. Assumptions must be made concerning variations between the current project and the one being used for comparison. These assumptions must be recorded in the test management file, so that it can be shown later what the estimate was based upon.

This technique is suitable if there is little information available, such as at the start of a new development stage. The only information available then, for example, might be the goal of the test project, overall information on the requirements and a general plan of the development project. On the basis of these, an initial base estimate can be created.

The big advantage of this method is that the total test project is gauged at once, with all the activities it involves. The test manager therefore cannot forget to include any important items in the estimate, such as hours required for test management, reviewing and configuration management.

This method also has a number of weak points:

- Technically complex steps in the test project may be overlooked. For example, the introduction of new test tools that are not yet completely stable in this environment. Such issues can easily increase the total budget required.
- Testers are not involved in drawing up a top-down estimate, despite being the ones who can help in providing the most realistic estimate of hours required.

Using this method can only lead to an initial, rough estimate of a test project. This means that the test manager must plan to reconsider the estimate at certain points and adjust it if necessary.

6.2.2 Bottom-Up Estimating

Bottom-up estimating is based on detailed information. The tasks necessary per phase and product are described, based on a work breakdown structure (WBS). A WBS consists of a product hierarchy and an activity hierarchy. The product hierarchy indicates how the various components (modules, subsystems, routines, etc.) of the information system are linked, while the activity hierarchy indicates which activities must be carried out with particular components. By grouping the tasks in this way, a picture is created of the range of tasks that have to be carried out and their interdependencies (Figure 6.2). Subsequently, an estimate of the time required can be coupled to each individual task. Naturally, the people who will eventually carry out the tasks have an important say in this. This creates involvement in the test project, and makes for a more realistic estimate.

The times estimated for the various tasks are added together and so form the total estimate of the test project.

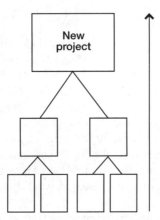

Fig. 6.2. Drawing up a bottom-up estimate

Since this method requires detailed information to be successful, it is less suitable at the beginning of most test projects (this certainly applies to new builds) – even less so, since sufficient information must be available at the time of estimating to determine the individual tasks. However, adjusting the estimate during the project is always possible with this technique, with more detailed information being available.

If certain tasks are not yet identifiable, this can lead to too tight an estimate of the total test project. To avoid this, allowances can be made for it in the estimate by leaving a certain margin.

This method is based on the individual tasks. It can be determined reasonably accurately whether a task is complex, and therefore whether it will take a relatively long or short time to complete. This will reflect in an accurate estimate, as opposed to the top-down method of estimating.

This method has its weak points, however:

- It takes a fair bit of time to draw up a bottom-up estimate. This is not necessarily bad, but the time must be planned for.
- There is a risk that certain overall tasks will be overlooked, such as test management, reviewing and configuration management. A checklist is a good solution here.

6.2.3 Using Percentages

Another way of drawing up an estimate is to use a percentage. Possibilities include using a "market percentage" or a percentage based on experience within the test manager's organisation. We discuss the two possibilities below.

Using a "Market Percentage"

Many organisations seek a way of estimating that will produce the best results for them. When an organisation first starts to consider drawing up a reliable test estimate, it may use a standard "market percentage". For example, the black-box testing for a test project takes 30–40% of the total budget for setting up the functional design up to and including putting an information system into production. Of this, 10–15% is required for the preparation and execution of a system test, and 20–25% for the preparation and execution of an acceptance test (Pol et al., 1998). In the absence of past figures, these percentages form a good starting point. As soon as an organisation starts to build up its own figures from experience, it can adjust the percentages to suit its own situation.

The advantage of a market percentage is that an organisation can quickly put an estimate together the moment the required information is available.

Disadvantages are:

- The test manager must have the right information available. The test estimate is only as accurate as the estimates made concerning the other phases. If a wrong estimate is made of the number of hours required to set up a functional design up to and including when it is put into production, the test estimate will also be wrong.
- Evaluation of the estimate can take a fairly long time. It also takes time to investigate variations. And if the variations are clear, an adjusted percentage must be maintained in the subsequent phases.
- The above-mentioned percentages are based on the testing of systems developed according to a linear development method. With development according to an iterative method, the cycles of development and testing

are shorter. The percentages cannot simply be adopted. The pace of development is faster. Using a fixed percentage thus means that less time is estimated for testing. This is wrong: the functionality being built is the same, or perhaps even more complex. The maturity of the development language also plays a role here.

Example: Testing and Estimating in New Environments

"Faster, faster, faster". It's on everyone's lips. People want immediate access to information and to be able to work with it directly, too. Where it used to take weeks for a consumer to find a mortgage, it is now possible to find many mortgage providers, compare their offers and even to conclude a mortgage in the space of an evening – all without leaving the house, via the PC or the mobile telephone!

It doesn't need much explaining that the expectations of consumers have a direct impact on methods of system development. The speed with which applications are put on the market is considerable and the life cycle of a version of an application is increasingly reduced. Where one maintenance release every six months sufficed, in the current economy life cycles are measured in weeks, and sometimes even in days (e.g. popular websites). Among other things, this places heavy demands on the maintainability of the software produced.

Testing is perhaps the part of system development that is hit the worst by the new economy. Even less time than before; complex architectures that hardly anyone understands and that considerably reduce the testability; rushed marketing people who call for the product to get onto the market otherwise market share is lost – these are all matters confronting the testers. Although there are certainly technical variations within these new architectures in comparison with the traditional situation, the challenges for the testers lie mainly in the area of human activity. This particularly concerns the relationship between the tester and his client, and the tester's area of focus.

The Tester and the Client. One of the most difficult aspects of test management is estimating the time required for testing (the time spent effectively as well as the actual duration). There are few hard and fast rules in regular system development: in most organisations, nothing more than a classic decomposition and perhaps the execution of a function point analysis (IFPUG, 1999) are used, and they largely rely on past experience and the gut feeling of the project manager. In testing, it is often no different.

One method that is regularly used in budgeting for the test effort is the allocation of a fixed percentage of the development effort to the testing phase. This method can provide a reasonably reliable indication, provided that the percentage is supported by metrics and regular adjustment is made based on new metrics. To illustrate, if the development of a system takes 1,000 working days, applying an often-used percentage of 30% means the testing is estimated to take 300 days.

However, this percentage applies mainly to development in classic environments (COBOL, C) and classic development methods (Waterfall, SDM), in which sufficient experience has been built up. In new development environments, however, the development effort is increasingly decreasing (both as regards time spent productively and the duration). Does this mean that the test effort, too, will show a linear decrease? A lot of managers seem to think so!

This creates difficulty for the testers as they attempt to obtain a realistic budget and timetable. By introducing new tools/development environments, systems can be developed faster and, in line with the above relationship, less time and money is set aside for testing (with a direct relationship between development and testing time). But testers know that if a modern development environment is used, the time required for testing remains absolutely the same, or is even longer! This certainly applies in today's society, where everything is measured in "web time" and the life cycle of an information system is weeks, rather than years. The biggest challenge in testing lies therefore not in the technology, but in expectations: how can testers make it clear to line managers and project managers that the relationship between the development effort and the testing effort is not what it once was, and that it is even possible for more time to be required for testing than for development?

This is a challenge that many test managers are faced with, and it is a challenge that largely lies in the area of communication. The testers must convince the managers responsible. With the aid of the arguments below, a discussion can be started in which the time that is spent on testing is no longer the standard percentage of the development effort, but may be based on other factors:

- The new technology is often unfamiliar, so it is more difficult to determine the test effort (certainly in the first phases of the test cycle);
- The functionality of a system remains the same. For a web-based developed system that has the same functionality as a COBOL application, the same test preparation, test analysis and test execution are necessary. Therefore, it does not follow that the reduced development time leads to lower testing effort in these testing activities;
- More emphasis may be placed on quality attributes besides "functionality". With web applications, for example, more emphasis is placed on "efficiency" and "security". Although in the traditional systems some attention was given to quality attributes other than functionality, it was usually insufficient. Since the clients for this system were usually internal, the consequences of not testing the other quality attributes often remained behind closed doors. This is no longer the case, and the slow response of a web page means that

customers are lost. There are more aspects to be tested, therefore requiring more time;

- Integration aspects play an important role in the information systems of today. Architectures are being extended with, for example, web applications that do not immediately fit into the present architecture. Much attention therefore has to be paid to the integration of current systems and traditional systems. The only way to be certain of the correct operation of this is by carrying out external integration tests (two systems communicating with each other) or chain tests (tracking a business process from beginning to end with the help of test scenarios);

- The development tools that are used and the architecture are complex and in many cases not transparent (to the developer as well as to the manager and the tester). It is therefore of great importance that the testability of an information system is given an important place during development. For if a system is not testable (where are data recorded and how are they approached, how do we test interfaces with third parties, etc.?), there is an increased risk of incorrect operation during and after implementation. Testers are in the best position to work on this.

Another factor that plays a role in the relationship between the client and the tester lies in the area of the test strategy. This is established in consultation with business, testers and other interested parties (stakeholders). As regards web, mobile and other channels that are to be addressed, there is often insufficient clarity in organisations on the place of these new distribution channels within company operations. If it is new and trendy, it must be used. Through a lack of clear vision, it is an almost impossible task to determine which areas the test strategy should emphasise. This is reinforced by the fact that due to a lack of vision, there is often no available documentation. Instead of using the traditional test techniques, the testers are required to develop new techniques to help the client arrive at a test strategy. This can be done, among other ways, by organising workshops, in which the parts to be tested are prioritised and in which the test strategy is refined. A method for realising this is Joint Testware Development (JTD^{TM}). Within the concept of JTD, the basis is not formed by documentation but by expertise and the knowledge of the experts present (CMG, 2001).

Using Percentages Based on Long Experience

Organisations, which for many years have been using the same technique and the same method of working, can usually indicate quickly the time required for testing. When many changes have been made over time, a large amount of testing has been carried out and the documentation has been kept up to date, then the developers, the testers, and everyone else know what has to be done. Furthermore, the testers are able to use available testware. This makes it possible to calculate quickly how much time will be involved in the preparation and execution of the test. This applies to organisations, for example, which for many years have been using information systems that run on mainframes.

6.2.4 Estimation by Analogy

In estimating a new test project, the reasoning can be based on analogies taken from previous, comparable projects. Time and costs are based, therefore, on past experiences.

An international organisation with headquarters in The Netherlands is rolling out a new information system for invoicing. It is doing this for every country in which it has branches. The test manager and the test team, based in The Netherlands, are responsible for testing each version of the system in each country.

The first rollout of the new system took place in Johannesburg. The test manager knows that the preparation and execution of testing for Johannesburg cost € 275,000 (see Figure 6.3). The next country on the list is The Netherlands. Owing to country-specific settings, the complete test must be carried out again. Because of variations in the functional design between Johannesburg and The Netherlands, 5% of the information system must be adapted. The changes consist of amendments to the existing information system; there is no new development. This means changing 5% of the test: the test manager adds € 13,750 to the initial estimate. However, the test team in The Netherlands is already familiar with the system and the various functionalities. The testers can make use of (part of) the testware of Johannesburg. The test manager decides that he can deduct 40% from the estimate, since the testers in The Netherlands are more experienced. Naturally, he must justify the percentages used on the basis of the variations in functional designs and the knowledge and experience of the test teams. This gives him an idea of the number of tests that can be reused. This eventually results in a budget of € 178,750.

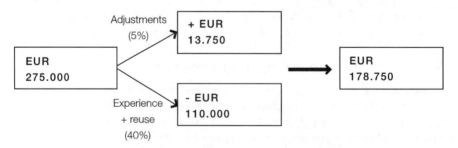

Fig. 6.3. Example of estimating based on analogy

To be able to use this technique, the test manager must have details from comparable projects and insight into the structure of the actual costs and number of hours involved in these projects. He must be in a position to gauge the differences and the consequences of these differences for the estimate relating to the current project.

6.2.5 Expert Judgement

A complex environment can be a good reason to involve experts.

Someone with a lot of knowledge and experience with an information system that has to be amended can obviously provide an important contribution to the estimation of the test project. Explorers are in a position to assess the consequences of variations from past projects, such as the consequences of using a new technology, new interfaces or of relationships with new information systems. Such an expert can determine whether knowledge and experience is required that is not available in the organisation at that point. In this way, the expert is a help in drawing up a reliable estimate. Experts can be recruited from within the organisation, or from outside if the project is entirely new to the organisation.

There is an immediate weakness here. An expert may be prejudiced; he may have a particular point of view that he may allow to exert a significant influence on the estimate. Perhaps he has a lot of experience with one particular part of the information system, whereby the emphasis in the estimate is placed on this part. It is possible that he has overestimated the knowledge level of the other employees: "Everyone knows that!" The judgement of an expert is therefore not always completely objective. Also the expert may not necessarily be the resource undertaking the work, so more time must be allowed for.

To obtain more objectivity, it is better to involve several experts. This creates a balance between the various subjective expert opinions. There are various ways of doing this:

- The test manager can combine the experts' individual results and take the average. This is the quickest method.
- The test manager can organise a brainstorming session and invite various experts. In this way, he gets not only an arbitrary average, but a well-considered basis for the estimate. The success of this session depends very much on the moderator. If he is not assertive enough, one of the stronger communicators among the experts may perhaps "force" his opinion on the others. A wrong choice of experts can influence the final estimate.
- The test manager can use the Delphi technique (Helmer, 1966). With this, he asks each expert to submit their anonymous estimate on paper. He collects the results and places them into a single document. This document is distributed again among the experts, with the request that

they again submit their comments and estimate anonymously. These steps are repeated until all of the experts largely come to a consensus. In this way, an objective estimate is obtained. The experts have all given their opinion: various views are represented in the estimate. Others have not influenced the experts in that they do not know who submitted which estimate and viewpoint. The advantage of this method is that the estimate does not get bogged down in endless discussions. Naturally, the accuracy of the estimate here depends on which experts are invited.

6.2.6 Fixed Budget

It sometimes happens that the client has already fixed the budget. The client indicates, for example, that the testing may take X number of hours or must stay within a Y budget, and that the final date is also fixed.

A test manager cannot and must not simply agree to this. He could get his fingers badly burned during the test project. At the start of the project, for example, it is not yet known:

- what all the requirements are;
- which functionality is and is not established;
- when the developers will deliver the information system to the testers;
- how many testers are available.

If the client gives a fixed budget, there are two possibilities:

- Make an estimate based on the client's goals and compare it with the one given.
- Calculate backwards from the given budget.

With either option, the product risks must of course be discussed. If the test activities do not fit within the fixed budget, this will have consequences for the goals and agreements of the test strategy.

We discuss both possibilities below.

Determining the Necessary Budget Based on the Goals and Comparing This with the Given Budget

When the results of the quick scan are approved, there is agreement on the goals and the results to be delivered. The test levels and depth of testing are agreed in the test strategy. On the basis of this information, an initial estimate can be drawn up by means of one of the previously mentioned methods. The result must then be compared with the budget given by the client.

If the results are fairly similar, there is no problem. But it is possible, of course, that they differ considerably. In practice, it often happens that the given budget is too tight to achieve the goals of the test project. The test manager must discuss the differences with the client; the client has the final decision on what is to happen. There are five possible responses:

- The client decides to adjust the goals and the associated results; in view of the current possibilities, the goals were perhaps too ambitious initially. Perhaps the client wants to rearrange the test project so that one test level is examined, rather than several levels.
- The client and the test manager together with the stakeholders determine what may be changed regards to the extent of testing. This must remain acceptable.
- The client makes more hours and a bigger budget available. If the client and the stakeholders wish to keep to the test strategy drawn up, this will have to be the solution.
- The client may tell the test manager that he will have to "make do" and carry out all the testing activities within the given timetable. He must then clearly communicate the consequences of that decision to the client and the stakeholders. In this way, no false expectations are encouraged, or accusations made in retrospect.
- The client decides to stop the test project. The testing requirements obviously do not fit within the budget that the client is able to provide at this time.

Calculating Backwards from a Given Budget

The test manager can, of course, approach the fixed budget from the other side (Figure 6.4). If it is known how many hours and what budget are available for testing, the possibilities are clear. Some realism is necessary: we are concerned with the most feasible options. Therefore with a reverse calculation, the number of test runs form the starting point, for testing is never complete after one test run; there are always issues which are handled and then require retesting, and this is a pattern that can repeat itself a number of times. The number of test runs necessary can be determined on the basis of experience with similar projects in the organisation.

The initial agreements made in the test strategy on scope and depth must be kept in mind. The starting date of testing can be calculated from the fixed final date – the date on which the developers must deliver to the test team the information system to be tested. On the basis of the number of hours and the budget, it can then be indicated what the possibilities are and where adjustment may be necessary with regard to the scope and depth of testing.

There must be communication with the client and stakeholders on this, as well.

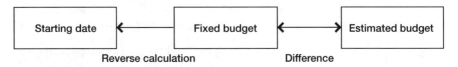

Fig. 6.4. Fixed budget

Apart from the fact that this method sets clear conditions for the test project, it gives something to go on. The client signals to the test manager the limits within which the test project must operate. Discussion with the client can continue on the basis of this.

6.2.7 Test Effort Estimation Model (TEEM)

An important reference point for a new project can be, as already said, found in the past. If the current project is comparable with the previous one, the estimate for the earlier project can be compared with the actual duration and costs. The combined details provide a better idea of the budget required for the current test project. Note, however, that there are many factors underlying the earlier budget that can change. A change in any of the factors will change the overall required budget.

It is possible to make the results of previous projects measurable. In this way, the test manager can justify how he came to a particular estimate. The model used in this is called the Test Effort Estimation Model (TEEM).

In consultation with the client, the test strategy is used to determine upon which information the estimate is to be based. The test strategy contains a summation of the quality attributes that are important in a particular test project. Different quality attributes may require different information on which to base the estimate. Suppose that these quality attributes are "functionality" and "efficiency". With "functionality" the number of test runs might be important in coming to an acceptable level of risk. Which level this is, is determined in the test strategy. The number of testers that get to work on the preparation and execution of the test does not make much difference in this case. On the other hand, this information *might be* of importance in the testing of efficiency. The point is to test the efficiency with the largest possible group of users,[2] with these users performing various operations simultaneously.

It is therefore important to register the information that will serve as a more accurate estimate for a subsequent project.[3] In the remainder of this book, we will speak of metrics.

By keeping a history of metrics, a picture is created of the progress of the estimate. There may be a discernible trend. This information can be used when drawing up an estimate.

However, a problem arises here. After completion of a test project, the project tasks do not carry on, at least not in this project form. Keeping

---

[2] In this example the performance test consists of demonstrating the workings of the information system with a large group of users carrying out all kinds of operations simultaneously. The time a particular transaction requires may also be tested. For example, one can test whether the generation of a report is completed within the specified 15 seconds. This last form is not what is meant here.

[3] An accepted method of determining which metrics are required for a (test) project is the goal–question–metric method. A description of this method is included in Appendix F.

metrics is therefore only useful for a subsequent project. The organisation within which the test project takes place must be convinced of the usefulness of metrics and determine which metrics are required for making a better estimate in the future. This means that the keeping of metrics must be embedded in the organisation, e.g. in a central test department.

As previously indicated, various quality attributes may require various metrics. The results of identical metrics will be different for these attributes. In testing functionality, practical experience demonstrates that there are more test cases per test condition than with a performance test. Therefore, to gain as good a perspective as possible on the estimate, the organisation must determine the metrics per quality attribute. Depending on the content of the test project, the organisation can use the metrics of the quality attributes that fall within the test project. By adding up the estimates of the various quality attributes, one arrives at a total estimate.

Naturally, in practice many metrics can be defined at various levels. We will explain in the following example which metrics may be kept.

In drawing up an estimate, simply put, there are two aspects: count something and multiply it by something. This outcome is an estimate. The test manager and the client determine a number of factors that are easy to count. Also the factors in the multiplication, the so-called calculation rules, must be easy to determine. Take factors that appear clear from the project. The calculation rules are the result of keeping metrics.

Test Effort Estimation Model: An Example

The test manager draws up the first estimate after he has recorded the results of the quick scan, the test plan and the test strategy. A number of "factors easy to count" are to be found in these documents. For example:

- the expected number of clusters;
- the expected number of test runs;
- the expected number of testers.

In this example, to test the quality attribute "functionality", we assume eight clusters, three test runs and five testers. These factors can be thought of as the variables of a formula. With these, the estimate fits with the chosen test approach and test strategy. The more the various activities surrounding the testing connect with each other, the more manageable the project will be.

Now the calculation rules. Below is a list of rules a test manager can use. These are like the constants of a formula. It must be emphasised again that this is just an example. It may be copied into practice, but it is advisable to determine first which metrics are important to the organisation.

- Average number of test conditions per cluster.
- Average number of test cases per test condition.

- Average percentage of issues (as against the number of test cases executed).
- Average design time per test condition (in hours).
- Average design time per cluster card (in hours).
- Average number of manually executed test cases per hour.
- Average follow-up time per issue: administration etc. (in hours).
- Average number of test cases for retesting after the first test run.
- Average time for setting up the test environment (in hours).
- Average waiting time for available test environment (per tester in hours).
- Average design time per test case (in hours).
- One FTE (Fulltime-Equivalent) in hours.
- Average time required for setting up a final report (in hours).
- Additional percentage for test management.

The first time a test manager records this information will be at the start of a new test project. In this example, the test project involves testing of the quality attribute "functionality". The test manager will assign values to these factors on the basis of experience, for he cannot yet make use of any other frame of reference (see Table 6.1).

Table 6.1. Example of calculation rules

R1	Average number of test conditions per cluster	20
R2	Average number of test cases per test condition	3
R3	Average percentage of issues (as against number of test cases executed)	5%
R4	Average design time per test condition (in hours)	0.5
R5	Average design time per cluster card (in hours)	2
R6	Average number of manually executed test cases per hour	6
R7	Average follow-up time per issue (in hours)	0.25
R8	Average percentage of test cases for retesting after first test run	25%
R9	Average time for setting up test environment (in hours)	80
R10	Average waiting time for available test environment (per tester in hours)	80
R11	Average design time per test case (in hours)	1
R12	One FTE expressed in hours	1,500
R13	Average time required for setting up final report (in hours)	40
R14	Additional percentage for test management	20%

We now come to the calculation as shown in Table 6.2. The column headed "Calculation" indicates the rules and factors used in the calculation. The factors counted are indicated in the grey area. Besides the factors already mentioned, there is also quality assurance. This is the time (in hours) that the test manager thinks will be necessary to carry out reviews and audits. He must gauge how many hours this will take.

Table 6.2. Example of calculated estimate using TEEM

			Calculation
B1	No. of clusters	8	
B2	No. of test runs	3	
B3	No. of testers	5	
B4	Test approach	16	B1 * R5
B5	Test design: test conditions	80	B1 * R1 * R4
B6	Test design: test cases	480	B1 * R1 * R2 * R11
B7	Test design: environment	80	R9
B8	Issue management	6	B1 * R1 * R2 * R3 * R7
B9	Test-obstructing issues	400	B3 * R10
B10	Test execution: first run	80	B6/R6
B11	Test execution: subsequent runs	40	B10 * (B2–1) * R8
B12	Test finishing: final report	40	R13
B13	Quality assurance	25	Estimation
B14	Gross total	1,247	Sum B4–B13
B15	Test management	249	
B16	Total	1,496	B16/R12
B17	FTE	1.0	

At the end of the project, the test manager can compare the actual hours spent against the estimated hours. In the example, 80 hours have been estimated for setting up the test conditions. This is for eight clusters, with an average of 20 test conditions per cluster and an average time of 0.5 hours per test condition. In reality, a total of 90 hours was spent and there turned out to be an average of 25 test conditions per cluster. With a constant number of clusters, this means that the average time per test condition is not 0.5 hours, but 0.45.

The test manager can now amend line R4, the average time per test condition (in hours).

In the following test project, he uses the amended calculation rules as a starting point. At the end of the test project, he again examines which rules should be amended. For each subsequent project, he can take the new average from the calculation rules. In doing so, he may decide to leave the first estimate out. This estimate was not, after all, based on actual hours spent.

In our example, the first estimation of the average time per test condition is 0.5 hours. At the end of the project, it turns out to be 0.45. This information is used for the next project. At the end of this project, the average time comes out at 0.49. For the third project, we then take the average of 0.45

and 0.49 (i.e. 0.47) as the rule. By always taking the new average, the value of the calculation rules, and with those the estimate, become increasingly more accurate (see Figure 6.5).

Calculation rule

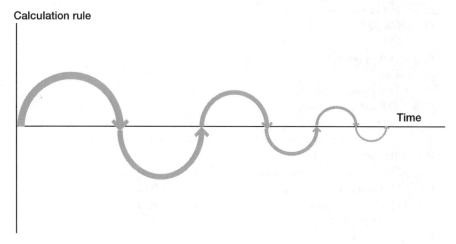

Fig. 6.5. Increasing accuracy of the calculation rules

6.2.8 Combining Various Methods of Estimating

So far, a number of methods for drawing up an estimate have been described. These methods all have their strengths and weaknesses. Using several methods can compensate for the weak points of a method. The time required to use an extra method and to compare the results of both methods must of course be included in the budget and the plan.

A few examples of combined methods:

- For a new release, a test manager draws up an estimate using TEEM. With the previous releases, he kept metrics of the most important elements that are of influence in the estimate. He now uses these to draw up the estimate for the current release. To be able to confirm that the right metrics have been used, he invites two experts to a brainstorming session to draw up a top-down estimate.
- The client gives a test manager a fixed budget. He wishes to know whether this budget is adequate for carrying out the test project. Using analogy, he examines what budget he requires for the project in light of past experiences.
- Via the bottom-up method, a test manager has drawn up an estimate for a test in a complex environment. There is little chance that he has omitted any difficult technical components. But the possibility exists that some aspects at the level of the total project are being overlooked. For this reason,

he asks one or more experts to draw up a top-down estimate. By coming in at this high level, the experts will cover matters such as integration.

If several methods deliver a corresponding result, this provides confirmation of the quality of the estimate. The estimate then provides a good idea of the means necessary for carrying out the test project.

The situation is different if the results vary significantly. The source of these variations must be investigated. It is possible that the wrong method has been used for the current situation. Perhaps an expert has placed a particular slant on the estimate, or certain assumptions might have been wrong at the outset. Seeking the causes of the variations and solving them will eventually lead to a better estimate.

6.2.9 Summary of Estimating Methods

In this chapter, seven methods of estimating have been described. As a reminder, Table 6.3 provides a summary. For each method, a brief description is provided of the situation to which the method is best suited. In addition, a brief summary of each method's strengths and weaknesses is given.

Table 6.3. Overview of various methods of estimating

		Strengths	Weaknesses
Top-down estimating	Use for a first estimate at a high level when little detail is available.	High level	Degree of detail Stability
	Consider at the beginning of a test project	Efficient	Low involvement of testers
Bottom-up estimating	Best use if detailed information is available	Detailed basis	Estimate is only as good as the detailed information
		Stability	Overall tasks may be overlooked
		Involvement	Takes more time
		Well founded	
"Market" percentage	Use as starting point of estimate in the absence of past figures in internal organisation	Efficient	Evaluation takes time
		"Pilot" provides good link	Dependent on accuracy of estimate of phases prior to testing

Table 6.3. (continued)

		Strengths	Weaknesses
Percentage from experience	Use if the organisation has been employing the same technology and methods for many years	Efficient	Dependent on employees
Estimation by analogy	Use if comparable projects exist	Optimal use of similar projects	Representativity of similar projects
Expert judgement	Use in complex situations	Judgement of representativity of future estimates and factors influencing the future	Prejudiced estimate
			Only as good as the experts
Fixed budget	Frequent situation whereby test manager is set limits concerning time and budget	Creates client acceptance	Restricts testing activities
Test effort estimation model (TEEM)	Precise method that can be used in a test organisation prepared to keep metrics	Well-founded estimate	Only suitable for use in structured testing
		Better historical insight	Defining the right metrics

6.3 Factors that Influence the Estimate

Experience has taught us that many factors influence the test project. The impact of the various factors must be reflected in the final estimate. This impact can be represented by a percentage. A team of junior testers has a negative effect of, for example, 10% on the estimate: since they have a lot to learn, their productivity will be lower at the start of the test project. As the project progresses over time, they will learn and their productivity will increase. The overall effect is set at 10%.

A test manager may discover that little documentation is available and that the quality of the available documentation is poor. The testers then have to consult the domain experts to collect the right information and so need more time than average in setting up the tests. This time must be included in the estimate.

A factor can of course have a positive effect on the estimate. When, for example, there is a new release of an information system, the same testers can be made available to the test manager as with the previous release. These testers are aware of the available documentation, have built up experience with the system under test, and are familiar with the set-up of the test set. It is therefore possible to benefit from the learning curve of the testers.

If a test manager is involved in a consecutive series of releases of an information system, it is worth the trouble of recording the influence of a factor and using this experience in the next project.

Table 6.4 contains a checklist of the most important factors that can influence an estimate. The test manager can fill in this checklist for the purpose of his project. A brief explanation is provided for each factor.

Table 6.4. Factors that can influence the estimate

Factor	Influence (positive/negative)
Effective working time	
Test management	
Quality control	
Scope of the test project	
Learning curve	
Reusability of testware	
Availability of documentation	
Test data maintenance	
Complexity of the test environment	
Complexity of the information system	
Time to repair issues	
Transfer	

6.3.1 Effective Working Time

People never work for the full eight hours they have available per day, and testers are no exception. Research shows that in an eight-hour working day, people work on average about five and a half hours effectively. This must therefore be taken into account when drawing up the estimate (DeMarco & Lister, 1999).

6.3.2 Test Management

Hours spent managing the test must be included in the estimate. The hours a test manager spends cannot always be linked directly to testing an information system! For example, the hours spent drawing up the estimate and plan. Experience shows that test management, compared with project management, takes up around 20% of the test budget. We should point out here that most of the test management hours are in the preparation and setting up of the test project, in creating the conditions for testing the information system.

The hours spent by the test manager must clearly show up in the estimate. In this way the test management hours can be controlled as well.

6.3.3 Quality Control

To measure the quality of the testware, reviews must be carried out. The testers must carry out reviews on the related documents and on their own testware[4].

Also a project audit may be carried out. In this, the emphasis is on the process. However, it takes time to carry out reviews and audits, and, as before, the time must be included in the estimate.

6.3.4 Scope of the Test Project

The scope of a project is likely to change during the execution of the testing. However well the scope of testing has been established in advance, there will always be changes to the functionality. During development of (a new version of) an information system, legislation, for example, might change, leading to a functionality change. A case in point is OPTA (the Dutch telecommunications authority), which subjects the telecommunication industry to all kinds of regulations. It can also happen that with new insight, users decide that changes are required. Or changes to the software environment may be required: a slightly different configuration can mean that testing has to start all over again. By reserving time for this, all of these changes to the scope of operation can be accommodated without too much difficulty within the test project.

6.3.5 The Learning Curve

An inexperienced tester learns a lot from the moment he starts on a test project. He will have learned a fair amount of theory on courses, but, lacking practical experience, the preparation of the first test will take some time. With good coaching, the tester can quickly work independently, and within a short time he will be able to tackle more complex tests.

An experienced tester may find himself in an unfamiliar environment. For example, if he has only ever carried out functional acceptance tests in

---

[4] There are different kinds of reviews, for example, in increasing formality: technical review, walkthrough and inspection.

a Windows environment, and the project requires him to participate in a system test in a Unix environment. The tester will need time to familiarise himself with the specific aspects of the test level and the environment.

Even a very experienced tester follows a learning curve in a new project. No matter how experienced the tester, at the start of a project he is in a new situation to which he must adapt and which he must get to know. He must bear in mind such things as the functionality of the test object, the technical environment, the tools employed, or the use of automated testing.

Experience shows that working out a test case takes three times as long at the start of a project than at the end of the learning curve.

General advice is therefore: in drawing up the estimate, make allowances for the effects of the learning curve.

6.3.6 Reusability of Testware

The project can use a method for structured testing. This method ensures that the testers all document their tests in the same way, the relationship between various test documents is visible and the version is easily ascertained. This makes the testware easy to adapt. The existing testware can then be reused without too much difficulty, which certainly offers advantages when testing new versions of a particular information system. Even when there are a number of changes, there are also large parts of the system that remain unchanged. If the testware is set up in a structured manner, the testers can find this information easily and use the tests again.

Much knowledge is often contained in existing testware. After all, when the testware was set up, documentation was used and domain experts were consulted. The experts' knowledge is therefore already present in the testware. Their input is only required again for changed parts of the information system.

If the testware was well set up, it can easily be reused, which will have a positive effect on the estimate.

It is also possible that testware is completely absent. In that case, much time will be required to set up the testware. The testers must then create the test documentation, and in doing so they will need to consult the domain experts. It will take time to select a testing approach and perhaps to train the testers. For the sake of securing the advantages mentioned above for a subsequent project, all of the testers will have to document their tests in the same manner. Between these two extremes, there are of course many possible variations.

6.3.7 Availability of Documentation

The same thing applies to documentation as to testware. There may be a lot of documentation available, or none at all, or anything in between. The testers base their tests on the documentation present, e.g. functional designs, technical designs and user manuals. Depending on the test levels that fall within the test project, the testers require particular documentation. If this is sufficiently available, they can quickly get to work. Naturally, it is important that the documentation relates to the current version of the information system. The documentation must be up to date, complete and accurate. Only then is it of real use to the testers in setting up the tests.

Where there is no documentation at all, the domain experts form the information source for the testers. The experts know how the information system works, and the testers can use this knowledge to set up a reliable test. However, the experts must be available, or at least have enough time at their disposal, to supply input. The test manager must allow for the experts' time in his estimate.

6.3.8 Test Data Maintenance

The maintenance of test data can influence the estimate. What is the convention within the organisation concerning the storing of data? There is a link here to the maintenance organisation. The organisation has placed the storing of data under a maintenance organisation, and the test project will have to keep to this arrangement as closely as possible. If data maintenance is not set up, the test manager will have to work on this. Setting up the maintenance does not necessarily have to be a part of the test project. The test manager has only to note this and pass it on to the client, who can then decide who will deal with it.

It is easier if the data can be stored and processed in a central location. The testers can then find all the data easily, and, furthermore, it is simpler to maintain the data this way. However, the testers do not always have full control over all the data, as for example with a startup database, an important item in a test project. Are the testers able to set this up themselves, or does it require the department that maintains the test environment? If all the information is at a central location, the test manager has only to agree with one party concerning who will maintain the data.

It is different when the test project involves storing and processing on different systems. The test manager then has to come to an arrangement with various departments, and these departments will have to (be willing to) cooperate with each other during the preparation and execution of the test. This requires a plan that includes all the parties involved. A rush job in any one of these departments can then significantly disrupt the plan. Also, all the departments must be motivated to help in the testing. One department that is not convinced of the need for testing, or that does not entirely commit itself during the execution of the test, can cause the test execution to falter.

When drawing up the estimate, allowance must be made for the way in which data maintenance is set up. Recording and processing on different systems can lead to a higher estimate.

6.3.9 Complexity of the Test Environment

The complexity of the test environment can have a bearing on the estimate. The results of a test only give a reliable indication of the quality of an information system if they are obtained in a representative test environment. If the test environment is very complex, it will take a lot of time to set it up at an acceptable level. Here, too, the testers will possibly require the help of experts.

The more complex the environment, the more time is required to set up a reliable test and mirror the live environment where possible.

6.3.10 Complexity of the Information System

The more functions an information system has, the more complex it will be. When the functions influence each other, the information system will be even more complex. Functionalities that are interdependent can make it difficult for the testers to oversee an information system. Which functions influence each other, and what are the consequences of a particular output for the function that is subsequently used? Only sufficient insight into the functions will result in a reliable test set.

Good documentation and the input of domain experts here can help to grasp the complexity.

The complexity may of course also depend on the functions themselves. For example, the batch functionality, where a batch may consist of the execution of various calculations, the setting up of various reports and the making of forecasts. The testers must get to grips with this total functionality in order to set up a test. A standard administration system will involve fewer problems in testing than a new system that has interfaces with other systems.

6.3.11 Time to Repair Issues

This factor can best be explained by means of Figure 6.6.

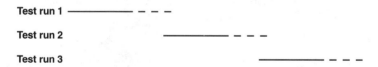

Fig. 6.6. Example of time repair issues

In this figure, the full line represents the testing time and the dashed line the repair time needed by the developers.

The testers start by carrying out the first test run. Say they have found issues during the test execution. Perhaps they could not even execute all the test cases because of test blocking issues. At the end of the test execution of the first run, the developers go to work on solutions for these issues. After that the testers start the second test run etc. The repair time of the developers is the waiting time for the testers. This does not mean, of course, that the testers do nothing at all. They can use this time to perform other tasks. Suppose that the test time in this example is always 3 weeks and the repair time 1 week. If only the effective working time is counted, the estimated time taken for testing will be 9 weeks. However, the testers are needed for 12 weeks. In many situations, it is not possible to send the testers away after 3 weeks and call them back a week later.

To obtain a reliable estimate of the number of hours that the testers will require, the test manager must estimate the developers' repair time.

6.3.12 Transfer

The time required to make the transfer between test levels and the end of the project must also be estimated.

Figure 6.7 clarifies this. In this example, the test project consists of executing the system test (ST) and the user's acceptance test (UAT).

Fig. 6.7. Example of transfer

The testers are involved in the setting up of both tests. With the UAT, however, a considerable input is required from the users in the preparation and execution. Before the UAT begins, the results of the ST must be transferred (represented by the dashed line). What issues were found in the ST? Which issues have been solved, and which ones remain outstanding? Were there any problems with the test environment? A successful transfer between the ST and the UAT can perhaps prevent similar problems.

The more transfers there are and the longer the transfer takes, the more time must be included in the estimate.

6.4 Conclusion

The resulting estimate shows the number of hours of work linked to particular activities. This eventually results in the total estimate. These activities must then be set out in time and it must be determined who will do what. Planning is therefore required, with a focus on the starting date, completion date and timetable.

Setting up the planning is the subject of the following chapter.

7

Planning

An estimate has been drawn up: the number of hours allocated is linked to the activities that need to be performed. These activities must now be set out in terms of time. It must also be indicated which interdependencies exist between the activities, who is going to carry out the activities and which results are expected from them. Activities are given a start date and a completion date. In the course of the test project, the plan will become increasingly detailed.

The quick scan has delivered a first impression of the test project. The risk analysis has delivered an overview of the test project risks, the product risks and their importance. The test strategy indicates which stakeholders have an interest in testing the information system, which test levels fall within the test project, which product risks will be covered and what the scope and depth of the test is. All of this has resulted in an estimate in which the activities and number of hours assigned to them are described. It is now time to set out these activities and hours in terms of time – this is the planning phase. When activities can start depends on the plan of the total project and on the time when the developers deliver the documentation and the information system.

The test plan should form a part of the total project plan. The plans of system development and of testing have to connect. Ideally, the test manager should be involved from the start of the project. Together with the project manager, he can then ensure that the developers start with those modules that relate to the highest product risk. In this way, the riskiest part is built first and can also be tested first. Indeed, these are very often the most important parts of the information system.

Planning demonstrates when various steps are being taken, how long they will take and who is taking them. The test manager consults with the testers as to whether an activity has been carried out. He will have to check continually whether the test project is on schedule. An aid to keeping a good overview of the progress is the earned value method.[1]

Just as with estimating, planning is also surrounded by uncertainty. This uncertainty only increases, the further into the future the test manager tries to plan. For this reason, it is better to make a detailed plan for the activities in the immediate test phase and a global plan for the rest of them. After finishing the detailed planning activities, the experience gained is used in the detailed planning of the subsequent activities. This method is known as evolutionary planning (Gilb, 1988).

To obtain an even better overview, the total test project needs to be broken down into smaller parts. For each part, both the test preparation and the test execution must be planned. On completion of each part, a decision can immediately be made concerning the covered product risks pertaining to that part. The test manager is thus able to demonstrate added value from an early stage, and management is easier opposed to all the test execution is planned right at the end of the test project.

There are various tools that can be used in drawing up and maintaining a plan. For instance, tools which can link people to activities and hours, and tools with which reports can be generated and the critical path defined.

The choice and use of a tool depends on the standard used in the organisation. The extent of the test project also plays a part. A warning is not out of place here: a test manager should not spend more time on using the tool and monitoring the hours than on managing the test project!

A plan is also a good means of communication. At the start of the test project, a plan can serve to inform the client of all the steps that will be taken. The preconditions and assumptions should accompany this description of the steps. The plan can also be used to show the client the progress of the test project: the steps that have been taken, the steps that have been completed within the timetable and the steps that are behind schedule. If there is any delay, it must be indicated what the cause of this delay is, for it may influence other parts of the plan. An unstable test environment might also present problems for any subsequent test levels. The preconditions and assumptions are also a means of control. If changes occur in these, it can influence the plan.

7.1 Planning Versus Estimating

This book contains a separate chapter on estimating and another one on planning. This appears to suggest that drawing up a plan and drawing up an

---

[1] With the earned value method (EVM), the planned budget is only declared to have been realised when the activity is 100% completed. This avoids the "90% completed syndrome". Another advantage of EVM is its predictive capacity. A comprehensive description of EVM will follow in Chapter 10.

estimate are two entirely separate activities. Of course, this is not the case. It is difficult to draw up an estimate without having in mind the various activities and the times at which they are performed. And it is not advisable to draw up a plan without making allowance for the estimate; the test manager must continually check whether the plan still corresponds to the estimate.

In practice, these activities appear to be carried out more or less simultaneously. Depending on the situation, it is preferable to start with the estimate one time, and to start with the plan another time.

If a *fixed budget* is involved, an estimate has to be drawn up first. In this case, it is not advisable simply to go along with the budget offered, but to draw up your own estimate for verification (see Chapter 6, Section 6.2.6). The result is an inventory of the activities together with the hours required for the test project. Then comes the planning: the activities are set out in time. The plan might show, for example, that more activities can be carried out in parallel than was assumed in the estimate. The duration of the project is then reduced, but more employees are required. These types of choices must be put to the client.

If the client states a *fixed date of completion*, a plan has to be drawn up first. A fixed date of completion may be determined externally, as for example with a change in legislation due to take effect on a particular date. It is also possible that it may be commercially attractive to keep to a certain fixed completion date. In banking, as a rule in the savings products market, the first one to put a new product on the market gains 75% of the market for it. Going onto the market later therefore can result in a big loss.

If the date of completion is fixed, it is necessary to extrapolate to the date when the test would have to begin. Between the start and completion dates, all the activities necessary to achieve the goals must be planned. The allocated number of hours for these activities results in an estimate. The estimate and plan must be discussed with the client. The conclusion may be that the test project is starting "too early": the developers will not finish building the information system in time. The starting date for testing will therefore have to be moved, and this means that additional testers will be required in order to carry out more activities in parallel. It may also turn out that the starting date has already passed, or that the estimate does not correspond to the client's expectations. In each of these cases, there must be a dialogue with the client concerning any changes in the set-up of the (test) project.

If the test project is dependent on many parties outside of the project, it is also better to start with the plan, in particular by agreeing the time slot within which these parties can offer their products or services. This information is then processed into the plan and results in an estimate. These parties may be found both inside and outside the organisation. An internal party might be, for example, a central test department. The test manager must then indicate when testers are required, which skills they must possess and when they must be available. The central test department reports on whom it has available, when, and at what skill level. Only then can the plan be made for the test project.

An external party might be, for example, a hardware supplier. The plan will then have to take notice of the date when delivery of the hardware can take place. These agreements can be laid down, e.g. in a contract.

Despite the strong relationship between the subjects of estimating and planning, the chapters on them are separate. In this way, each activity together with its own specific characteristics can be explained without creating confusion. The rest of this chapter will focus on the planning of a test project.

7.2 Setting Up the Plan

Figure 7.1 shows how the plan of a test project often looks. In dynamic testing, a test team starts designing all the tests and relevant test data per test level. Then test automation follows, if necessary. The test environment, too, must be set up before test execution can begin. These things can partly be carried out in parallel.[2]

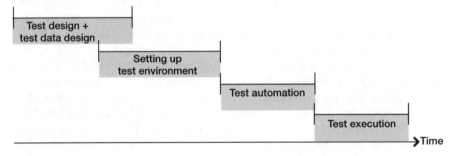

Fig. 7.1. Example of a plan of activities within a test level

However, there is a disadvantage with this way of planning. Should the test project, for whatever reason, be interrupted at an early stage, a large number of test conditions, test cases and possibly test scripts cannot be carried out. A verdict cannot yet be given on the quality of the information system. This will only be possible after completion of the test execution. The added value of the testing then only becomes apparent at the end of the test execution within a test level.

The various activities surrounding testing also quickly land on the critical path. A problem with one of the activities at the beginning of the execution

---

[2] Running across all these activities are planning and monitoring of the test project. These activities are not relevant to this figure.

phase of a test level immediately puts pressure on the subsequent activities. All the pressure then comes to bear on the test execution, exactly where all eyes are fixed. And only then can a judgement be made concerning the outstanding and covered product risks and the quality of the information system.

There is a way to avoid this problem: evolutionary planning.

7.3 Evolutionary Planning

Planning is accompanied by much uncertainty. The longer a test project takes, the more difficult it is to plan realistically. In the course of a test project, events are always taking place which influence the plan. One way of managing this is to use evolutionary planning. This is aimed at delivering added value at an early stage in the project with a strong focus on the users of the information system.

7.3.1 Detailed Planning Versus Global Planning

One of the principles of evolutionary planning is that activities in the near future are planned in detail, while those further in the future are only planned globally. Activities taking place in the short term are easier to oversee and therefore allow more realistic and detailed planning. Those that will only be performed after some time are dependent on the outcome of the short-term activities. In addition, all kinds of unforeseen circumstances can arise which influence the plan. This certainly applies to projects of long duration. By continually planning small parts of the early phase in detail, the experience gained can be incorporated into the detailed plan of the subsequent phase.

A travel organisation plans to develop a new service for its customers on the Internet. Customers who have booked a trip are given a user ID and a password. This gives them access to information on their trip. At the end of the total development project, which will take one year, customers will be able to obtain information on their trip (flight/bus/private transport), their hotel, apartment or bungalow, events taking place in the vicinity of their resort, the 5-day weather forecast for the region and information on car hire and public transport. A test manager is asked to draw up a plan for testing this information system.

After carrying out a quick scan, the test manager knows that the developers are going to deliver the system in various modules. The modules relate to the functionalities indicated. The travel organisation as yet has no experience with information systems on the Internet.

Development of this information system starts on 1 April 2002. The developers' plan is shown in Table 7.1.

Table 7.1. Example of a travel organisation's plan

Module	Starting date	Finishing date	Description of content
1	01 Apr. 2002	01 July 2002	User ID + password
			Travel information (flight, bus,
			private transport)
2	01 July 2002	01 Sept. 2002	Information on holiday resort
3	01 Sept. 2002	01 Jan. 2003	Events
			Car hire + public transport
4	01 Jan. 2003	01 Feb. 2003	Weather forecast

The project manager has also allowed time for retesting the latest issues and testing in a production environment. He has also allowed a margin. The planned end date is 31 March 2003, so the information system is ready in time for the summer holiday season.

The test manager makes a detailed 3-week plan for the first module. For all the subsequent phases, he makes a global plan, also in 3-week periods. In reality, the testing of the first module takes 5 weeks, because the quality of the information system was not as expected. The developers have little or no experience in programming Internet applications and need more time to develop and document the programming. Consequently, the test team took longer to set up the various test cases: they had to carry out a lot of consultation with domain experts. For the following module, the test manager plans a 4-week slot instead of 3 weeks. He also amends the global plan. The modules containing events, car hire and public transport will take 4 weeks. However, the test manager expects the last module to take no longer than roughly 1 week. He assumes that, by that time, the teething problems will be out of the way, the testers will have gained a lot of experience and productivity will be higher.

With evolutionary planning, the test manager can remain closer to the real situation. The test project proceeds along the lines of the original plan (see Figure 7.2). At a certain point, circumstances appear to require a change in the plan. Since the test project is planned in small, manageable steps, the test manager is able to adapt the plan accordingly.

Evolutionary planning also contains a number of other principles:[3]

- Projects are driven by multiple objectives.
- Added value is delivered at an early stage.
- Design, analysis and test execution (and test automation, if required) within each iteration.

---

[3] The original model for evolutionary planning is mainly aimed at system development. The model therefore has more specific characteristics than mentioned here. We have included the most important ones for the purposes of test projects.

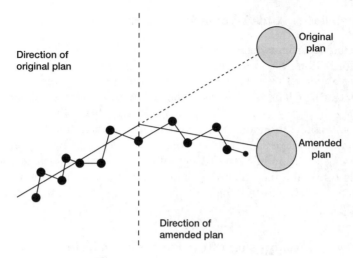

Fig. 7.2. Evolutionary planning

- Focus on the user.
- Focus on the result instead of the system development process.

We discuss these characteristics below.

7.3.2 Projects Are Driven by Multiple Objectives

Many test projects have the goal of testing the functionality. But increasingly, non-functional quality attributes are playing a role – for example, efficiency, usability and maintainability. In the testing of a website, for example, performance, security and understandability are important, as well as functionality. If it takes too long for the next page to appear, people will move on to another site: the irritation level is quickly reached and the competition is often just "one click away". It is frustrating when customers buy their products from a competitor for that reason. Security also plays an important part. Customers will only order products from a particular site on the Internet if they are sure that their credit card details will be safe there. An unclear structure means that people are unable to find quickly what they seek: the level of understandability is low. In that case, too, customers will move on to another site in search of the product concerned.

The test strategy contains a description of the quality attributes that are important to the testing of a particular information system. These quality attributes must be included in the plan, but not all of them are easily tested. Testing the functionality is usually self-evident. But how is a test team to test maintainability? For this reason, the testing of non-functional quality attributes is often brought under a separate test type. The various test types can then be executed in parallel when the information system is sufficiently stable.

7.3.3 Delivering Added Value at an Early Stage

The test manager may delay designing and executing the test until the complete information system has been delivered, but in that case the test team will not be able to test the quality of the information system dynamically until a late stage. The test manager should try to deliver added value at an early stage by agreeing with the developers that they will deliver the system incrementally, in modules. The test team will then be able to report on each module in stages and indicate which product risks are covered. Also, after testing each module, the team will obtain a better idea of the quality of the total information system. This means that the team must prepare and execute a suitable test for each module. The plan must accommodate this.

7.3.4 Design, Analysis and Test Execution Within Each Iteration

In long-running projects, there is always a risk that the requirements of the information system will change regularly: at the start of a project not all the information is available. The test team seems to be constantly engaged in designing the tests and amending them!

By planning in small test cycles, a measurement of the quality can be given after each module. The developers can use this experience in developing the subsequent module, and the users also gain insight into the operation and quality of (part of) an information system after each module.

We can gather the early, frequent delivery and all the test activities within one iteration under the term "logical unit of test" (LUT). An LUT is a collection of related activities that together form a whole, from test design to test execution. The test manager defines the LUTs so that upon completion they contribute added value to the (test) project.

Each cluster of testware can be planned as an LUT. The activities for a cluster then range from design to execution. The test manager first plans all the activities for cluster 1, and subsequently for the following cluster. He continues in this way until all the clusters have been planned. The clusters that cover the highest risks are planned first. The priority of the clusters is determined in the test strategy.

The activities for one cluster are shown in Figure 7.3.

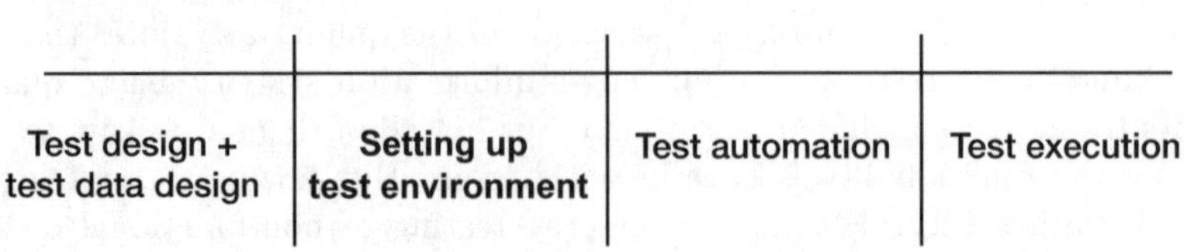

| Test design + test data design | Setting up test environment | Test automation | Test execution |

Fig. 7.3. Example of activities within one cluster

This categorisation of activities corresponds to the activities in Figure 7.1. But the activities mentioned there are for a complete test project, yet here they refer to activities within one cluster. Various clusters are usually defined within a test project.

Figure 7.4 shows the plan for a test project in which, for example, the system test consists of three clusters. In this, cluster 1 has the highest priority and cluster 3 the lowest. The activities within a cluster correspond to the activities as shown in Figure 7.3.

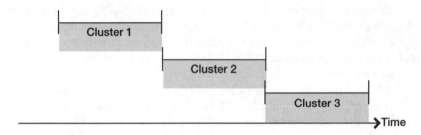

Fig. 7.4. Setting out the clusters in terms of time

Test execution is only one of the activities per cluster. The added value can be demonstrated early in the test project, after execution of each cluster. After completion of cluster 1, and therefore of LUT 1, a measurement is already possible on the product risks that are covered by this cluster. In this way, a prediction can also be made concerning the quality of the total information system. Users also gain an early impression of the operation and quality of an information system if they are involved in the execution of the tests for each cluster.

After the testing of a cluster a part of the information system could be delivered, if the clusters connect to the modules that the developers are delivering. This certainly applies if the project is working with prototypes, where the modules consistently provide a working prototype. The advantage here again is that the test project quickly delivers the optimum added value.

7.3.5 Focus on the User

One of the most important aspects of evolutionary planning is that it is focused on the user. In many test projects, the plan focuses on achieving goals that only relate to the information system. Is the functionality as agreed? Are the developers delivering on time so that the test team can start the test execution in time? Will the deadline be met? An evaluation of the test process follows at the end of the test project. During this phase, users are often completely forgotten. Does the result actually satisfy their requirements? With evolutionary planning, users are involved at every iteration: their assessment is important. If the information system does not live up to their expectations, then relatively little time has been spent on developing and testing. And it is easier to adjust the goals earlier on in the project.

The decision of whether to modify an information system lies in the end with the client. If the client wishes to include the users' requirements, he will instruct the developers to modify the information system. With the execution of the tests in the subsequent iteration, users can indicate whether the system is developing more along the lines of their expectations.

An information system to be built has to provide better organisation of all the material in a library. This will make it easier to show which books and which other materials are available. The end users want to be able to search for books, videos and CDs under author and title, but also want to be able to look up the latest titles by an author or artist.

The developers make a prototype of this information system. The end users are satisfied, particularly with the fact that the latest titles are presented clearly. These users have another idea: they would like to see the latest titles acquired by the library. The client wishes to comply with this request, and the information system is modified to accommodate this latest requirement.

So a new prototype can inspire end users with new ideas. Perhaps these users would like to know whether the library contains any reviews of the various titles in their collection of newspaper clippings? The client must continually make decisions on whether to include these requirements in the information system, as this has ongoing consequences for the (test) project and for the developers and testers involved. The goalposts are always moved a little, the results to be delivered are different, and therefore the estimate and plan have to be constantly adjusted. The changes in the functionality also have consequences for the testing. And the test manager will have to adjust his estimate and plan. The testers need time to adapt the tests and execute them. They will also have to carry out a test that demonstrates that the unchanged functionality still operates correctly: namely, a regression test.

7.3.6 Focus on the Result Instead of the System Development Process

In development, there is often a lot of focus on the process itself. Is the project following all the defined steps and tasks? Are the steps being carried out correctly according to the applicable standards? There is a risk that actual results are lost from view. By using evolutionary planning, it is easier to remain focused on results. The project consists of a series of short iterations. Each iteration consists of the design and execution of (test) activities. The user is involved in every step and decision within the test project from the beginning. It is therefore possible after each iteration to examine whether the project is still on track to achieve the desired goal, and to make any necessary adjustments.

7.3.7 Advantages of Evolutionary Planning and Logical Units of Test

A combination of evolutionary planning and LUTs has the following advantages:

- The various completed parts ensure that added value can be delivered quickly. After completion of each part, the test manager is able to give an overview of the product risks that are covered.
- After each completed iteration, the client is able to make an informed go/no-go decision. Is the quality good enough to continue? Does the tested part of the information system meets the requirements of the users?
- If the client decides to proceed, he feels reassured concerning the achievement of the set goals, since the users are involved with each iteration.
- Planning in small, complete iterations allows effective management of the test project. Breaking down the total test project into sections provides clearer insight.
- The outlook for the test project is more realistic, since the immediate iteration is planned in detail, while the following iterations are only planned globally. Experience gained during the first iteration is used to plan the following iteration in detail.

7.4 Distinction Between Test Project Preparation and Execution

As with drawing up an estimate, in drawing up a plan, a distinction must be made between test project preparation and test project execution, for these two phases have a different planning basis. Planning both phases collectively and lumping everything together would result in loss of clarity and transparency.

The preparation includes those activities that set the conditions for the test project. When these activities have been completed, the testers can be set to work.

The activities referred to are as follows:

- The execution of a quick scan, a test project risk analysis and a product risk analysis.
- Writing a test strategy and a test plan.
- Setting up an estimate and plan.
- Setting up a test management file and the test organisation.

These are activities which the test manager has control over. He will carry them out for every test project. The input of the stakeholders is a requirement here, but from his own experience the test manager will be able to indicate the length of time he will need to carry out these activities.

It is different with the execution of the test project. The test manager is then dependent on a variety of other parties. Whether or not the testing goes to plan depends, for example, on:

- the quality of the information system to be tested;
- the availability and stability of the test environment;
- the number of issues and the necessary repair time;
- the actual amount of time the domain experts are able to spend on the test project;
- the quality of the documentation.

The test manager's activities during the execution of the test project consist of monitoring and reporting on progress. When the testers have set up the testware, the execution of the tests begins. In setting up the testware, the testers are dependent on the availability, completeness and quality of the domain experts and documentation. In executing the tests, the testers are dependent on the quality of the information system under test. The quality of the system influences the number of issues found. In turn, these issues influence the activities of the testers. They have to record all the issues and eventually carry out retesting. The number of issues also influences the developers' repair time and the time required for a retest. In the test execution, the testers use a test environment. The quality of this test environment also determines progress of the test execution. Has the person responsible set up the test environment appropriately and on schedule? Is the test environment stable?

The test project is therefore dependent on factors beyond immediate control. This makes planning the test execution more difficult.

No information system is ever fit to go into production immediately after a single test. At least one retest is necessary, and often several more. To make allowances for this in the plan, the test execution per test level can be divided into various steps:

- the intake test;
- the basic test;
- the complete test;
- the final test.

The intake test actually forms no part of the test execution. This first step is meant to provide an initial indication of the quality of the information system to be tested, and of the test environment. Successful completion of the intake test is one of the entry criteria for commencing the actual test execution. This consists of the basic test, the complete test and the final test.

It does not matter whether the test manager identifies three of four steps. The important thing is that, in his plan, he makes allowances for the fact that there is no such thing as a fault-free information system. By planning for only one test per test level, the test manager leaves no time for carrying out retesting. The test time may seem short, but he will eventually require more time in order to carry out the retest(s), and so creates problems for himself in this way. It may be sufficient to carry out an intake test, a complete test and a final test. The intake test is necessary to establish that at least the basic functionality of the information system works. During the complete test, the testers execute all the tests. The final test is the one that results after all the issues have been resolved as agreed.

If the quality of the information system and the stability of the test environment are unsatisfactory, it is advisable to plan for an extra test cycle, namely the basic test. The test manager's experience of the information system under test will help this decision.

This division into various steps influences the plan. After the testers have executed the test cases once (the *basic test*), the developers can go to work solving the issues. The testers therefore cannot immediately carry on with the next step of retesting (the *complete test*). The test manager will have to consider other activities that the testers can carry out in the meantime.

If, with each subsequent retest, significant parts of the testing have to be carried out again, the test manager may decide to set up a *regression test* during the project. In this, the test team demonstrates that the unchanged functionality is still working correctly. In addition, within each step tests can be carried out that are more specifically aimed at the solved issues.

In the following sections, a brief description is provided of the content of the various steps in retesting.

7.4.1 The Intake Test

An information system that stagnates with each action causes much delay in the test execution. Not only does the system have to keep going back to the developers for repair, but also there is a big chance that the testers have to keep starting the test execution all over again. The information system has to be adjusted (to include changes and additions), and this might introduce faults in the unchanged parts of the system.

To avoid testers having to execute tests repeatedly, the test team carries out an intake test. This is a test to examine whether the information system complies with the starting quality as stated by the test team. In the intake test only the basic functionality is tested. This must not take long – from half a day to 1 day at most.

Customers may place orders via an ordering system. Apart from the customer details, products and suppliers are necessary. The intake test for the functional acceptance test could for example examine whether a new product and a new supplier can be entered into the system. The placing of an order could also be tested. If this intake test is completed successfully, the test manager will accept the information system and the testers can start on the actual test execution. If, however, the information system does not pass this intake test, the test manager will take it back to the developers. Naturally, the test manager must agree this procedure in advance with the party or parties involved.

If the test team consists of various members, it is advisable to have this intake test carried out by only one tester (Kaner et al., 2002). The other testers carry on with their current tasks. Only after approval of the intake test will the information system be installed for all the testers, who then test this version. In this way, not too much time is lost.

The intake test ends when the information system to be tested is correctly installed, the basic functionality has been tested and the results are as expected and agreed.

7.4.2 The Basic Test

The purpose of the basic test is to carry out all the tests that have been specified. This does not mean that all the tests have to be successful! It will happen in practice that the testers will be unable to execute a number of test cases because they run into issues. Other test cases can perhaps only be partly executed.

After analysing the issues, the client and stakeholders must be consulted on any measures.

Of course, there will also be test cases that can be completed successfully.

For the ordering system referred to previously, the following test conditions have been specified for the functional acceptance test:

1. Can a new supplier be entered into the system?
2. Can a new product be entered for an existing supplier?
3. Can a new product be entered for a new supplier?
4. Can an order be entered for an existing product?
5. Can an order be entered for a new product?
6. Can product details be changed?
7. Can supplier details be changed?
8. Can product details be deleted?
9. Can supplier details be deleted?
10. Can an order be changed?
11. Can an order be deleted?

When changing the product details (test condition 6), the testers discover that all the details can be changed except the colour of the product. However, according to the specifications this should be possible.

When changing the supplier details (test condition 7), the testers discover that the information system crashes. The whole system has to be started up again before they are able to continue with the subsequent test conditions. It then appears that all the details that have been entered are lost. This is a fatal issue that merits a high priority to be solved quickly by the developers. The testers document the issues. At this point the developers start to resolve the issues.

The basic test is complete when the testers have tried to execute every test once. The developers solve eventual issues.

7.4.3 The Complete Test

In the complete test, the testers can carry out all the tests. The developers have solved the fatal issues. Of course, other issues may arise. It is agreed with the client, the stakeholders and the developers which issues must be solved throughout the test project on the basis of the product risk.

The developers have solved the issue relating to changing the supplier details. When the test is executed, this functionality indeed appears to be correct. However, the testers find a new, non-fatal issue when entering a supplier's details: the postal code consists of five characters instead of six. And the colour of the product still cannot be changed.

The complete test is accomplished when every test has been executed once and no fatal issues have occurred. Where in the basic test fatal issues obstructed the execution of a number of test cases, this is not the case at the end of the complete test. All the test cases *must* be executable.

7.4.4 The Final Test

During the final test, the testers execute all the test cases and examine whether all the issues that were supposed to have been solved have indeed been solved.[4] It is possible that a number of minor problems remain in the information system when it goes into production. These are usually issues that are found in the test conditions with a low-priority product risk. These are the "known errors".

The stakeholders have indicated that the field length for the postal code is important: the developers have solved this issue. The stakeholders have

---

[4] See Chapter 11 for a complete description of issue management.

given the colour of the product a low priority and this issue will not be solved during this phase. The testers execute the tests again and see that there are no longer any issues, apart from that relating to changing the colour of a product.

After the final test, the test manager sets up a report on the tests within the test level concerned. The known errors are also included in this report. The following phase of the test project can begin.

7.5 Template Plan of the Test Project

Figure 7.5 shows what a template of a test project plan might look like.

In this plan, test management activities are included together with activities carried out by the testers. The template plan is suitable for any test project. The figure does not give realistic values for the number of days to be spent, as this varies greatly from one test project to another.

Example Planning

This is a case description of a department within a line organisation where problems have occurred with the testing of an information system on time. One of the causes was found to be the resourcing.

This case shows how a national government institution, which we will call LINST, gained better control over its test process by, among other things, setting up effective planning. The case concerns a department within a line organisation, and not a test project such as we have been discussing in this book so far. The problem with resourcing is one of the differences between a line organisation and a test project: in a line organisation there is often a very long-term requirement of resources.

The department described here is responsible for the ongoing maintenance of applications, in both the adaptive and the corrective sense – for example, in the event of such things as changes in legislation. The whole environment consists of dozens of applications that are used both centrally and locally – a variety of platforms and various development languages. The majority of the applications are around 25 years old. The planning and estimating at LINST was particularly important in view of strict deadlines laid down by the government.

The biggest problem at LINST was that it was often impossible to get the amendments tested in time. This meant that the software regularly went into production despite not having been fully tested, with all the unfortunate consequences this involved. For this reason, it was decided to engage a test consultant.

The instruction to the consultant was as follows: solve the two biggest problems, namely:

- Too many production breakdowns (owing to insufficient testing).
- The employees having to carry out too much overtime to reach the deadlines.

After an initial investigation, the focus quickly shifted to two points of concern:

- The plans that were issued were not feasible (capacity not available, environment test not available, construction delays, etc.).
- It was unfortunately not possible to redeploy testers, whether or not temporarily. They could only test their "own" application.

From these perspectives a number of potential improvements were defined. Of interest to this case is:

- Basing the planning and estimating on the release strategy, and learning from previous experience.

The most important question here was: how can I see to it that I will know **when** something has to be tested by someone, and **what**?

To find this out, one of the things to look at is how a tester's tasks are currently built up. The role of the tester at LINST is a combined one: testing the application, maintaining the application and solving production breakdowns.

First, it was examined and recorded how much time the average tester spends on each activity, to establish the actual time he spent on testing. In parallel with this enquiry, a work group was set up to implement and/or professionalise the plans and estimates. One of the decisions adopted was that a plan was henceforth to be issued per application (in relation to the changes). This plan resulted in the required capacity. On the basis of the required capacity and the tester's defined tasks, the available capacity was examined for sufficiency.

Prior to this, when the available capacity did not suffice, the following measures were applied:

1. The deadline was postponed (5%).
2. The available capacity was increased by removing capacity from maintenance or solving production breakdowns (15%).
3. Simply not testing (80%)!

The easiest step was to make the testers redeployable. With the introduction of redeployment alone, the 80% mentioned in point 3 was reduced to only 40%. With the aim of reducing the other percentages as well, a test script was introduced, containing the procedures and templates for drawing up an effective plan. It fully described how a test was to be executed, from intake to aftercare. In this case, only a number of sections from this script will be dealt with, i.e. those of relevance to drawing up the plan:

1. The section on impact analysis.
2. The section on weight of changes.
3. The section on allocating activities and plans.

1. Impact Analysis. When the designers have set up a general functional design, each system is examined to see which functionalities are being changed and in which programs these changes have to be carried through. On the basis of the type of change, it is examined to see which functional change belongs to which cluster, and therefore to which test. Table 7.2 refers to this.

Table 7.2. Impact analysis

PROGRAM	FUNCTIONALITY			
	Payments		Relation	
	func 01	func 02	func 03	func 04
INV 01		X	X	X
INV 02				
INV X	X		X	
WIJ 01		X	X	X
WIJ 02	X			

2. Weight of the Changes. To arrive at a reliable estimate of the test duration, it is also important to determine the weight of the function. The changes can be divided into three categories in terms of weight (heavy, medium and light). Table 7.3 refers to this.

Table 7.3. Weight of changes

	Input	Output	Weight	Remarks
Payments				
Func 01	3	2	Heavy	
Func 03	1	1	Light	
Func x	1	3	Medium	
Relationship				
Func 03	1	2	Medium	
Func y	1	2	Medium	

Usually, the number of hours is given that is required for testing the changes. With the aid of Table 7.3, the number of hours per function can be corrected upwards (heavy) or downwards (light). This allows more realistic planning. Eventually, the hours per function can be added up and the total test time required per cluster can be defined.

3. Allocating Activities and Plans. With the aid of the impact analysis and weight definition set up in the previous sections, the plan below is filled in. In each project, it is indicated for each cluster who will work on it, the start date, the completion date and the capacity. Each test coordinator is individually responsible for this. The test manager collects and combines all the overviews. This makes it possible to see whether employees have been doubly deployed or perhaps not at all. The activities are divided by cluster into phases of preparation, execution and completion. Within the completion activities is a users' check. This enables users to accept the programming quicker after the end of the project.

When it has been determined what and how much is to be tested, the amounts are entered into tables (see Table 7.4). After each phase, it is checked whether the plan still corresponds to the real situation. If the real situation differs from the plan, the test manager will have to take action.

Besides improving the plan, a number of useful rules of thumb were initiated:

- When junior employees are deployed, the required capacity is multiplied by 1.25.

Table 7.4. Allocation of activities

Preparation (design + environment set-up)				
Cluster	Executed by	Start	Finish	Capacity
Payments	Jb, al, mm	1 Mar. 2002	30 Apr. 2002	3
Relationship Xx	Rg, al	1 Apr. 2004	31 May 2002	2

Execution				
Cluster	Executed by	Start	Finish	Capacity
Payments	Mb, mm	30 Apr. 2002	31 May 2002	2
Relationship Xx	kb	31 May 2004	30 June 2002	1

Completion				
Cluster	Executed by	Start	Finish	Capacity
Payments	Jb	31 May 2002	30 June 2002	0,5
Relationship Xx	Rg	30 June 2004	31 July 2002	0,5

- Occasionally an outline plan is required at an early stage, and the general rule here for the testing is that the number of hours required for setting up the functional design is multiplied by 3.
- When the functional design is available, the required time per cluster can be calculated. To obtain an accurate estimate, the following rule is used: preparation represents 50% of the testing, execution 40% and completion 10%. As stated earlier, the figures are checked continually and adjusted if necessary.

By introducing the improvements previously mentioned, LINST succeeded in delivering more or less all of the systems within the deadline and thoroughly tested. Furthermore, since the implementation, the budgets have rarely been exceeded (almost no overtime).

Of course, important points remain that demand extra attention, as follows:

- Discuss in advance what a release should contain.
- It is a good thing that people are redeployable, but ensure that they also get the appropriate training.
- Keep a close check on progress and make any necessary corrections.
- Learn from the past; ensure that reporting on, for example, the comparison between the plan and the real situation is not just used for management, but use the figures also to improve your own test process.

7.6 Factors That Influence the Plan

Various factors can have an influence on the plan:

- The system development method.
- The way of transfer.
- (Un)familiarity with test automation.
- Necessary repair time.
- Time required for test management activities.
- Employees' experience.

7.6.1 The System Development Method

The system development methods can roughly be divided into two groups: linear and iterative methods. With a linear method, the phases are sequential. Only when a phase is completed, on reaching a milestone, does transfer to the next phase take place. Since documentation is always supplied on completion of a phase, the testers have a good starting point for the test design. However, there is also a negative effect. The test team is only supplied with

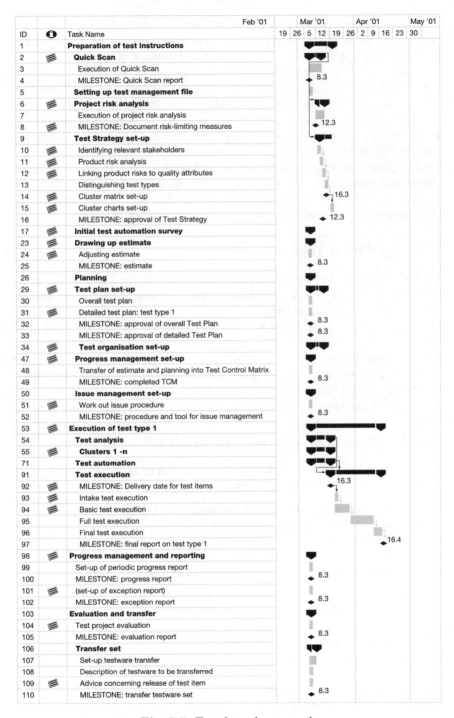

ID	ℹ	Task Name	Feb '01		Mar '01				Apr '01					May '01
			19	26	5	12	19	26	2	9	16	23	30	
1		**Preparation of test instructions**												
2	✍	**Quick Scan**												
3		Execution of Quick Scan												
4		MILESTONE: Quick Scan report			8.3									
5		**Setting up test management file**												
6	✍	**Project risk analysis**												
7		Execution of project risk analysis												
8	✍	MILESTONE: Document risk-limiting measures			12.3									
9		**Test Strategy set-up**												
10	✍	Identifying relevant stakeholders												
11	✍	Product risk analysis												
12	✍	Linking product risks to quality attributes												
13		Distinguishing test types												
14	✍	Cluster matrix set-up				16.3								
15	✍	Cluster charts set-up												
16		MILESTONE: approval of Test Strategy			12.3									
17	✍	**Initial test automation survey**												
23	✍	**Drawing up estimate**												
24	✍	Adjusting estimate												
25		MILESTONE: estimate			8.3									
26		**Planning**												
29	✍	**Test plan set-up**												
30		Overall test plan												
31	✍	Detailed test plan: test type 1												
32		MILESTONE: approval of overall Test Plan			8.3									
33		MILESTONE: approval of detailed Test Plan			8.3									
34	✍	**Test organisation set-up**												
47	✍	**Progress management set-up**												
48		Transfer of estimate and planning into Test Control Matrix												
49		MILESTONE: completed TCM			8.3									
50		**Issue management set-up**												
51	✍	Work out issue procedure												
52		MILESTONE: procedure and tool for issue management			8.3									
53	✍	**Execution of test type 1**												
54		**Test analysis**												
55	✍	**Clusters 1 -n**												
71		**Test automation**												
91		**Test execution**				16.3								
92	✍	MILESTONE: Delivery date for test items												
93	✍	Intake test execution												
94	✍	Basic test execution												
95		Full test execution												
96		Final test execution												
97		MILESTONE: final report on test type 1								16.4				
98	✍	**Progress management and reporting**												
99		Set-up of periodic progress report												
100		MILESTONE: progress report			8.3									
101	✍	(set-up of exception report)												
102		MILESTONE: exception report			8.3									
103		**Evaluation and transfer**												
104	✍	Test project evaluation												
105		MILESTONE: evaluation report			8.3									
106		**Transfer set**												
107		Set-up testware transfer												
108		Description of testware to be transferred												
109	✍	Advice concerning release of test item												
110		MILESTONE: transfer testware set			8.3									

Fig. 7.5. Template plan example

the information system at a late stage of the total project. This means that insight into the quality of the system is not gained earlier. An intake test is necessary and it is also advisable to plan for a number of retest steps.

With the iterative method, the developers deliver the information system in various modules. Each subsequent iteration consists of supplementary modules; in this way the developers build up the system incrementally. Evolutionary planning is perfectly suited to this. The disadvantage of this form of development is that there is often less attention paid to documentation: the prototype is considered as documentation. The advantage is that the work is done in teams containing all the necessary knowledge: developers, designers, testers and users. Thus the testers are told what is important to the users and they assign priorities accordingly. The testers can then start with the most important items within a time slot.

7.6.2 The Way of Transfer

Various measures exist concerning the manner of transfer between the delivering and the recipient parties. The test manager can, for example, arrange that he is to receive a final report from the delivering party (entry criterion). This is a measure that is relatively easy to implement. A much stricter measure is to let the test team observe or even participate in testing when the delivering party is carrying out testing. Each measure that the test manager chooses has an influence on the plan. First of all, there are the extra tasks that the test team has to carry out: observing or participating in the testing. A number of measures also provide increasing dependence on other parties.

7.6.3 (Un)familiarity with Test Automation

If the test execution is automated, this also influences the plan. Various problems can confront an organisation, such as:

- The test tool employed cannot communicate well in all areas with the information system under test.
- The test environment is not wholly suitable for test automation.
- Not all employees are familiar with test automation.
- The existing automated test scripts are immature.

This results in one or more extra risks for the test project.

To allow automation to proceed as smoothly as possible, the test manager is best advised to remove it from the critical path by planning test automation in parallel with the design and manual execution of the tests. Thus, the automation of the tests is placed outside the test project. If anything unexpected goes wrong, it will not have a direct influence on the test project; the tests can then be executed manually. In the meantime, the problems with test automation can be solved without endangering the progress of the test project.

Figure 7.6 shows an example of the parallel automation of the test execution for the first release of an information system.

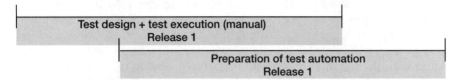

Fig. 7.6. Parallel development of test automation for release 1

The testers design tests based on the requirements for release 1 of an information system. When this is done, the test execution takes place manually. In the meantime, the test automation engineers can start on preparations for the automation of the tests for this release. Any problems with the test automation do not interfere with the testing of the release.

For release 2 of the same information system, the testers go to work designing the tests for this release. This involves the development of new tests and amending existing tests that relate to the changes in respect of release 1. On test execution, these new and amended tests for release 2 will be executed manually. The testers will now use the automation that was prepared for release 1 to execute the unchanged part automatically. In parallel with this, the test automation engineers set to work developing scripts for the changes in release 2 (see Figure 7.7).

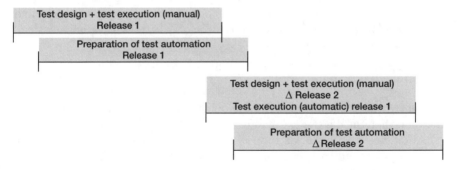

Fig. 7.7. Parallel development of test automation for release 2

It applies here too that the tests can still be fully executed manually in the event of problems with the automation.

By planning in this way, not only is the test automation removed from the critical path, but time is also saved in the test execution. With each release, a greater part of the testing can be carried out automatically. Thus an automatic regression test is built up. It is necessary, however, that the test manager always considers which parts of the test he wishes to automate and which not (CMG, 2001; Fewster & Graham, 1999).

In preparation for the test automation, a test tool must be selected.

This test tool must communicate as well as possible with the information system under test. A tool may also be used that the organisation has previously used in other projects. A technical test can subsequently be carried out to see whether the selected tool satisfies expectations and is able to communicate with the information system. If this is successful, the test automation engineers can go to work on the development of test scripts that execute the tests automatically.

The time required for test automation depends on the type of information system concerned. Most test tools can manage information systems that communicate with users via an interface screen. It makes no difference here whether the interface is character or GUI (Graphical User Interface) based because most tools can handle both. It is a different matter if embedded software is to be tested, e.g. televisions, measuring equipment or mobile telephones. There is in that case no direct interface with the software, so testing of this software is therefore more difficult. The testers will have to seek access to the system and in many cases this is not possible manually. Neither do many of the existing test tools offer assistance, so the testers are faced with a technical problem. Before the system can be tested, they first have to develop a test tool themselves that can communicate with this system.

The same problems apply to test environments. It is often difficult to install an embedded system in a test environment. The testers will need to seek a solution for this, too, with the help of technical experts.

In both cases, extra activities have to be included in the test project, and this affects the plan. However, it is often the only way to test such a system. Manual testing is not an option here!

7.6.4 Necessary Repair Time

The next factor that has an influence on the plan is the repair time. This is the time that the developers require to solve the issues.

Allowance was made for the repair time when the estimate was drawn up. An indication was given of the number of hours the developers need: this represents waiting time for the testers. During the waiting time, the testers should have useful work to do, such as preparing the next test run and expanding the collection of test cases. The testers could also try to find additional issues in areas where a lot of issues have already been found, by means of exploratory testing. Other activities could be updating testware or reviewing each other's testware. Testers can also be involved in reviewing, for example, requirements, functional and technical designs. Interim evaluations with the test team could also take place during repair time.

7.6.5 Time Required for Test Management Activities

It is sometimes forgotten to include test management activities in the plan. This refers to hours spent on executing the quick scan, setting up the test strategy and the test plan, the plan, the estimate, the setting up of the test organisation and of reporting and evaluations. Hours must also often be reserved for reviewing the plan and adjusting it after each iteration. The test manager will spend a lot of time communicating with his team and the people of interest.

7.6.6 Employees' Experience

If only experienced testers who know the organisation are carrying out a test project, the information system and the test method employed, little time needs to be planned for training. The productivity will also be high.

New, inexperienced testers who are added to the test project will first have to receive training to familiarise them with the work of the test project and the testing itself. This means theoretical training as well as practical training, which can be given on the job. With training on the job, the test manager himself or an experienced tester must have time for coaching on top of his own tasks. This can put considerable pressure on productivity.

The experience level of parties indirectly involved is another important factor. A maintenance department that gets the testware in the transfer phase has to be able to understand how the test team has set up the tests. All stakeholders should know what is expected of them. If they have to consider whether the test conditions provide sufficient coverage, they should know what that means. The same applies to the cluster cards, which they have to approve.

7.7 Conclusion

Besides the factors mentioned in the previous sections, there are many more; it is not possible to provide an exhaustive list. Below is a short list of other factors:

- Discuss with the client when the developers should be present during the (re)test execution.
- Ensure that the testers do not leave the team too early to join another project. At the end of a test project, testers are often required to finish off final tasks, such as updating all the test documents to the latest version.
- Plan time for feedback on the metrics to the organisation when the test project is finished. The organisation can use these for improving the test process and/or the development process.
- Plan time for closure of the test project.

It is always advisable to build in margins. Therefore, the test manager should not simply indicate the date when an activity will start and when it will end, but also indicate potential deviations: the bandwidth of the plan. The basis for the bandwidth can lie in the project risks. The test manager can indicate where the biggest threats to the test project lie and estimate the extent to which the plan may deviate. The same applies to the assumptions and preconditions contained in the quick scan and the test plan. If the assumptions and preconditions appear to be wrong, there are consequences for the plan, and a bandwidth for this can also be indicated for the relevant activities.

The test manager must indicate to the client immediately at the start of the test project what consequences the materialisation of project risks and wrong assumptions and preconditions has. This will reinforce the plan.

The test manager is now almost finished with the preparation activities of the test project. The last activity is setting up the test organisation. This and the relationship with the test project are the subjects of the following chapter.

8

The Test Organisation

The scope and depth of the test are set out in the test strategy. The test manager has based the planning and estimating on that information. The cluster matrix sets out which test levels will be carried out. A system test will largely be performed within the IT project, while an acceptance test will be carried out by the business side (a users' organisation or a central test department). The test organisation should be described in the test plans. Sometimes a reference to documentation already present in the organisation is sufficient.

In organising testing, the test manager should bear in mind the knowledge, experience and guidelines within the organisation. Some organisations have a department that is able to take over a number of test activities from the project. Furthermore a test manager will have to set up the structure regarding roles, reporting, meeting and the use of the test environment.

8.1 Project Structure

To be able to carry out a test project, various people are needed with various types of knowledge and skills. Which knowledge and skills the testers must have mainly depends on the level and complexity of the test environment. In a system test, apart from professional testers, for example, the test team will also consist of developers, since they have technical knowledge of the system. For an acceptance test, the team must include end users of the information system, since they know the business processes the system must support. When testing an embedded system, there must be sufficient software engineering expertise in the test team, and people who have knowledge of the system architecture and the hardware used. It is also possible that one or more of the test levels will be executed outside the project. This section discusses the various testing roles and the collaboration between the various parts of the organisation within and outside of a test project.

8.1.1 Test Roles

A number of different roles are possible in a test project:

- *The test manager.* The test manager is responsible for the testing within a project. This is an independent role, on the same level as the project manager. Among other things, he bears a budgetary responsibility for testing and quality.
- *The test team leader.* In large programmes that are characterised by various test projects, the daily management of a test project can be handed over to a test team leader. The final responsibility for the test remains, however, with the test manager. The role of the test team leader is similar to that of foreman in the test team, ensuring that everything is organised so that the team is able to carry out its work effectively.
- *The test analyst.* The test analyst creates the test design. He will build up the test set based on the product risks and requirements pertaining to the information system. In particular, the test analyst possesses knowledge and experience of test techniques and the domain area.
- *The test executor.* The test executor will carry out the test cases that the test analyst has made. Sometimes, the same person holds both roles of test analyst and test executor. In an acceptance test, the test manager will include end users of the information system in the test team. They will be asked to review the test cases during the test preparation. In the case of a system test, information analysts may be included in the test team.
- *The navigator.* If the results of the cost–benefit analysis of automatic testing are favourable, a navigator will create test scripts for automatic testing. He has knowledge of test tools and structured programming.
- *The test consultant.* The test consultant advises and supports the project members in the application of test methods, techniques and test tools. He therefore helps to give shape to test projects and to outline the test strategy. He also advises clients and project members on how to improve the testing within projects or organisations.

Appendix I contains a comprehensive profile description of the test roles.

8.1.2 Staffing the Test Project

A test team that possesses test knowledge, technical knowledge and business knowledge should carry out the test project. The members of the test team must also possess social skills.

A team that contains a good mix of people with varying levels of experience helps ensure the success of test project execution. If a team consists of only juniors, it will require a lot of attention and management. With a test team that consists only of senior testers, it will be difficult to maintain the motivation: the senior testers will be carrying out activities that are not exactly challenging to a senior. You should therefore examine carefully the profiles of the testers who will be included in the test team.

The test levels and test types also determine the desired profile of test team members. Since a performance test is usually executed automatically, it is necessary to include in the team a navigator, who possesses knowledge of performance test tools. In a system test, the testers should have technical skills. In an acceptance test, several testers with business knowledge will be required.

The test manager, like the project manager, may experience problems with the availability of project members. If testers with the necessary skills are not available, this will of course have consequences for the progress of the test project, and perhaps even the quality of the information system in the end. It is possible, for example, for the necessary resources to be tied up in another (test) project that is behind schedule. In that case, those testers will become available to the project later. The test manager will always have to indicate the consequences of this clearly and, together with the stakeholders, come to a decision. For example, can the project be rescheduled? If that is impossible and there are no alternative resources available, perhaps the only solution is to make concessions to the scope and depth of the test based on the product risks. The test manager will then propose removing the test clusters with the lowest priority from the scope of the test project. Clearly, if resources disappear before the test is fully completed, the same problem will arise: it will no longer be possible to test everything that was agreed upon. This is one of the reasons for executing the test clusters on a priority basis. Chapter 9 deals with the dynamics of test project execution.

8.1.3 Centrally Organised Test Services

An organisation that does not have much experience with structured testing will place much of the testing within the system development project itself. With this kind of organization, there is not always a department that maintains the testware at the end of the project. If the test is executed automatically, it will be done within the project. The cost of the necessary equipment will be met by the project. Team members who do not as yet possess knowledge of testing have to be trained, and a budget must also be set aside for this.

However, a number of these kinds of project activities in the area of testing (e.g. arranging licences for the issue management tool) are also of interest to other test projects. It may therefore be useful to organise these activities in a specialised department, offering services to the projects.

We can envisage various kinds of such departments. The two most important are a staff department that concentrates on managing and providing test expertise within the organisation, and a line department that actually carries out the testing itself. The first is often called a test competence centre (TCC), the second a test centre.

The Test Competence Centre

The tasks of such a department may include:

- Knowledge management of the test approach used in the organisation; advice and knowledge transfer, training, etc.
- The provision of test tools, e.g. issue management tools, test execution tools, etc.; arranging licences, maintaining contacts with tool suppliers and organising training and coaching.
- Maintenance of the test infrastructure, setting up test environments, placing the correct versions of programs in the environment, maintaining various connections between systems, keeping test data, etc.
- Providing resources with testing experience, e.g. the test team leader.

The advantage of a competence centre is that the wheel does not have to be invented repeatedly, and that testing knowledge is preserved within the organisation. For example:

> Issue management is done entirely within the project; on completion of the project, the issue administration ceases to exist and issues that remain open are often no longer managed. Continuity is also lacking and with each new test project, issue management is again set up and the wheel is invented again.

Complementary services are also created within a test competence centre: for example, a human resources (HR) policy to ensure that people with the appropriate test skills can develop and have sufficient career prospects. Test advising is an independent service, which is carried out by experienced test consultants. The project might, for example, develop along the lines of the dynamic system development method (DSDM). The test consultant will then be able to advise projects on setting up effective testing for this. These consultants can also initiate, conduct and implement test process improvements.

The existence of a TCC provides the test manager with various advantages. Many things are already organised and can be taken on board without too much time and expense. The people assigned to the test project have a test background. The TCC provides training. If a standard test method is used within the organisation, the testers can transfer from one project to another, without requiring training. This provides considerable flexibility in the event of over- or under-capacity in projects. In the areas where the organisation lacks knowledge, the test manager can put forward proposals for the project. The TCC can use the experience gained with this as input to other, similar projects.

A step beyond a TCC is an operational line department for executing tests, known as a test centre.

The Test Centre

The test centre prepares complete tests and executes them. It contains testing experience and has standard procedures and instruments available for issue administration and management. For smaller test projects, issue management can be organised centrally. For bigger ones, tailored issue management is set up based on centrally available knowledge and experience.

Testing may also take place partly within the project and partly within the test centre: for example, the technical tests within the project, and the functional tests in the test centre. The test centre would then only require having functional knowledge of the information system available.

The test centre can also take on a supervisory role, by issuing the test process with particular approval or certification before the information system is put into production. The test centre then functions as a quality control department for testing.

Within this variant, the test employees have a high level of knowledge of testing and the test manager will have more of a monitoring than a managing role. A big advantage of this organisational form is that after the project, the testware is maintained within the test centre. No transfer is therefore required and the knowledge is retained.

As with a TCC, there may be a question of "forced goodwill". This is good for the efficiency of the testing, but can lead to problems. When the project builds a new information system for which there is no knowledge present in the test centre, it is often more efficient to carry out the testing entirely within the project. It is then preferable to involve testers from the test centre in the project; in this way, the resourcing of the project and the transfer of knowledge to the test centre are done in one go.

8.2 Reporting Structure

The frequency and data with which the client desires progress reports vary from project to project and from organisation to organisation. It should be ensured at any rate that clear agreements are made regarding this. Different forms of test organisation call for different types of reporting. If the test manager, for example, has the preparation and execution of the acceptance test entirely carried out by a test centre, then that department will probably take care of the reporting itself. The test manager will then include this report within his own report on the test project as a whole. Chapters 10 and 12 go into this in more depth.

How the reporting takes place, to whom and with what frequency, must be established in the test plan. In Table 8.1, the target group, the purpose and the frequency in respect of various types of reporting are shown.

Table 8.1. Types of reporting

Type of report	For whom	Purpose	Frequency
Progress report	Project manager	Reporting progress in respect of time, money and quality	Usually weekly, but always by agreement with the project manager
Phase report (milestone report)	Project manager	Transfer from one test phase to the next	At the end of each test phase except the last. The final report follows at the end of this
Final report	Project manager, stakeholders	Advising on putting into production	Once only, at the end of the test project
Exception report	Project management, stakeholders	Emergency report when the test project is influenced by the extent of the total project planning or the quality of the information system being under threat	Based on previously defined criteria in the test plan (e.g. with x% deviation from the planning)

It must be ensured that all the stakeholders are kept well informed on the quality of the information system. This can be a source of tension with project management, therefore independence must be guaranteed. Make sure that the reporting presents a realistic picture of the situation: not over-positive, but not too negative either.

The test manager can set up objective reporting by reporting on the outstanding and covered product risks. When the decision has been made to use the RRBT approach, the test manager must examine whether the reports offer the possibility of reporting on the product risks. If not, he should consider whether it is better to deviate from the standard.

Example Test Organisation

While setting up a test organisation, the test manager must bear in mind the complexity and extent of the project. In large projects, a clear project organisation and good communication with the appropriate reporting structure are essential. This case describes a possible project structure and shows how a formal reporting structure can prevent communication problems.

This case concerns an implementation phase of a new way of evaluating stock in a Dutch supermarket chain, called here "The Grocer". The new evaluation has significant consequences for the systems in which the stocks are registered. Moreover, not only is the system at head office to be adapted, but also those of the distribution centres and all the shops. New software has to be developed, and the infrastructure and the relevant interfaces must also be adapted. The entire project will take around 3 years, and has been given the title MONEY.

The biggest challenge in setting up the test organisation for the MONEY project is its very wide scope. Many different departments, systems, infrastructures and interfaces are involved. MONEY is being introduced in phases with related functionality. If systems change at the head office, the supplying parties, such as shops and distribution centres, will have to attune their systems to this. For this, therefore, the local software must also be adapted at the same time.

Figure 8.1 shows the set-up of the organisation around the testing.

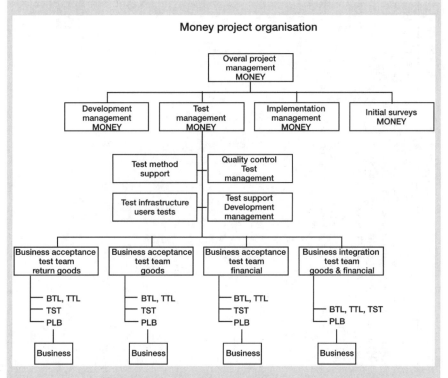

Fig. 8.1. MONEY project organisation

To set up the test organisation in this way, among other things a number of standard roles will have to be delegated. A description of the roles as taken up at The Grocer is shown in Table 8.2.

Table 8.2. Roles within MONEY

Role	Title	Tasks	Remarks
TM BTL	Test Manager Business Team Leader	Overall coordination and management of users' tests Test planning, *functional* support for the test preparation and test execution	One TM is appointed for MONEY A BTL is appointed per test team. The BTL bears the final responsibility for the testing and accepts and approves the test result on behalf of the business. He works closely with the TTL
TTL	Test Team Leader	Test planning, *technical* support for the test preparation and test execution	A TTL is appointed per test team. The TTL is responsible for the timetable and the day-to-day management of the test team. He works closely with the BTL
TST	Tester	Test preparation and test execution (functional and/or technical)	
TTI	Test Team Leader for Infrastructure	Test planning, set-up and provision of test infrastructure	TTI supports the various users' test teams in areas of: • Provision of test infrastructure • Use of test environment and test tools • Test management (transfers, version management) • Test coordination (across parties)
TMS	Test Method Support	Test method support	TMS supports the various users in the areas of: • Test method • Test techniques • Test infrastructure
TSP	Test Support (technical)	Supports the users' tests from development management	
PLB	Project Leader Business	Test planning, *business* support of the test preparation and test execution	PLB supports the various users' test teams in the areas of: • Concept monitoring (business) • Business expertise input • Coordination of business matters (over the test team) • Quality control of test products

Because this is a project with a 3-year duration, it has been decided to split it into various phases for the sake of manageability. A complete project group will be set up per phase. This means that there is also a test team required per phase. Within the project, it has been decided to appoint not one, but two team leaders: one team leader from the business side and one from the test discipline. Known within "The Grocer" as "tandem management", these team leaders are jointly responsible for the daily management of a test team within the MONEY project.

A potential problem that arises is that three camps will emerge, which will play off against each other. We mean here the users, the testers and the developers. The formal arrangement is that the users report to the testers and the testers then report onwards to the developers. However, the prevailing organisational culture within "The Grocer" is such that people are used to dealing directly with each other, and so the test teams are often left out. This results in, among other things, the various issues not being registered, with all the consequences this brings. To ensure that the project is not jeopardised, and also that everyone is satisfied, a number of extra consultation situations have been introduced and extra conditions applied to the reporting.

Table 8.3 sets out the three most important reports.

Table 8.3. Roles within MONEY

Type of report	For whom	Purpose	Frequency
Progress report	Management, users, developers	To keep everyone informed of progress	Weekly, distributed on Monday before 10:00
Issue report	Testers, users, developers	A technical document to supply insight into faults	Weekly, discussed during the issue consultation
Phase report	Project manager, stakeholders	To supply insight into completion of the phases	After every phase

The experience of "The Grocer" is that the setting up of a good organisational structure, with appropriate procedures, is essential to the success of a project. MONEY is one of the larger projects, but the problems that arise here often occur in smaller projects, too. Also, the time lost in the beginning through poor communication among all the groups, and the confusion regarding status – as to how, what and when – were entirely made up for later through the introduction of a clear (test) organisation. Thanks to this measure, the entire project was successfully completed according to plan within the 3 years.

8.3 Meeting Structure

It is of the utmost importance that the test manager is part of the regular project meetings. After all, this is where the most important decisions are made, decisions that might affect the risks with the information system (product) and in the project. In the test team meetings during test preparation, progress will be one of the subjects handled. During test execution, the subject of issues will be added. There will also be issue meetings in the course of the test execution. Apart from the test manager, the stakeholders, project leader and the developers will also attend these meetings. The stakeholders then decide what is to happen concerning the outstanding issues, using the product risk priorities.

If improvement of the test process is part of the test manager's task, meetings on this subject may also be set up.

The types of meeting and communication structure required depend on the type of project and the project organisation.

Table 8.4 shows the various meeting types, the participants, the purpose and the frequency.

Table 8.4. Types of meetings

Type of consultation	Participants	Purpose	Frequency
Test team meeting	Test manager, test team	Discuss test progress and issues	Weekly
Issue meeting	Test manager, key stakeholders (during acceptance tests), developers' team (during system tests)	Discuss and prioritise issues	Usually daily, during test execution
Project meeting	Project leader, test manager, project members	Discuss project progress, quality and risks	Weekly
Test process improvement meeting	Test manager, test team, test consultant, client	Improvement of test process	Optional and only when test process improvement is part of the test manager's tasks

8.4 Infrastructure

By infrastructure is meant all the provisions necessary for the preparation and execution of tests, e.g. test environments, test tools and workstations.

To enable the test team to perform its tasks, the necessary arrangements must be made in the organisation. For example, the testers must have at least a workstation with a PC and access to the test environment. They will also require access to the issue administration and other necessary applications.

8.4.1 Test Environments

The test manager must ensure that the test team has a test environment at its disposal in which it can execute the test.

Below is an explanation of the various test environments:

- *Development test environment.* For the execution of technical (white-box) unit tests. This environment is used for testing the technical operation of (parts of) the software. The setting up and maintenance of this environment is the responsibility of the developers of the application. They will carry out the unit test on their own software in this environment.
- *System test environment.* For technical (white-box) and functional (black-box) system tests. The purpose of this environment is to subject the application to technical and functional tests; it must be logically separated as far as possible from the development environment. This makes it impossible for the developers to carry out actions on the test environment while the testers are executing tests, a situation which could influence the test results. The maintenance of the software, documentation and testware must be prescribed and set up.
- *Acceptance test environment.* For acceptance tests by users and (functional and operation) managers. An acceptance test environment must be logically and physically separate as far as possible from the other environments. The developers may not change the environment. In short, the separation of systems and responsibilities must be guaranteed. The acceptance test environment must be set up to reflect the final production system. This is sometimes impossible, owing to links with other systems. If these links cannot be realised in the acceptance test environment, the use of simulators is an option for consideration.

The separation of test environments must guarantee that:

- Users and managers can carry out an acceptance test independently in a separate environment.
- Developers can carry out tests without getting in the way of the testers; the approved software cannot be changed by the developers before it is transferred to a subsequent environment.

- The test environment represents the goals of the test to a satisfactory degree and demonstrates the correct infrastructure prior to production.

If various projects are using the same test environment, the test team does not always have full control over it. Since the test results of different projects can influence each other, clear agreement is essential. If the test environments are managed by a test centre, it will coordinate them.

A number of steps are involved in the setting up of a test environment:

1. *Definition of the requirements of the relevant test environment.* An indication of these is given in the cluster cards. The product and project risks created by differences between the infrastructure and the final production infrastructure are defined and supplemented with the measures to be undertaken. A plan is also set up showing the timetable of the required activities and contingencies of the environment set-up. It is possible that the required infrastructure cannot be realised according to plan. In that case, the project plan and the test plan will have to be adjusted, since no (dynamic) test execution can take place in the absence of a suitable test environment.
2. *Specification of the test environment.* The required test environment, consisting of applications and technical components, is further worked out in a plan set up specifically for that purpose. Agreements with the suppliers and specialists are established and the planning is refined.
3. *Realisation of the test environment.* The test environment is set up with the aid of the plan and the overall planning. This is typically a process that can be difficult to manage if the test team is dependent on the input of suppliers. It is then especially important to monitor the agreements and relevant planning.
4. *Intake and acceptance of the test environment.* Following set-up, it should be clear whether the test environment is suitable for executing the tests. The completeness of the test environment is tested with the aid of a checklist. A trial test is carried out on the application. Shortcomings are noted, new agreements are established and the planning is adjusted. The intake of the test environment should take place well in advance of testing the application, so that the planned start of the test execution is not jeopardised. As soon as the test environment is approved, it can be released for use by the test team.

When these steps have been taken, the actual test execution can begin. During the test execution the infrastructure specialists must be available on call to carry out tasks such as running batches, making a back-up or restoring it, exporting test data, maintaining tables, etc. In a very formal organisation, Service Level Agreements (SLAs) are made with the department that maintains the test environment.

At the end of the test project, the test manager can release the test environment for other projects. If the test environment was set up within the project, it has to be transferred to the maintenance organisation (see Chapter 13).

8.4.2 Workstations and Facilities

If the testers are from the organisation itself, they will often have their own workspace. For the sake of good communication, it is practical to site them close together. End users should preferably not remain in their own department, as they will be distracted too much. It is advisable to locate them near the development team, for communication between testers and developers is very important, and it is through this collaboration that the desired level of quality of the information system is to be achieved.

In many test situations, it is necessary to test apart from the organisation's network. A network has therefore to be set up in a separate test area. In addition, other facilities are required, such as photocopiers and printers.

8.5 Conclusion

When the test manager has determined the test organisation of the project, he can complete the test plans. It is now known what is going to be tested, who is going to do it, how much time and money are reserved for it and how the project is set within the organisation. The execution of the test project can now begin. This obviously is not static, the project itself and its surroundings being continually in motion. This results in considerable dynamics in the testing, and this is the subject of the following chapter.

9

The Dynamics of Testing

Following the preparation, it is time to go on to design the testware and eventually to perform tests on the information system. The test strategy and the test plan have been developed and signed off by the stakeholders. Nevertheless, in practice, the analysis and test execution do not always proceed according to the predictions made in the test strategy and test plan and based on the information that was available at the time. The project and its context are always in motion. Within the dynamics of the test execution, the test manager's attention shifts away from creating conditions to controlling the situation. Everything must be geared towards achieving a successful result, for testing is not something you do "on the side". It is a specific profession. The management required and the potential problems demand specific knowledge. During this phase, the test manager has the opportunity to demonstrate his added value.

The test should result in well-founded advice on the quality of the information system regarding the product risks involved when it is put into production. The basis for this is laid down in the test strategy, which sets out exactly what is to be tested in order to cover the product risks sufficiently. When the testing is over and all the results have been considered, the test team is able to indicate which product risks are covered and which are outstanding. The reasons why a product risk is not covered, or only partially covered, may vary. Possibly the test team was unable to carry out certain tests for technical reasons to do with the test environment. It is also possible that the test manager has had to make assumptions during the preparatory work that have proved to be incorrect, or has laid down preconditions in the test plan that could not be complied with, owing to various circumstances.

If it is not possible to free up more time or budget to measure the quality described in the test strategy, it must be decided together with the stakeholders which parts of the test set the test team should still carry out and which not. Precisely because a basis for this has been laid in the test strategy, the organisation is able to make an informed decision.

Apart from an overview of the product risks, there must also be an overview of the project risks, since they can influence the progress of the (test) project. Measures should also be identified with which these situations can be prevented. The project risks and their countermeasures are included in the test plan. Risk management must also take place, so that any new risks that arise or others fall away can be monitored.

Unforeseen situations can always arise during a test project, and a test manager must be able to respond quickly and adequately to unexpected situations that disrupt the project: the domain experts who were to provide support in carrying out the users' acceptance test now have urgent work to carry out for production; upon delivery, the quality of the software appears different from what was agreed. What now?

In the first part of this chapter, we deal with the manageable factors of time, money and quality that the test manager has in his control. We have also collected a number of situations that have often arisen in a large number of test projects. Each of these situations is described in the subsequent sections, together with their possible causes and potential impact on the test project. Measures are then described that can be taken in response, together with the consequences for time, money and quality. Naturally, not all of the proposed measures will be successful in every situation in every project. They are meant to be seen as tips.

9.1 Management of Time, Money and Quality

A project manager can manage four factors: time, money, quality and functionality – the "eternal quadrangle". A test manager can only exert influence over the functionality of the information system at the beginning of the project – the design stage. He can, for example, point out that functionality which cannot be tested owing to a shortage of time should not form a part of the information system. As the project progresses, he can exert less and less influence on the functionality. Once the test execution stage arrives, the biggest part of the information system has already been built and functionality is no longer subject to management. At most, requests for changes can only be rejected for reasons of time, complexity or the fact that they would lead to unacceptable product risks.

This means that, as far as the test manager is concerned, usually only three controls are subject to management: time, money and quality (Figure 9.1). These three business controls cannot be separated: the higher the quality of the test set (and with that of the information system) must be, the more time and money are required. If time is at a premium, then more money will perhaps be necessary to measure the same quality.

We will take a closer look at the three business controls below.

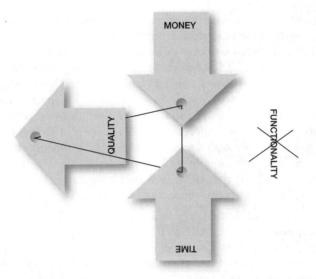

Fig. 9.1. The test manager's "eternal triangle"

9.1.1 Management of Time

"We absolutely must go into production at the end of next week. The only way to achieve this is to have the test teams work at night and as much as possible at the weekend." Sounds familiar? The execution of a test often comes at the end of a project, and consequently there is a shortage of time. This means that the test team has to work overtime to catch up with the backlog that arose in the earlier phases. But is this really effective?

Overtime can be a solution, but only for a short period: working overtime demands a lot of energy and if employees are required to work overtime over a long period, it results not only in resistance but also in increased chances of mistakes, such as overlooking discrepancies. Even more important is the feasibility of the set goal. If, with 1 week's overtime, the test is carried out completely according to plan, then overtime may even provide a sense of satisfaction. But if it does not go according to plan, it will do little for the employees' motivation!

Also, when testing is being carried out, it often requires others to be present. If testing occurs at the weekend and there is no support organisation available – to restore a database, for example – there can be very little progress. Imagine that a test team is mobilised to come in and test on a Saturday morning because a new version has been delivered. The information system gets stuck at the second test case because on Friday afternoon the installation was not completed. The test team will not be happy with this. All the supporting parties must be present or within reach if overtime is worked. It is therefore only advisable over short periods, when the aim is achievable and when all the support departments are present, such as development, functional management or database administrators.

A good alternative is working in shifts. Two or more teams can work in alternate shifts so that all the tests are carried out more effectively over each 24-hour period. This avoids the situation whereby the whole team becomes exhausted, and the effectiveness of the overtime is destroyed. But with shift work, the condition also applies that the support must be available. There must also be at least one senior tester in each team who can provide daily progress reports. Even a test manager can only be in one place at a time!

No matter how early on the test team gets involved in the project, the fact remains that a large part of the test execution can only take place at the end of the project. Test execution is therefore always on the critical path.

The development team has delivered the information system and would like nothing more than to hear that it is fine, and where any adjustments might be required. Therefore, after the system has been delivered there is great pressure on the test team. The whole organisation nervously awaits the first issues. If, after a day, no issues have been reported, it begins to get a little impatient. Often, some adjustments to the requirements are made during the development phase and so the test team will not always be fully prepared with the complete test design. Pressure on the test team increases.

How can pressure on the test team be reduced? One way, for example, is to report a number of issues as quickly as possible. This shifts the pressure onto the development team, and the test execution is no longer so critical. The development team will have to analyse and solve the issues.

To allow reporting on a part of the information system, a plan must be set up in small units by means of evolutionary planning.

It can happen that the cluster card relating to a part of the system with a low priority has not yet been completed, while all the test conditions (logical test design) and test cases (physical actions to be performed including data input and expected results) have been fulfilled (and also carried out) relating to a high-priority cluster.

9.1.2 Management of Money

If the same level of quality has to be realised in less time, more money is required – to recruit more employees, for example. Instead of carrying out a test with two people in four weeks, for the same budget the test manager could test for two weeks with four people. Unfortunately, this calculation does not always add up. There will be more need of organising and consulting to coordinate tasks and progress successfully. In the end, it might require a bigger budget. There is also the risk that people will get in each other's way. Four painters can paint one room, taking one wall each. Any more painters and they would be more of a hindrance than a help.

If money is not the problem, but the test environment is, investment in an extra environment can drastically reduce the duration of test execution. This extra environment can be realised by introducing another machine, but also, for example, by creating separate environments on one network server in the form of separate files. Each tester, or each test team, must then know precisely what their own tasks and responsibilities are. The management of the environments will involve more staff and consequently more money.

Allowances must be made in planning for situations where idle time is created because of unforeseen circumstances. This time must be put to good use, for there is nothing less motivating than waiting for the day to end while there is no work to be done! It is better at such times to elaborate test cases for low-priority aspects. It must be clear, however, that these are extra activities and not replacing planned tasks. These hours can be logged under "waiting time", for example, giving the test manager insight into the time that has been lost and who was responsible for it. In this way, no call is made upon the budget.

If the test team comprises persons who have been hired on a contractual basis, the test manager can expel them from the project temporarily and call on them again at a later stage when they are needed. However, these breaks should not be of long duration, since there is a risk that these people will get involved with another project in the interim. A good alternative is to set up test resource pools which can be drawn upon at the point when they can immediately go to work effectively. The setting up and use of this type of resource pool requires a mature test organisation with testware documentation of such a high standard that every tester can step in to prepare and carry out the test without much introduction. Furthermore, the testers would have to possess sufficiently broad expertise to be able to work quickly and effectively in various projects.

The budget can also be spared by using the just-in-time (JIT) method. This means that for example an expensive scanner is only rented and set up at the very last moment. While taking on people and equipment far in advance may provide a greater degree of security, it also costs more money. The disadvantage of the JIT approach is, of course, that there may be the risk of people or equipment being unavailable at the point when they are needed, but much in this area can be established by contract and agreed with the parties involved (particularly as regards the purchase of hardware and software).

9.1.3 Management of Quality

The test plan assumes that overrun in the system development leads to overrun in the testing. If the developers of (a part of) the information system deliver a week later than planned, the consequence is that the testing will be completed at least a week later than planned. Other disruptive and delaying factors arising outside the test team's sphere of influence during the planned test period will lead to a delay in delivery of the information system. It happens occasionally that the delivery date is hard and fast (as with the millennium problems, the introduction of the euro or a change in legislation set to take effect on a particular date, for example) and the test project can then come under severe pressure.

During both preparation and execution, it may be necessary to make choices because the test team is no longer able to perform everything that was planned at first. During the preparation and execution stages, it must be determined in consultation with the stakeholders, on the basis of the product risks and their allocated priorities, what can possibly be cancelled if there really is not enough time to carry out everything as planned. This means that tests with a high priority are developed and performed, while tests with a low priority are the first to be cancelled. This can be taken to the point where the product risks the organisation would run are not acceptable to the stakeholders. In the end, with less time there will also be less testing carried out. The completed test therefore provides a lower degree of coverage than that described in the test strategy, but this does not automatically mean that the quality of the information system is compromised; there is merely insufficient insight into the quality of some parts of the system to assess whether it is adequate. We call this method of managing the execution of the test project the strategic test slicing method (STSM), see Figure 9.2. For an explanation of this method, see Chapter 2.

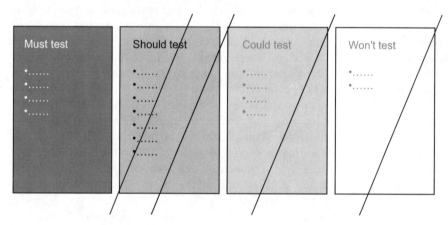

Fig. 9.2. The strategic test slicing method (STSM)

The stakeholders decide not to carry out any preparatory tasks concerning a cluster with the priority "Won't test" (Table 9.1). Concerning a cluster with the priority "Could test", it is decided that the test team will only define the test conditions and no test cases. For clusters with the priorities "Should test" and "Must test", both the test conditions and the test cases are defined. Agreements can be made in the same way concerning the execution of the test.

Table 9.1. Example of an STSM choice

Cluster importance	Preparation
Must test	Test conditions and test cases
Should test	Test conditions and test cases
Could test	Test conditions
Won't test	–

Communication with the stakeholders is very important. Matters must be clarified as early as possible in the test project concerning the manner of slicing to be used on occasions when there is time pressure. There is enough time and opportunity at the early stage of the project to decide objectively what should happen if there proves to be less time available than was first planned. If it proves necessary to apply the STSM, everyone should be aware of what is to take place and there is no need for long discussions. A minimum requirement should be established in the test strategy, to allow the test to cover the degree of acceptable risk for production purposes.

9.2 Situations That Influence the Test Project

In the following sections we describe nine situations that often arise during the preparation and execution of tests. We describe briefly the problem, the possible causes, the measures that the test manager can take and the impact on the business controls of time, money and quality.

The situations are as follows:

1. The cluster cards are incomplete.
2. The stakeholders do not feel (sufficiently) involved.
3. Incomplete documentation.
4. Domain experts are unavailable or do not have enough time to spare.
5. Changing insights lead to changes in the requirements.
6. Insufficient knowledge on the part of test professionals.
7. Late delivery of the information system.
8. Poor quality of the delivered information system.
9. The test environment is unstable or even unavailable.

9.2.1 Cluster Cards Are Incomplete

In Chapter 5, it was mentioned that when setting up the cluster cards, it is not necessary for all the information to be available at that point. Figure 9.3 shows an example of a number of cluster cards from a test strategy in which a number of the spaces have not yet been filled in.

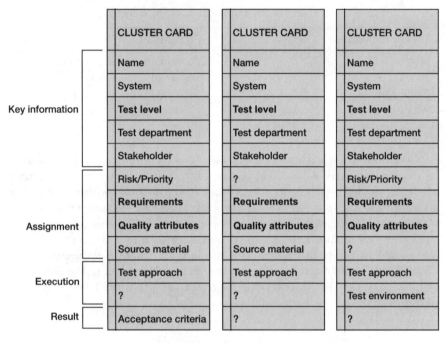

Fig. 9.3. Example of filled-out cluster cards

The parts relating to the key information should always be complete.

There may therefore be blank spaces in the other areas (assignment, execution and result). The first action by the testers at the start of test designing is to fill in these empty spaces. If one or more of the parts mentioned are not completed, this will result in one or more project risks. If, for example, the test environment is not yet known and it later appears that this environment is so complex to set up that at least 3 months will be required to do it, a problem quickly arises if the test team is due to begin within 2 months. For the project risk, contingency plans should be made available as soon as possible.

Possible Causes

These spaces are often not filled in because not enough information was available at the time of setting up the test strategy, which after all is set up at an early stage of the project. It is therefore possible that, for example, the source material for the test is not yet (fully) available. At the time when the test team starts the test preparation there is more time and many more details should then be available, allowing the empty spaces to be filled in. If, however, there is still an absence of source material, the test manager will have to take action.

Possible Actions

Since some omissions are less important than others, the measures taken might depend very much on the blank spaces that remain. In Figure 9.3, in the second cluster, the product risks and their significance are not known. This is a situation that can only arise if, for example, the stakeholder has indicated that the system's time behaviour is very important, and he does not explicitly mention what might go wrong if the requirements for this are not sufficiently met. The test manager can play devil's advocate here: why does the stakeholder want the quality attributes related to this cluster tested if there appears to be no product risks? In other words, if he really wants this cluster to be tested, the stakeholder will have to indicate which product risks at the very least have to be covered by the test. Without this information, the test team cannot start with the test design using RRBT. If the test team does begin the test design, it will not be clear whether the most important parts will be tested.

If the test environment is not known, as in the first cluster, the test team can still start on the test design. Often, it will become clear from the test design itself which environment is necessary.

Some information, such as that concerning product risks and requirements, is essential. The test manager can agree with the client and the stakeholders that the test team will not start the test design without the essential information. In that case, the test manager must discuss with the stakeholder responsible for the particular cluster what information is minimally required and within what time frame the stakeholder must supply the information.

Other parts can sometimes be dealt with by making assumptions. An assumption concerning a test environment may be made based on the test level, the product risks to be tested and the associated requirements. Such an assumption should of course be clearly communicated to the stakeholders, for it could result in other project risks. If it later appears during the test design or execution that a wrong assumption has been made, this can influence the progress of the test project (in terms of time and money) or even the quality of the information system. The additional project risks associated with any assumptions must be added to the list of established risks and included in the progress report. If the project risks relating to empty spaces or those filled in on the basis of assumptions are too high, it may be decided not to start the test design.

Impact on the Project

If essential information is only available at a later stage, this naturally influences the time factor. The test preparations for the cluster concerned have to be started later, and this may have consequences for the total planning. If certain information never becomes available, this will be reflected in the quality of the test, and with that possibly also in the quality of the information system.

9.2.2 The Stakeholders Do Not Feel (Sufficiently) Involved

During the test project, the test manager may come up against various situations in which it can be seen that the organisation does not feel sufficiently involved in the (test) project. When the test strategy was set up, a list was drawn up of who had an interest in what and who was responsible for what. Significant changes in requirements can result in other product risks and their importance and lead to associated changes in the stakeholders; therefore it must be examined what impact this has on the test strategy and also for the plan and the budget. It also sometimes happens that other parties who play a vital role in supporting the test project do not deliver the support that is required. Not all the stakeholders attach the same importance to testing, and there may even be conflicting interests.

In an insurance company, support for test database data entry is supplied by the service centre department, which also carries out maintenance and management of the production databases. At a certain point, a request comes from the test project to reload the test database, returning to the starting position to allow a new critical path test to be carried out. However, at the same time a very small production fault materialises. The service centre indicates that the testers will have to wait until the problem in the production environment is solved, for the rule within the service centre is: "Production always has priority!"

Possible Causes

Stakeholders often do not feel involved in the test project because they are unfamiliar with it or with testing. Involvement may also decrease because a project takes too long and/or other projects have been started which also require the stakeholders' attention.

The first action to undertake is to establish why the stakeholder no longer feels responsible. Why is support from the systems administration department inadequate? Is it because it also has to manage production as well as projects, and production problems always have priority? Does it lack time because it is involved in various projects, or has insufficient budget been allocated?

Possible Actions

The following measures may help to promote involvement:

- Do not wait until the last minute of the project before involving the stakeholders. The earlier they are involved the better! By asking them to assist in identifying the product risks and acceptance criteria as the test strategy is being set up, the importance of the test project will soon become apparent to them.
- Emphasise the importance of their input. Bear in mind not only the interests of the project, but their interests, as well (WIIFM: What's In It For Me; and WIIFY: What's In It For You?). The stakeholders may well be interested in having a voice in the requirements and product risks to be covered.
- Ensure that it is clear to all the parties concerned what the project and the selected test method involve. Do this by providing information in the form of presentations or newsletters. If necessary, also provide training on the application of the test method.
- Make sure that it is clear to everyone which tasks, authorities and responsibilities they have. This information forms part of the test plan.
- Deliver testware and results quickly, so that everyone sees the added value of testing. Consider structuring by means of LUTs.
- Involvement has to come from two directions. In other words, management has to be involved, but also the people on the shop floor. Therefore, do not focus all attention on the management, but involve the shop floor in the project as well.
- Supply reports in language everyone understands, describing the status of the project and what is expected of those involved. Make it explicit; nothing will happen on the basis of implicit assumptions.

If the degree of stakeholder involvement remains low, a drastic solution is *not* to continue with the cluster. Naturally, this will have to take place in agreement with the client.

Impact on the Project

Reduced involvement of the organisation can in the end exert a lot of influence on time, money or the quality of the test project. The influence on time can come about because other parties in the organisation are not extending enough cooperation. If a support department cannot or will not cooperate sufficiently when setting up a test environment, it can lead to such a delay that the testing cannot be started on time. If it appears, for example, that insufficient budget resources have been allocated for the test project, the organisation will have to release more money for management of the test environment.

If stakeholders are not sufficiently conscious of the importance of the project, it can have consequences for the completion of the cluster cards. Much time can then be lost, as the information will still have to be gathered. This can have direct consequences for the quality of the information system.

9.2.3 Incomplete Documentation

It may be the case that there is no good system documentation available. The quick scan can allow the test manager to spot many situations where source material is lacking, for this is where he determines which documentation can serve as source material and which alternative methods he will use if he finds the material lacking. However, a test manager carries out the quick scan early on in the project. During this phase, everyone is usually convinced that documentation is either immediately available or will surely be put together and will suffice as source material. However, during the later, more thorough, examination of testability and completeness of source material, it can appear that some things are missing after all, or that the documentation was not updated to correspond to the latest release of the information system.

Possible Causes

Everyone has probably experienced legacy systems, whereby the documentation represents a mere fraction of the knowledge held by that one member of staff who has been working for the company for over 10 years. Even when great pressure is brought to bear on the development team to deliver it as quickly as possible, the source material may be incomplete or inadequate. Also, it is possible for the development method to be such that documentation or other source material is delivered only at a late stage, as, for example, with a method like the dynamic system development method (DSDM).

Test levels can also have consequences for the preparation (and execution) of the test. The test team can make structured preparations for a system and program test with the available documentation. At this point, the test analyst can largely predict the input and output from the source material.

In an acceptance test, the testing shifts in the direction of processes. It is more difficult here to predict the output.

A functional design provides excellent detail, but often it is on the basis of system parts and not on the process that the information system is to support. Descriptions of working procedures are therefore also required in addition to the functional design, but in many organisations these are not up to date.

Possible Actions

The first instinctive response is that without good source material, there can be no test design. The poorer the quality of the source material, the greater the risk of ambiguity and the need for changes to the information system during the (test) project, and therefore also to the testware. Even during the test execution, it can turn out regularly that wrong design decisions were taken during the development of the information system owing to lack of documentation. Doing nothing, however, will result in a situation in which the test team has to wait until the required documentation is available. Because of this, testers will have to derive test cases using other means to determine the outcome of a test, if necessary!

One possible solution is to gather information from the development team concerning the information system and its functionality. After all, the information analysts designed the system and the programmers built it, therefore it is to be expected that they will have insight into its operation. They can also often indicate which parts of the system led to problems during development and where things went wrong in the tests they carried out themselves. The danger here is that the testers may carry over design and build faults from the developers. The development team must not, therefore, be the only source. The test team must be sure to approach the end users as well.

To allow the test design and the test execution to start in a structured manner, the test manager can employ the technique of Joint Testware Development (JTD) (Janssen, 2000) in all of the situations described. Experts are necessary during the preparation and execution of the tests created, to predict and check the results. During short workshop sessions, the participants can set up parts of the testware based on their collective knowledge. Not only test conditions and test cases, but also the test environment, the defining of product risks and the set-up of a test scenario should be borne in mind here.

Impact on the Project

Waiting until the correct source documentation is available does little for the time-to-market. It is in the organisation's interest that the information system goes into production as quickly as possible. If domain experts are involved in the preparation and execution of the testing, it will naturally have an effect on the planning and duration of the test project. Allowances must therefore be made for this at the planning stage.

9.2.4 Domain Experts Are Unavailable or Do Not Have Enough Time To Spare

While setting up the test plan, the test manager agrees with the organisation which domain experts will work on the test project. He also provides a task description and an indication of the number of hours per week these people should be available to the test team. A change of circumstances may mean that when the test team actually needs to make a start on the test preparations or test execution, the domain experts are not able to give as much of their time as was agreed.

Possible Causes

It is often the case that participation in a test team is an extra chore for the experts on top of their normal workload. It also happens that the "real" experts are not available; they are indispensable to the day-to-day business. The organisation then makes others available who are of less value to the project. The test team is then unable to set up a test properly, or carry it out within the set time, particularly if the available documentation leaves something to be desired. This results in delay or reduced quality of the test.

Possible Actions

It is necessary to make the organisation (in particular the departments that supply the domain experts) aware of the importance of the experts' involvement in the whole of the (test) project. After all, they are often also the ones who will eventually have to work with the system. Their input into the project as a whole, and also during the test project, therefore guarantees the quality of the information system. An information system then not only meets the requirements, but also will work satisfactorily in practice. Involving the domain experts in the (test) project ensures that they gain familiarity with the new information system. Additional training is then often unnecessary. The experts can pass on the knowledge they have gained to other colleagues within the organisation, thus ensuring that the information system is accepted more easily. The test manager should therefore emphasise the importance of these people to the (test) project, and also emphasise their own interest in participating in it.

Together with the client and the line manager concerned, the test manager should try to find a way of involving the domain experts for the test project. For example, could any of their daily tasks wait, or could others (perhaps temporary workers) carry these out? He should determine when these domain experts will really be needed, and make as efficient use as possible of their knowledge. He can agree, for example, that questions will be collected on a daily basis, so that they can all be answered in an hour. In this way, the test team members do not have to disturb the experts every half-hour with just one question.

Impact on the Project

Of course, the influence of the availability of the domain experts on the (test) project depends on what phase the test project is at. With a system test, it does not have any great consequences; another (external) party can also set up and carry out the system test. This also applies to the users' acceptance test. For this test level, however, the input of the users is always necessary.

They will at least have to confirm that the test was successfully completed as far as they are concerned.

If the test team has to delay the test preparation or execution until the domain experts are again available, more time will be required to complete the former according to the test strategy. If it is not possible to use domain experts, this will have an influence on the quality of the test and, thus, on the quality of the information system. A lot depends, of course, on the quality of the available documentation.

9.2.5 Changed Insights Lead to Changes in the Requirements

During the course of every project, changes of insight lead to changes in the information system. Both during the development and the test phase, these changed insights may lead to changes in the requirements. As the information system takes shape, things that were unclear at the beginning become clearer, and therefore better described in the requirements. It is of course important that the test team is kept fully informed of these changes.

When the requirements are changed, this can lead to adjustments in the test conditions, test cases and test data. Traceability from requirements to product risks and testware is therefore of the utmost importance, otherwise the testware will not be up to date and test results could prove useless. It should be established in the test plan who is responsible for informing the test team concerning changes and how the test team is to proceed with these changes. The changes must also be carried out to the requirements. By constantly checking the latest version number and date of change, the test manager can gain an insight into possible adjustments. However, it regularly happens that during testing the information system reacts differently from the testers' expectations based on the requirements.

Possible Causes

With new products in particular, where much is as yet unclear, the requirements can change regularly. This situation often occurs when the pressure of time on the project is at a peak. The development team quickly implements the requested changes in the information system, but communication with all the other parties involved (including the test team) is lost along the way.

The development method may also be the reason why changes to the system are communicated late or incorrectly. With a completely waterfall-oriented development, the chances of undocumented changes are somewhat lower than with a development method such as DSDM. Requirements may also change because projects are of long duration (changes in the organisation or environment lead to new wants and needs) or because not all the stakeholders were involved in the setting up of the initial requirements.

Within a large bank, a system is in use to define and register credit limits. The users have defined the requirements for this and the development of the system has been started. However, since this concerns financial data, the internal security (IS) department communicates extra requirements concerning the degree to which data can be traced and protected. However, IS was initially not involved in the project and must now make its wishes known retrospectively. This has consequences for the previously created requirements, which will change – for example, the requirement for the terms of agreement – and new ones will be added. It must now be ascertained what consequences there will be for the test project's timing and budget.

Possible Actions

As soon as the test team discovers that, despite all the measures and procedures followed, unexpected changes have taken place in the requirements, it must immediately ask the development team what exactly has been changed and what documentation is available relating to this. On the basis of this information, an impact analysis can be carried out concerning the necessary changes in the testware and the consequences of these for the duration of the test project.

In an (interim) evaluation, it will have to be discussed whether and how agreements on communicating changes have to be adjusted. After all, a large number of unprepared changes are detrimental not only to the duration or quality of the test project, but also to the motivation of the test team. Locating the development team and the test team close to each other can make a big difference, allowing them to communicate better with each other.

Impact on the Project

The test manager must, as with the notified changes, indicate what impact the unexpected changes will have on the testware, and also consult with the project manager and the client concerning the measures to be taken. Together they will have to decide on how the changes are to be dealt with within the project. If the test team is unable to carry out the necessary changes within the time available, this will mean in principle that there will be a delay in putting the information system into production. If another solution is possible, such as deploying more people to process the adjustments in the test set and to support the rest of the test preparation and execution, it will have consequences for the budget. If the test team carries out fewer tests than was originally planned in the test strategy, the quality of the information system may suffer.

9.2.6 Insufficient Knowledge on the Part of Test Professionals

It is true for every project that the availability of good employees is essential to its success. This is no different with a test project. At the start of the test project, the test manager will therefore do his best to ensure that he gets the right people with the right knowledge and skills for the project. He sets up profiles describing the knowledge and experience the test team members must have, and also which personal skills are required. Unfortunately, it is not always possible to find a test employee who exactly fits the profile.

Possible Causes

Despite the many available means of finding good test team members, it is by no means always possible to attract the "ideal" test employee to the project. Testing is a job apart, and each level of test has its different approaches and points of focus. A tester whose expertise is in functional analysis and the use of testing techniques is usually not the person most suited to carry out a performance test, and vice versa.

In addition, testing is still too often seen as a training ground for other "more important" functions: this is how the future developer gets to know the information system well. And that is why many organisations believe that everyone can do testing "on the side", requiring no separate training. The result is that the "tester" overlooks important test cases and does not employ a thorough testing process.

Staff turnover is another possible cause. A good tester leaves, for example, because of better prospects elsewhere. The chance of staff turnover, particularly during lengthy projects, is something to take into account.

Possible Actions

It is important to look at ways in which the team can deal with any shortcomings in knowledge. Possibilities include, for example, training courses or redistributing tasks within the team.

Having been a member of the test team for 6 months, John is given the chance to be team leader on another project. He was responsible, among other things, for the peer reviews of the test conditions and test cases. Angela, who now has several months' experience in the test project, can take over this task from him. A new tester has been taken on and will take over Angela's test duties. Another possibility is to recruit specific expertise on a part-time basis (e.g. methodical support).

It is always preferable in any case to retain a more experienced tester in the team. A team that includes many inexperienced workers will require a lot of time for training and coaching. An alternative is for testers to work in pairs. Two heads are better than one, and this also takes care of the reviewing arrangements. They also form each other's back-up. The test manager must always be aware of whether the various team members find their work sufficiently challenging. Is more variety required, do they want a broader range of tasks, or do they want to rotate them? In seeking an appropriate range of tasks, the test manager must make allowances for the team members' level of learning and for their ambitions.

From an HR perspective, it is necessary that testers have career prospects. It is therefore advisable to organise periodic reviews, in which the test manager and tester consider the challenges facing the tester now and in the future.

Impact on the Project

Naturally, an inadequate supply of skills or knowledge will influence the duration of the test project. Not only does the transfer itself takes time, but also newly recruited members will not immediately be able to work at the same pace as their predecessors. If team members require training in order to fit the profile, this will cost not only extra time, but also extra money for training that was unplanned. On-the-job training also extends the duration of the project. The more experienced tester will be unable to spend all of his time on testing. Coaching a colleague takes up a lot of time. In many cases, therefore, the planning and budget require adjustment.

9.2.7 Late Delivery of the Information System

Every test manager sooner or later experiences a test project in which the information system to be tested is not available on the due date. Naturally, the delivery date was included as a precondition in the test plan. If this precondition is not complied with, this has a knock-on effect.

Possible Causes

The information system may be delivered later than planned. Reasons may include developers leaving, problems with the development environment, requirements were changed, or the information system and its development turned out to be more complex than was originally expected.

Possible Actions

The testing will still require the same amount of time, therefore the date on which the test project was due to be completed will have to be extended by the same length of time. Depending on the reason, the test manager may even request more time than originally estimated. If the system turns out to be more complex than expected, more testing will be necessary. If many requirements have been changed, extra time will be required to carry the changes through into the testware.

The test manager can also start with an incomplete system, but only on condition that the parts of the system to be tested are set up in modular fashion, with relatively few connections, and that they are stable – otherwise this approach will only lead to frustration in the test team and, at worst, to unreliable test results.

If the problems have arisen as a result of obstacles while setting up the development environment, it makes sense to learn from these experiences when it comes to setting up the test environment. Perhaps it is necessary to start earlier. It may be possible to carry out part of the test design in the development environment, so that progress can already be made in that area.

Impact on the Project

Time exerts the biggest impact on a test project. The same amount of time, or even more, is still required for the (re)design and execution of the test. This means that the test project will release the information system later (for a subsequent phase of testing or for going into production). The plan, and very likely the budget, will need to be adjusted accordingly.

9.2.8 Poor Quality of the Delivered Information System

When setting up the test plan, the test manager agrees and establishes certain criteria with the supplier that the information system must comply with for the test manager to accept it for testing. These are called the entry criteria. On delivery, it may appear that one or more of the entry criteria have not been complied with. It cannot therefore be demonstrated by the party who has delivered it that the information system meets the required level of quality. If the information system is not of the desired quality before the start of testing, the test manager can no longer guarantee that the test team will realise the quality agreed in the test strategy within the planning and budget!

Possible Causes

Non-compliance with the entry criteria could be due to various reasons:

- The team ran out of time in the previous phase.
- The wrong quality was delivered at the previous phase.
- The set transfer measures were not carried out or were not carried out correctly.
- The development team did not possess sufficient testing knowledge, with the result, for example, that no unit tests were carried out.

- The testers, in accepting the system themselves, have supplied and/or carried out the wrong test conditions for determining the quality.
- It was not possible to carry out an intake test in the absence of a test environment.
- The development team assumes that the testers will find the faults and they consequently focus only on the development, hardly ever performing the unit tests.

It is not just on delivery from a previous phase that the quality of the information system may not come up to expectations. This may also occur during the course of one of the test runs. It must be agreed that during and after each test run, the development team first of all solves the issues having the highest priority.

However, when solving issues, often the first consideration is how quickly they can be solved; at the test execution stage, there is much pressure on the development team as well as the test team to find solutions quickly so that they can supply a new version for the next test run. The test manager therefore has to make sure that everything is clear, and that the most important faults are solved first and retested.

Possible Actions

It is important to agree clearly with the development team in advance the responsibilities of both the test team and the development team. Agreements must be made concerning the unit testing and the quality of the information system on delivery. The test manager sets these agreements out in the entry and exit criteria of the test plan.

If not all the criteria have been complied with, the test manager can assume that the quality of the system as delivered is inconclusive. He must then establish its quality as quickly as possible.

If the quality does not satisfy the agreements in the test strategy and the test plan, there are three possible responses for the test manager:

1. He refuses to accept the system, indicating that the party delivering it must first comply with the agreed entry criteria before the information system is accepted for testing.
2. He accepts the system. Since it is highly likely that other issues will arise, more time will be necessary for retesting. The plan and/or budget will be adjusted in accordance with the current quality level of the information system. With this, delivery of the system will be delayed or more funds will be required.
3. He accepts the system and keeps to the original planning and budget. This may, however, be at the expense of the final quality of the information system.

Impact on the Project

Depending on the decision taken, a lower starting quality means that more testing time is necessary, or that the start of testing will have to wait. If the number of testers remains the same, the delivery date will at any rate be later than planned. By making use of the predictive character of the EVM, which will be explained further in the next chapter, the test manager can indicate what the impact will be on the required time. If delay is not an option, then the manageable factors of money and quality must be used to find a solution, so that the delivery date is maintained.

9.2.9 The Test Environment Is Unstable or Even Unavailable

A completely new information system often also requires a completely new test environment. The set-up of this environment demands specific knowledge and is by no means always a simple matter. If the information system is a PC application that can run on a standalone basis, then the set-up of the test environment will not be too problematic. However, the more complex the architecture of the information system, the more complex the environment, and if connections to other systems and platforms are required this can present considerable difficulties.

Possible Causes

An unstable or unavailable test environment may be the result of, for example:

- A new architecture.
- Unfamiliarity with parts of the architecture during the setting up of the environment.
- Lack of time on the part of the support department.
- Lack of clarity concerning responsibilities for setting up and managing the environment.
- Failure to keep to the script for setting up the environment and installing the information system.
- Late delivery of components of the environment (e.g. software, hardware, and also things like telephone lines etc.).
- Connections that do not work properly or that are not set up properly.
- More than one team using the same environment and data.

Possible Actions

If it takes too long before the test environment becomes available, the test manager can check whether the testers can carry out tasks outside of the test project, to alleviate pressure on the test budget.

If the testers are not yet finished with test preparations, they could work out the clusters with low(er) priority according to test conditions and test cases.

It is difficult to provide a single solution for dealing with unstable test environments, for it is strongly dependent on the cause of the instability. The best thing is for the test manager, together with the project manager, to examine where the cause of the problems lies and what the impact is on the test project. Possible solutions are:

- Carry out a test of the environment in advance of the planned tests of the information system itself.
- Make use of another similar test environment where it is possible to carry out the tests. This alternative may avoid too great a delay.
- If the problems are the result of a shared environment and/or test data, come to an arrangement with other test managers concerning use of the environment. If the situation can be resolved by agreeing on who uses which coding and which ranges of test data, this will have little or no consequences for the availability of the environment. It may affect the test cases already set up, however, for if the test data to be used in certain test cases have to be changed, the test team will need extra time to adapt the cases. If agreements have to be made concerning the times that the environment is in use, it may be the case that the environment is not permanently available, possibly lengthening the duration of the test project.
- Determine which expertise is required for setting up and managing the environment. Together with the client, consider whether it is possible to recruit this expertise and to assign it permanently to the project.
- Bring in a support group especially set up to support the test environment.
- If certain tests are impossible in a test environment, consult with the client and stakeholders on whether the risk involved in omitting the tests is acceptable. In that case, a trial production run may be necessary.

Impact on the Project

Every disturbance of the test environment has an influence on the duration of the testing. If they occur regularly or for lengthy periods, the margin built into the timing of the plan can no longer accommodate them. Adjustment of the plan will then be necessary.

Example of Set-up and Management of a Test Environment

Within a bank a survey among project managers, developers, administrators, test managers and testers has been carried out to locate the most significant bottlenecks within test projects. Among the many bottlenecks, **obtaining the appropriate test environment** was mentioned most often. We went in search of the causes of this, and they appeared to be of both a technical and an organisational nature.

Technical Causes. It took a lot of time, and therefore a lot of money, to set up the test environment, since almost everything was done "manually". Nor was it possible to keep the test environment up to date, since the developers had no insight into the implementation of new releases of applications, communication software or even infrastructure in the production environment. And if this insight was present, implementation was often only carried out in a few test environments, because it had not been clearly established where each test environment was and for whom it was set up.

Test environments were barely delineated, and therefore various projects were making use of the same environment. If a particular project wanted to restart a test environment and carried this out, the other parties were no longer able to test. Also, the data in the test environment were incongruous and inconsistent. A customer that was assigned customer number 124 in system A was assigned customer number 456 in system B, while in system C the customer did not exist at all. This came about partly because projects manipulated each other's data. This also meant that the testware could only be used once.

Organisational Causes. The setting up of the test environment was something the developers did incidentally. It wasn't actually their job, but since no one else did it, they had to do it themselves. They had to make and maintain contact with a large number of parties outside the project to set up the test environment. This often involved between eight and ten people from various departments and also various external contacts. The developers had to be patient, since the setting up of a test environment did not always have the highest priority with these parties and the tasks involved had to be fitted into overfull agendas. It sometimes took a month to set up a database.

The developers did not feel responsible for the test environments, which did little for the quality of either the product or the process. Usually, the test environment was set up once, with no further maintenance during the course of the project (other than placing new versions of the application they had themselves developed), so that there was no continuity for subsequent projects. During these projects, the developers were obliged to completely update or, in the worst case, start afresh on building and reinventing the wheel each time.

Furthermore, there was no one in the development projects with an overall perspective of the way in which a test environment should be set up. The developers naturally possessed sufficient knowledge of the application they themselves were building, but their knowledge of the adjacent systems was marginal, to say nothing of their depth of knowledge of the hardware and middleware in use.

In summary, it was unclear who had which tasks, responsibilities and authority. No one was owner of the "test environment problem", and so no one could be approached concerning this. Technically, people demonstrated willingness, but it was "handiwork" that took up many hours. The test project was thus on the critical path within the larger project.

Impact on the Business Controls. The aspects mentioned had a negative influence on the factors concerning time, money and quality within each test project.

- **Time**
  1. Because of many mistakes in the test environment (poor set-up, see also section on quality), test execution often came to a standstill, causing delay to the whole project.
  2. Through not having planned the tasks surrounding test environments into the test project in advance, they always had to be fitted in at the last minute. Since other tasks had priority (as pointed out, test environments were not "core business") it often took a long time before the setting up of the test was commenced.
  3. Because a lot of work was carried out manually, the tasks were not really performed efficiently.

- **Money**
  1. Inefficient use of products and knowledge and having to reinvent the wheel each time meant that a lot of investment was wasted.
  2. Lots of staff were needed to set up the test environment, making great demands on the budget.
  3. Because of the absence of insight into (the planning of) tests, each project purchased its own hardware, which led to a surplus. This meant that one project bought a server while another had no need of its server during the period when the first project had to carry out testing.

- **Quality**
  1. Faults that materialised during the test execution appeared, following a lengthy investigation, not as a result of the software, but from a badly set-up test environment. A lot of expensive time was wasted in searching for the cause of the fault, and the search turned up nothing in the end, much to the frustration of both the developers and the testers.
  2. There was a "false sense of security". Tests proceeded faultlessly, but when the information system went into production, it appeared not to function properly, because old versions of other information systems had been tested in the test environment. During the creation of the test environment, those versions had been represented, but not in the subsequent phases. Often during

the project, a new version of an information system was put into production that was never implemented in the test environment.

Solution. To solve these problems, a central test environment was set up, including an organisational unit which was assigned the core task of facilitating the establishment and managing of test environments. This was a major challenge, partly because it concerned a centralised approach in a very decentralised organisation. The set-up of the test environment and test organisation was aimed at:

- Delivering measurable, quantitative added value for the projects (faster, cheaper).
- Delivering qualitative added value (less trouble for the developers, who would be able to focus on their core task, namely designing and developing information systems).
- Delivering added value quickly (no Big Bang scenario, but gradual expansion so that advantages could be capitalised on quickly).
- Delivering phased added value (building in clear go/no-go moments to enable timely management).
- Carrying out "hands-on" implementation without coercion, determining together with people involved in the projects the optimum way of working and trying to achieve results on the shop floor through cooperation. No ivory tower approach!

Technical Solution. A technical solution was set up in the form of a master test environment containing the central information systems required in more or less all of the projects (see Figure 9.4). Whenever a project requires a test environment, a copy is drawn from (a part of) the master environment following specification of the required configuration. These copied environments are logically separated from each other by authorisations, so that dedicated test environments are supplied with a 1:1 relationship between project and environment. This prevents contamination from other projects.

Duplication procedures were also developed to ensure the generation of test environments. The test environment is thus produced in a factory-like style. Naturally, a number of checks still have to be carried out manually, and a test has to be carried out prior to delivery to check whether the environment meets the requirements of the project.

There is also a connection with the distribution procedures as applied within the bank's organisation. That means that all the components from configuration management (hardware, middleware, operating systems, software, data) are also delivered to the central test environment. In this way the master environment keeps pace following its rollout with the most recent production environment as well as the copied environments.

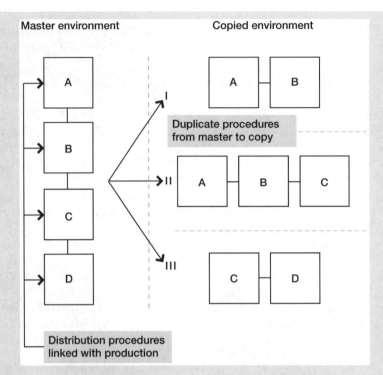

Fig. 9.4. Technical solution for test environment

In the area of data, an unambiguous set of test starting data is defined, which can easily be restored to its initial state. This can also be done easily with separate test environments, since it doesn't interfere with other projects. The data were reconciled in all the systems and procedures developed to keep them synchronised and to enrich the test database on changes in systems. As new functionality is built into an application, extra data is often required to allow it to be tested. This also has the advantage of the opportunity to reuse the testware.

To summarise, by setting up a master environment (including fixed and synchronised data) and establishing accompanying procedures, the knowledge of the architecture and the information systems is secured, and there is the possibility of reusing the test environment to the maximum. The end result is lower costs, shorter duration and a higher quality of test environments.

Organisational Solution. Within the line organisation a separate department was set up which was fully dedicated to the arranging and managing of test environments. This department was called the Test Bureau.

Whenever a project starts, arrangements are made with the Test Bureau concerning the test environment, when it is to be delivered and the time it should be active. The agreements are established in an SLA (Service Level Agreement), so that it is clear to both the client (the project) and the supplier (the Test Bureau) what exactly is to be supplied. Any ambiguities or omissions then appear at an early stage and can be managed in time.

An important task of the Test Bureau is to ensure that the test environments are always up to date throughout the duration of the project. When new versions of information systems go into production, the test environment must be adjusted accordingly. This prevents the environmental changes making their first appearance in production (and the extra expense involved). Since the Test Bureau knows exactly which test environments have been supplied and which configurations of information systems are running in them, it can update them simply and consistently.

The Test Bureau has all the resources available for setting up the test environment, as long as it concerns information systems that it manages itself, otherwise it has the contacts to make arrangements with other parties concerning the supply of various system requirements. The Test Bureau then functions as a single point of contact (SPOC) for all the development projects. It is irrelevant to the development team how many parties are eventually involved, as they only have to deal with the Test Bureau. The Test Bureau maintains and manages the SLA's that are agreed with other parties outside of its own organisation.

Because the Test Bureau has insight into all the tests being carried out, it is able to allocate resources effectively and efficiently, regarding both staffing levels and machine resources. This planning and explicit allocation of people and resources make it possible to carry out the same tasks with lower capacity.

Results. The introduction of the technical and organisational solutions delivered excellent results. In summary:

- The length of time taken to set up a test environment was reduced by between 50% and 90%.
- The costs involved in setting up and maintaining a test environment were reduced by 65% on average.

- The number of faults that materialised during testing owing to incorrect set-up of the test environment was negligible (a 95% decrease).
- Faults no longer materialised through cross-contamination of test environments (they are separate).
- Practically no faults materialised in production through testing of the wrong version of the information system; those faults that did materialise were often the result of management data that were not always distributed (90% decrease).
- Almost all of the test environments were delivered on time (95%).
- Thanks to explicit planning, 50% less hardware was required.
- Project leaders and developers needed only to contact one person regarding the test environment and were therefore able to concentrate on their core tasks.
- More test levels were possible through data synchronisation across systems.
- The number of opportunities for reuse of the testware had increased through using repeatable test data.

9.3 Conclusion

If the test manager has set up a good way of managing the test project, he will be able to handle all emerging problem situations. The following chapters of this book focus on the activities the test manager carries out during execution of the test project. Progress management is the first important instrument for continuing effective management of the test project.

10

Progress Management

The preparations for the test project are completed. The budget is available, the project and product risks have been surveyed and the test organisation is ready. The stakeholders have approved the test strategy, and the plan describes the activities together with their relevant resources and time required. Everyone knows what has to be done. The execution of the test project can begin, starting with the test preparation. This chapter shows how the test manager monitors the test project and how he is able to provide timely information and advice to the client concerning bottlenecks and possible consequences of risks that materialise.

The business controls that a *project manager* has at his disposal are time, money, functionality and quality. A *test manager* has no influence on the functionality to be delivered; what the information system is required to do is not determined in the test project. Quality, on the other hand, takes on an extra dimension for the test manager – it can be divided into quality of the test project products (the testware) and of the products to be tested (the information system).

An overview of the status of each of the business controls should enable the test manager, and thereby the client, to answer the question: can we provide an indication of the quality of the information system, promptly and within acceptable costs? It is also important here that the test manager shows which product risks established in the test strategy are covered by the test. The combination of the demonstration of covered requirements and the coverage of product risks is dealt with in depth in Chapter 2.

As already mentioned, time, money and quality are the only business controls at the disposal of a test manager. To maintain awareness of the status of each of these, he must be able to answer at least the following questions:

- Is the test project supplying the desired information quickly enough?
- Is the test project keeping within the budget?
- Is the test project providing sufficient insight into the quality of the information system (what product risks are outstanding at this time)?

This chapter first of all looks at each of the business controls of time, money and quality, and then presents a method whereby these interconnected elements can be tracked.

The earned value method is used to monitor progress. Details of progress, budget and quality can be shown in relation to each other in the test control matrix (TCM) developed by LogicaCMG.

The work method and instruments presented in this chapter provide the test manager with:

- Insight into the status of the test project at any given moment.
- No "90% completed" effect; progress is measured and managed on added value for the project instead of on hours spent.
- The opportunity for pro-active management and the ability to make well-founded, realistic prognoses.
- Clear communication of information to the stakeholders and the client, with everyone speaking the same language and expectations managed unambiguously.
- Learning benefits from the project that can already be capitalised upon during its course.

Good progress management leads to insight into the test project and, with that, provides a firm basis for the management of the business controls of time, money and quality.

10.1 The Earned Value Method

The earned value method (EVM) (US Air Force, 1978) is an excellent progress management method available to the test manager. The basic idea is to measure progress not only in terms of hours spent in relation to the budgeted hours (money), but also in terms of actual progress, i.e. the prompt delivery of products (time). Budget spending and progress are therefore separated from each other, providing more insight and more management possibilities if there are deviations from the plan.

A product is only completed when it complies with certain standards and criteria (quality). During the test preparation, the focus is on the quality of the test products delivered. The test clusters, for example, could only be considered completed when they had been subjected to a peer review. An alternative is to consider the clusters completed only when the stakeholders have reviewed them. During the test execution, the focus is on the quality of the information system being tested: to what extent can it be demonstrated that the requirements for the information system have been met, and that the product risks have been covered? With EVM, the premise is that a product – such as a document, report or test clusters – has no value while it still has to be completed. Therefore, no progress is registered regarding a product that is not yet fully completed. The budget is said to be realised only when the product is 100% completed, for the proportional contribution of the product to the total project has not been increased by spending more hours on it.

Using EVM puts an end to the biggest problem that faces test and project managers: the "90% completed" syndrome. People who are asked to indicate how far they have progressed in carrying out an activity often give an over-optimistic estimate. If they have to say how much time is required for an activity, they often do not make allowances for setbacks. The sting is usually in the tail, since we have a natural inclination to leave the difficult things to the end, and the realisation of that last percentage often costs relatively more time than expected. This makes progress management a difficult activity for the test manager.

Activities cited as "90%" offer a rose-tinted perspective on a project. If the test manager uses these estimates in his resource planning or in giving an estimated completion date, he will probably have to revise the agreements a number of times. Over time, this will be very detrimental to his own credibility and that of the whole test project. Figure 10.1 shows the course of the estimated completion percentage of the project over time. It can be seen that after a slow start good progress is made, but towards the end it becomes an uphill struggle. It takes 5 weeks to realise the last 10% of a project that lasts 11 weeks in total. Activities may also be said to be "90% completed" because the test team is *unable* to make any progress, e.g. because it had to wait for an X25 connection to be set up in a test environment, which takes a couple of weeks. In that case, no hours are spent on completing the last 10%.

With the help of EVM, as realistic a picture as possible of progress is obtained, thus allowing timely intervention. By extrapolating the information provided by EVM, the impact of deviations from the plan can be quickly determined and communicated. EVM already yields learning benefits within

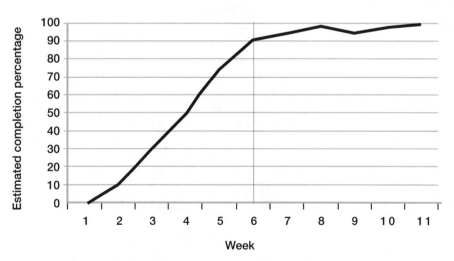

Fig. 10.1. The 90% completed syndrome

the project. If it takes 10 days to make 10 test cases while 5 were planned for, the test manager can incorporate the new information into his amended plan concerning the time required to make test cases. He does not have to keep repeating the process of drawing up a new estimate and plan (with an ensuing loss of credibility in the eyes of his client).

An added advantage of EVM is the increased motivation of the test team to complete products when the data (diagrams) are published.

Following on from this, we will show the value of EVM by discussing the various steps and instruments that go with them.

10.2 Progress (Time)

10.2.1 Setting Up Progress Monitoring

With the test project plan as a basis, the test manager sets up EVM to monitor progress. The planning can be in the form of a standard planning package, for example in MSProject®.

In Figure 10.2 it can be seen how the planning can be converted to EVM. All the activities are reproduced, including the number of hours estimated to complete the activities, and the week of completion. Next to this, note is also kept of when the activities are actually realised.

The work method is as follows. Copy the activities and the associated tester's name from the planning into, for example, a worksheet in a spreadsheet program. Next to the activity, note how many hours have been esti-

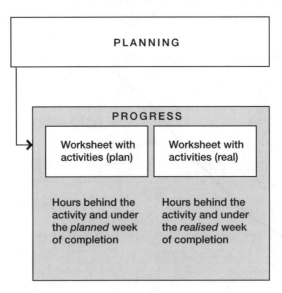

Fig. 10.2. From planning to EVM progress

mated for it. At the week in which the activity should be completed according to the plan, note the estimated number of hours (see Table 10.1). If it is desirable to keep a link to the planning, include, for example, the identification number of the activity from the planning in the spreadsheet as well.

Table 10.1. EVM activity planning

Planning Activity/week	Tester	Hours	18	19	20	21	22	23
Design cluster 1	Iris	25	25					
Design cluster 2	Bob	15		15				
Design cluster 3	Iris	20		20				
Execute cluster 1	Iris	5				5		
Execute cluster 2	Bob	5				5		
Execute cluster 3	Iris	5					5	
...	...	...	...	...	...	...	...	...

In order to maximise opportunity for correction, the activities listed should not be too extensive. Larger activities have the disadvantage of fewer opportunities for checking, so that it is difficult to make corrections at an early stage.

The frequency with which progress can be measured can vary for each project, but this is usually done on a weekly basis. A second worksheet may be used to register progress. Many details will be identical to those in the planning worksheet, in which case links can be used to the first worksheet. Changes in the planning on the first worksheet will then automatically be carried over to the second and any other worksheets.

An Example

A test manager fills in the completed activities each week. In week 20, the progress that was made in weeks 18, 19 and 20 is entered in Table 10.2.

Table 10.2. EVM activities during the realisation

Planning Activity/week	Tester	Hours	18	19	20	21	22	23
Design cluster 1	Iris	25	25					
Design cluster 2	Bob	15						
Design cluster 3	Iris	20			20			
Execute cluster 1	Iris	5						
Execute cluster 2	Bob	5						
Execute cluster 3	Iris	5						
...	...	...	...	...	...	...	...	...

From this overview, set against the activity planning of Table 10.1, the test manager can infer that Bob has not yet completed cluster 2, which he should have completed in week 19. It is irrelevant here whether he still requires 1 hour or 10 hours. If the test cluster is not 100% completed, no progress has been realised. Also, Iris has completed cluster 3 a week later than planned. These details are reason to investigate what is going wrong and to take measures if necessary.

A diagram can be made to show the situation by setting out the accumulated columns from the planning sheet and the progress sheet next to each other. The situation in week 20 is shown in Figure 10.3.

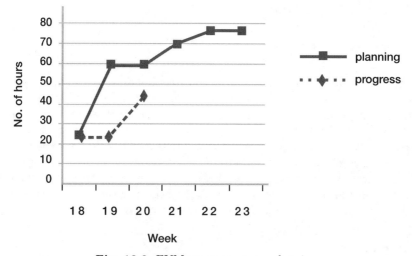

Fig. 10.3. EVM progress versus planning

Another Example
The elaboration of a number of test conditions into test cases has been estimated to take 40 hours and will be ready in week 32, according to the planning. However, in week 32 this activity is not yet complete; it is "90% completed". What is the progress made in week 32? According to EVM it is zero, since the expected product has not arrived. It is completed in week 33, however, and a total of 46 hours has been spent on it. Progress of 40 hours is then recorded. The other 6 hours are an overrun of the plan and represent a budget expense. The test team would also record 40 hours of progress if only 35 hours had been spent. This would represent a saving of 5 hours on the budget. In both cases, there can be said to be a 1-week delay, irrespective of the number of hours spent.

When all the activities are completed under or over budget, the test manager will have information that will enable him to make better estimates and to predict when all the other activities might be completed.

Of course, in most cases each product to be delivered will not be an equal part of the total. But even though the parts vary in size, this method supplies a good view of progress. It answers the question "Will we be finished on time?", although it remains necessary to keep an eye on interdependencies. The progress of a crucial activity, can, for example, halt the entire progress of a project.

10.2.2 Allow for Interdependencies

Using such a method does have a disadvantage: the interdependencies of the activities are not visible, but the test manager must remain constantly aware of it. He should have noted these interdependencies in the form of project risks, which he monitors separately. To illustrate:

> A test team has to develop and execute three clusters. A test environment must also be set up, a test tool installed and action words programmed for automatic testing. The planning for this is shown in Table 10.3.

Table 10.3. Interdependencies between activities in planning

Activity/week	16	17	18	19	20	21	22	23
Design cluster 1			8					
Design cluster 2			16					
Design cluster 3					24			
Set up test environment				40				
Install test tool					8			
Program action words							32	
Execute cluster 1								4
Execute cluster 2								4
Execute cluster 3								4
...	...	...	...	...	...	...	...	...

> The realisation at the end of week 18 can be seen in Table 10.4.

Table 10.4. Dependencies between activities in progress

Activity/week	16r	17	18	19	20	21	22	23
Design cluster 1		8						
Design cluster 2		16						
Design cluster 3			24					
Set up test environment								
Install test tool								
Program action words								
Execute cluster 1								
Execute cluster 2								
Execute cluster 3								
...		...	...	...	...	...	...	...	...

The results of this are shown in the diagram in Figure 10.4.

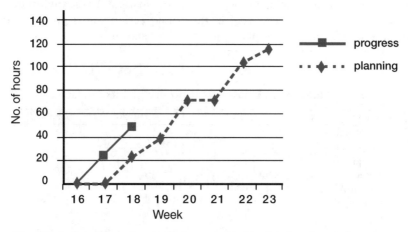

Fig. 10.4. Interdependencies between activities in planning and progress

At the end of week 18, it looks like the test project is ahead of plan. Cluster 3 has even been completed earlier than planned! However, it now appears that the test environment is not ready, and the test manager has heard that it will be available in week 20 instead of week 19. The testers cannot install the test tool nor begin the preparations for automatic testing. The whole project will therefore not be ahead of the plan, but will instead be pushed back by 1 week in relation to the plan.

10.2.3 Test Preparation and Test Execution

In the chapter on planning it has already become clear that test preparation and test execution should be planned separately. Test execution is partly dependent on the number of issues found and the repair time of those issues. The test project alone is not responsible for this, and this distinction must be reflected in monitoring progress. The test manager can monitor the test preparation on the basis of EVM, supplemented by an internal quality review of the test products. He must then monitor the test execution on the basis of EVM and the outstanding issues and covered risks of the information system under test. The products in EVM should be defined for the test execution as test clusters to be executed.

When a test cluster has been executed, this does not automatically mean that the test is completed. If significant issues remain outstanding following execution, the test team will have to test this cluster again after the development team has solved them. In the planning, this is noted as a test cluster to be executed in the following test run. Making an explicit distinction between an executed test cluster and a completed test cluster prevents the pressure in this phase of the project from being placed solely on the test team.

Example Progress Management

During execution of the test project, the test manager has to ensure that the test products are delivered timely and within the set budget. During the test execution, the test manager monitors the progress and costs of executing the test clusters. The following case describes the setting up and monitoring of the planning based on EVM for test execution.

This case demonstrates how a large international bank manages testing by employing EVM in progress management. It has been decided at European level that from 1 July 2003 the transaction charges for all euro payments within the euro zone should be the same as for national payments. The existing systems must be converted accordingly. This example concerns the "TRANSACTION" project. The software for this was developed by an external supplier, and the acceptance test was consequently very important. In this bank, EVM became the adopted standard for progress management during the course of the project.

In the TRANSACTION project, EVM was only applied during the test execution, since the method was not yet the standard during the test preparations. EVM was set up per test run, because the bank was always dependent on the external supplier for delivery. The complete test eventually comprised three test runs. The first test run will be discussed below, having a timetable of 15 working days. In Table 10.5, the planning is set out based on EVM. For example, tester John Smith will test the Macro regression cluster. He has 8 hours to do it in, and should have it completed on 19 March.

Table 10.5. EVM progress in TRANSACTION project

Activity	Person	Plan Hour	Plan Day	Day						
				19 March	20 March	21 March	22 March	23 March	24 March	25 March
Totals		108		24	0	24	44	0	0	16
Macro regression	John Smith	8	March 19							
Macro regression	Paul Jones	4	April 9							
Performance	John Smith	12	April 9							
Set-up	Paul Jones	8	March 19	8	0					
Account number	Paul Jones	4	March 27							
Authorisation	Andy Williams	4	March 25							4
Authorisation	Paul Jones	4	March 28							
Hashing	Paul Jones	4	April 8							
Conversion	Andy Williams	4	March 26							
STAP	Paul Jones	4	April 2							
Checking	Kees de Vries	4	March 26							
Export	Paul Jones	8	April 3							
FIN	Paul Jones	4	April 2							
Initial	Paul Jones	8	March 25							8
Importing	Andy Williams	8	April 8							
Multi-user	Andy Williams	16	April 3							
Scheduler	Andy Williams	4	April 4							
Scheduler Multi-user	Andy Williams	4	April 8							
Security	Paul Jones	12	March 27							
Table maintenance	Paul Jones	12	March 22				12			
Room maintenance	Paul Jones	4	March 28							

When the project starts, daily progress will be assessed and processed into the EVM progress table as seen in Table 10.6. This shows that John Smith has finished the execution of the Macro regression test cluster not on 19 March, but on 20 March. It also shows that on 19 March, only 8 hours of progress in total were realised within the test project, while it should actually have amounted to 24 hours. The cause of this was that the external supplier of the system had forgotten to deliver a number of modules, so John was unable to start until later that day. Although he could still have executed most of the cluster on the 19th, progress is not registered until the 20th in line with EVM. After all, he had not entirely executed his cluster until the 20th.

Table 10.6. EVM planning in TRANSACTION project

Activity	Person	Plan Hour	Plan Day	Day 19 March	20 March	21 March	22 March	23 March	24 March	25 March
Totals		108		8	8	6	30	0	0	26
Macro regression	John Smith	8	March 19							
Macro regression	Paul Jones	4	April 9							
Performance	John Smith	12	April 9							
Set-up	Paul Jones	8	March 19	8	0					
Account number	Paul Jones	4	March 27							
Authorisation	Andy Williams	4	March 25							
Authorisation	Paul Jones	4	March 28							
Hashing	Paul Jones	4	April 8							
Conversion	Andy Williams	4	March 26							
STAP	Paul Jones	4	April 2							
Checking	Kees de Vries	4	March 26							
Export	Paul Jones	8	April 3							
FIN	Paul Jones	4	April 2							
Initial	Paul Jones	8	March 25							
Importing	Andy Williams	8	April 8							
Multi-user	Andy Williams	16	April 3							
Scheduler	Andy Williams	4	April 4							
Scheduler Multi-user	Andy Williams	4	April 8							
Security	Paul Jones	12	March 27							
Table maintenance	Paul Jones	12	March 22							12
Room maintenance	Paul Jones	4	March 28							

Tables 10.5 and 10.6 together show the planned hours, as set against the realised hours.

As can be seen from Figure 10.5, the actual realisation is running somewhat behind the planning. The reason for this was that most of the testers in the test team were working with the information system for the first time, and had to familiarise themselves with it. The delay was made up for at a later stage. This diagram is hung up in the test room every day, and each tester is able to see the status at any given time. In practice, the tester usually feels more involved in the project and will also make a bigger effort to realise the plan. Even the project leader comes to take a look every day to see how they're getting on.

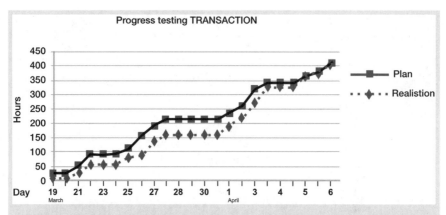

Fig. 10.5. Diagram of progress of testing in TRANSACTION project

The experiences of this bank were, among other things:

- In planning for the first test run, the expertise of a senior tester was used who was familiar with both the test set and the application. Despite his experience, discrepancies arose. The experience from the first cycle was taken into account for the planning of the second and third test run. Because of this, the second and third test run turned out to be more accurately planned than the first one.
- Initially, an estimate was made relating to the whole project. However, the test manager has no influence on some external factors. Delivery by the external supplier was repeatedly postponed. This would show as a flat progress line over a long period in the EVM realisation, and so the project clock was not started until the application was delivered.
- Clusters are registered in EVM as executed when all test cases that were planned to be executed have actually been executed. If some of the test cases could not be executed because of blocking issues in the application, the test team nevertheless completed the activity in accordance with EVM. An explicit distinction was made between an executed test and a completed test. They were not complete until the stakeholders accepted all the outstanding issues.
- Hanging up the progress chart in the project room facilitated communication. Both the testers and project management checked the progress every day. It was seen that whenever anything unusual arose, everyone reported it very quickly and it was possible to react promptly.
- EVM was only applied here to the execution of the test. It is advisable to use it also during the setting up of the test.
- EVM diagrams were easy to incorporate into the test manager's progress report.

10.3 Budget (Money)

It will also be of interest to the client whether the test team is carrying out the activities within budget. A record of spending is therefore kept per period, corresponding to the monitored periods in the timetable.

10.3.1 Setting Up a Budget Spending Record

The test manager can immediately see from the EVM diagram whether the project is behind schedule. To be able to see whether too much money is being spent, an additional overview within EVM is necessary. Here the testers can fill in the actual hours spent (see Figure 10.6).

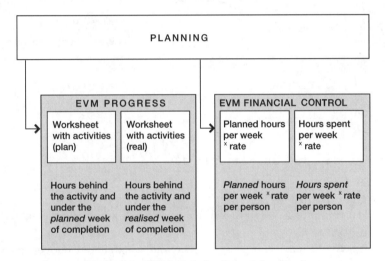

Fig. 10.6. EVM and the financial control

The worksheet with budget spending is shown in Table 10.7 relating to the example in Section 10.2.2.

As with monitoring progress, the test manager can also set out the planning and budget spending against each other in a diagram, as seen in Figure 10.7.

It may be concluded from this diagram that fewer hours have been spent than were budgeted for in this period. The EVM diagram and the diagram showing the budget spending together provide a good view of the status of the test project. It should be indicated in the progress report why fewer hours were worked than estimated. It may be, for example, that Bob was ill in weeks 18 and 19. This immediately explains the fact that Bob has registered no progress in those weeks.

A number of things can thus be learned from the diagrams. For example, if both progress and budget spending are behind schedule, the test project

Table 10.7. Budget spending

Budget spending Activity/week	Tester	Hours	18	19	20	21	22	23
Design cluster 1	Iris	25	25					
Design cluster 2	Bob	15			5			
Design cluster 3	Iris	20	5	5	5			
Execute cluster 1	Iris	5						
Execute cluster 2	Bob	5						
Execute cluster 3	Iris	5						
...	...	...	...	...	...	...	...	...

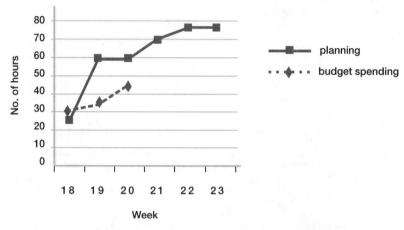

Fig. 10.7. Budget spending and planning

has a problem of capacity. If progress is behind schedule but budget spending is going according to plan, the cause lies elsewhere. It may be, for example, that the test team is waiting for a test environment, or that the test base is not yet complete. It may also be that the testers are less experienced than was expected. Each deviation from plan will have to be explained, and EVM flags these. Because a distinction is made between progress and budget spending, there is a sound enough basis for giving a realistic prognosis of the test project.

Within a project a group of three testers are responsible for the acceptance tests, and have been given 4 weeks to do them in. Unfortunately, the information system to be tested was delivered a week late. However, the test manager has a flexible plan, knowing from experience that this situation often arises. Each tester is scheduled for only 32 hours per week. They are asked to put in an extra effort, and by working 44 hours per week they manage to complete the tests on time. What are the consequences of this for the budget? There was a budget for three testers for 4 weeks at 32 hours each ($3 \times 4 \times 32$), making a total of 396 hours. In reality, the three testers each spent 44 hours over 3 weeks. With an average hourly rate of € 80, this means a deficit of € 960 in the budget. EVM would show that the plan was behind schedule in the first week, followed by acceleration in the subsequent 3 weeks. The net result is that the project is completed exactly according to plan. However, the financial overview shows that extra budget was necessary to achieve this.

A budget may be allocated in hours or in money. A budget in money has an extra complicating factor, in that the size of the budget allocated to a task depends on the hourly (internal or external) cost of the employee – unless, of course, a higher rate can pro rata be translated into fewer hours. Unfortunately, in practice it does not always follow that a 10% higher rate will mean a 10% reduction in the time budget. It is difficult to express experience in percentage terms in advance.

This chapter on progress management will premise budgeting in hours, and these hours are contained in the budget in the test management file. Naturally, not all of the budgetary costs can be expressed in hours – for example, the costs of the test environment, training and renting of conference rooms. These will form a separate item in the budget.

10.3.2 Monitoring Budget Spending

With smaller test projects, the testers register their own hours spent and test products realised. We are dealing here with a register of the number of hours that the employee has spent or realised on a particular activity over a particular reporting period in a particular role or function. With larger projects, a central registration of hours is necessary, and the details are subsequently incorporated into the progress reporting. The budget spending is monitored by adding up the hours worked per period per person per activity, and comparing this with the budget.

10.3.3 Utilising Idle Time

In practice, it often happens that development takes longer than expected while the test preparation is already completed. In that case, the testers have to await delivery of the information system to be tested. No further progress is registered in the test project, although the budget is being spent. It then appears in the progress report that the discrepancy between progress and budget spending is due to the development project overrunning.

This is a situation that often arises, and it is therefore advisable to plan to fill in the waiting time with lower-priority activities. These can be such things as refining the testware and carrying out "error guessing". Faults tend to be grouped around a particular piece of code or functionality (Hatton, 1995): in many cases, the testers will find further faults in an area where faults have already been found. The period between test runs is the ideal time to go on looking for these faults. It is also a very suitable time for an evaluation of the test project so far. This can result in points for improvement that may be useful within the current project.

There must be agreement with the client as regards the risk of idle time, which may result in budget overspend, or less opportunity for testing.

10.4 Quality

In a test project, quality can mean two things. On the one hand, there is the quality of the testware, such as the test clusters, and on the other hand there is the quality of the information system under test. We will discuss both of these definitions.

10.4.1 Quality of the Test Products

Earlier, we discussed the measurement of progress in terms of time. EVM assumes a 100% completion of the (intermediate) products to be delivered. But when is a product finished? Is it when the test analyst delivers it for the first time? When the project leader approves it? It would seem logical to assume that a product is finished when it meets the expectations of the recipient of the next phase of the project. One might also say that a product is only finished when it is transferred to maintenance. For test products, too, there must be acceptance criteria. These should be checked, for example, by peer review, inspection or other method of quality control. It is important whether the stamp of approval is given by the (test) project itself or by an outside party. This choice can have significant consequences for progress. These are matters that the test manager *must* settle. The review activities should be visible in the plan and in the progress reports. This will be further explained in the following example.

In the detailed test plan, it is indicated that the users' organisation will review the test clusters. At the moment the users' organisation has to contend with sickness and there is also a marketing promotion running, involving a high level of incoming telephone calls. The employees naturally have no time to review the clusters. If the test cluster is only marked as completed when the review has taken place, the progress report will show no progress on the part of the test team for some time, although it has indeed completed its part in the exercise. In such a situation, it may be better to mark the making of the product and the reviewing of it as separate activities in the plan.

That way, it is immediately apparent that the test team has completed the work, and it only remains for the stakeholders to approve.

10.4.2 Quality of the Information System

However important the quality of the test products may be, the main concern of the stakeholders will be the quality of the information system under test. The quality of the information system is measured by the degree to which:

- expected characteristics of the system (requirements) are shown to be present;
- product risks in operation are shown to be covered.

This combination of Risk & Requirement Based Testing (RRBT) forms the basis of the test management approach as described in Chapter 2. The scope and depth of the test is described in the test strategy. Figure 10.8 shows a complete overview of the test manager's three business controls. The illustrations relating to quality are further explained in this section.

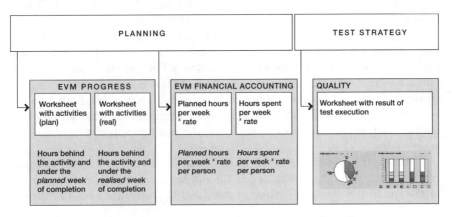

Fig. 10.8. Progress, financial accounting and quality

Demonstrating that requirements are present and satisfactory is a form of positive reporting. This contributes to a pleasant working atmosphere and a better relationship with the development team, as opposed simply to reporting faults. Test cases that have not yet been carried out are linked to outstanding risks in this form of reporting. This does not mean that the system is faulty, simply that the testers have not yet been able to demonstrate its quality.

Table 10.8 below shows that the testers are able to record the results of the test case execution themselves. The test cases can obtain the following results:

- G: Good. This test case was executed and no anomalies were found.
- T: Fault in Test. The test case was executed and an anomaly was found. On investigation, it appeared that the fault was not contained in the information system, but in the test case itself. In this case it is possible that the documentation was outdated or that the test analyst made a mistake.
- F: Fault in the application. The test case was executed and an anomaly was found. On investigation, it appeared that there was a fault in the information system.
- N: Not selected. This test case was not selected for this test run. It may be that it was deliberately placed outside the scope of the test owing to shortage of time and overrunning of the project. It is also possible that this sample was tested in earlier test runs, giving satisfactory results each time and now considered stable.
- S: Selected, not yet executed. These test cases still have to be executed. The test manager can check the progress of the test execution by the reduction in the number of test cases under S.

The results of the test are registered for the various test runs to be able to show or predict developments in the quality of the information system. In Table 10.8, R1 to R3 indicate the various test runs. They can be the basic, complete and final tests as discussed in Chapter 7, Section 7.4.

It is particularly important to distinguish between T and F when executing the test. If the information system gives a result other than expected in the test case, it does not necessarily indicate a fault in the system. A fault may have crept into the test case, or the test analyst may have misunderstood the requirements. The stakeholders must establish whether the fault is in the test or in the information system. If it is clearly shown that the test case was wrong, the test analyst himself can adjust the test set, without troubling the stakeholder.

The tester registers the result in the column relating to the test run concerned. This offers the test manager the opportunity to display the progress of the quality of the information system and the testware over the various test runs.

Across various test runs, the progress of the results can be made visible. In Table 10.8, for example, it can be seen that the second test run has produced issues that did not appear in the information system in the first test run. Test case CL06.TS1.T2C1, for example, went well in R1 but was faulty in R2. This shows that new faults are being introduced into the information system. This information on the progress of the system quality across test runs can be used to make a prediction of when the system will be good enough to go into production. The following situations could be automatically inferred in a tool from the results noted by the tester from various test runs:

- N: Not selected. These test cases are no part of the test run.
- S: Selected. These test cases are part of the test run, but have not yet been executed.

Table 10.8. Registering the test results

Document:	Generic functions		Not defined		Run	
Cluster:	CL02		Must test		G	Good
System/appl.:	Online payments		Should test		T	Fault in test
Version & date:	0,2 & 04 Feb. 2002		Could test		F	Fault in appl.
			Won't test		N	Not selected
					S	Selected, not executed

		R1	R2	R3
Test sheet	**CL06.TS1**	**Payment status**		
Test condition	**CL06.TS1.T1**	**If a bank employee amends the status in the Inmessage table, the status in the browser should reflect the same change**	**Must test**	
Test case	CL06.TS1.T1C1	Amend RES_STATUS from PAY1 to "Repaired" in the Inmessage table. The status in the browser must then be "Sent"	S	S	N
Test case	CL06.TS1.T1C2	Amend RES_STATUS from PAY1 to "Informed" in the Inmessage table. The status in the browser must then be "Rejected"	S	S	N
Test condition	**CL06.TS1.T2**	**The retain/restore screen should first display all the payments to be restored and then the payments to be retained**	**Must test**	
Test case	CL06.TS1.T2C1	Enter a payment and give it the status "to be restored". This payment should be displayed at the top of the retain/restore list	G	F	N
Test case	CL06.TS1.T2C2	Enter another new payment and give it the status "to be restored". This payment should be the first payment on the retain/restore list	G	F	N
Test case	CL06.TS1.T1C1	Enter a third payment and give it the status "retain". This payment should take the first place on the list after the payments to be restored	G	S	N

- GWF: Good Was Fault. The test case was successful, but was unsuccessful in an earlier test run. This fault is now solved.
- FWG: Fault Was Good. The test case was unsuccessful, but had been successful in an earlier test run. A new fault has been introduced.
- FNG: Fault Never Good. This test case has never been successful in any test run. This is an outstanding issue.
- GNF: Good Never Fault. This test case has never been unsuccessful in any test run. This is a proven requirement.
- T: Fault in test. This test case was not correctly executed, owing to a fault in the test case itself.

If no tool is employed, the codes must be derived by another method.

With the derived codes it is also possible to create overviews as shown in Figure 10.9. Following a test run, as many selected test cases (S) as possible must be executed. It is of course always possible that events surrounding the test project will prevent all of the selected tests from being executed; for example, problems with the test environment or sickness within the test team. The S category should decrease in the course of a test run. If T (Fault in test) arises, the test team will have to adjust the test cases. The part that is faulty in the information system should decrease over the various test runs; otherwise, the project is going in the wrong direction. If in a test run faults are found in test cases that were good earlier, new faults are being introduced. In that case, the test manager must consult with the development project leader on how this can be avoided. When information on the test execution from the various test runs is available, the progress of the quality of the information system can be made visible as indicated in Figure 10.10.

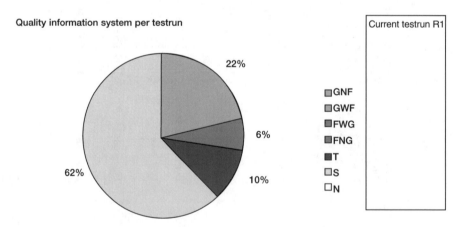

Fig. 10.9. Result overview of the test for a test run

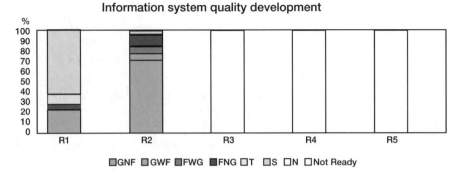

Fig. 10.10. Overview of test results across various test runs

10.5 The Test Control Matrix

Research has shown that the result of a project largely depends on the quality and strength of personnel and on the project management. With this in mind, there is a need for an instrument with which the test manager, together with the client, can get a grip on the progress of the project. It is necessary to come to grips with the plans, the dependencies within the project, the dependencies in the organisational context of the project and the testware to be supplied. The aim of the test manager is to gain insight himself and to provide insight to others into the connections between the activities, products, roles, costs, planning and progress of the test project and also the quality of the information system.

All the dependencies of the test project in relation to other phases in the project can be established in one clear overview: the test control matrix (TCM). The TCM provides insight into the status of the entire test project and contains all the information necessary for managing the test process.

The TCM includes the test manager's three business controls: time, money and quality. In this way, the TCM forms a dashboard for the test manager and is an instrument along with the methods described in the previous sections.

Table 10.9 shows an example of a TCM, displaying a sample of the information on tests, products, tools and roles that the test manager can store in the TCM. All the information on a horizontal line belongs together. The table shows, for example, that in the analysis phase, the test clusters were set up by the test analyst and reviewed by the test coordinator.

The TCM constitutes a part of the test management file, which is described in Chapter 4. As such, the TCM is transferred at the end of the project. It is pivotal in the test evaluation and can be an aid in collecting test metrics. These metrics provide useful information in making new estimates as described in Chapter 6. In the TCM, both the agreements and the compliance with them are established.

Table 10.9. TCM example

TEST DEVELOPMENT / TEST	Testing Activity	PRODUCTS	Testing Product	TOOLS	Testing Tool	ROLES	BM	PL	TC	TE
	Preparation									
	Carry out risk		Risk analysis report		Risk analysis template		–	R	X	–
	Establish test strategy		Test strategy report		Test strategy template		R	R	X	–
	Set up project test plan		Project test plan		Project test plan template		R	R	X	–
	Set up detailed test plan		Detailed test plan		Detailed test plan		R	R	X	–
	Analysis									
	Set up cluster 1		Test cluster		Test cluster template		–	–	R	X
	Set up cluster 2		Test cluster		Test cluster template		–	–	R	X
	Set up cluster 3		Test cluster		Test cluster template		–	–	R	X
	Set up cluster 4		Test cluster		Test cluster template		–	–	R	X
	Navigation									
	Execute technical test		Technical test report		Technical test template		–	–	R	X
	Set up navigation		Navigation structure		Navigation template		–	–	R	X
	Set up navigation script		Navigation script		Navigation template		–	–	R	X
	Realise engine		Engine				–	–	R	X
	Execution									
	Set up test environment		Sheet "General"		Test book template		–	X	X	X
	Execute (re)tests		Test findings report		Findings template		R	R	R	X
	Transfer testware		Transfer report		Transfer template		R	R	X	–
	Perform test evaluation		Final test report		Final report template		–	X	X	X

Test roles
BM=Business Manager
PL=Project Leader

TC=Test Coordinator
TE=Tester

Test roles
X=Execution
R=Reviewing

10.5.1 Setting Up a TCM

The TCM is a two-dimensional matrix, developed in a spreadsheet in which the most important details of a test project can be contained compactly, on one page. Filling in the TCM is flexible and it can be adjusted to suit the needs of the test project and its organizational context. The TCM can, for example, be built up from the following indicators:

- System development (project phasing).
- Testing (test project activities).
- Products (to be delivered by the test project).
- Clusters (weekly planning per test cluster).
- Roles (of persons involved in the test project).
- Budget (hours per test level).
- Planning (in weeks).
- Realisation (in weeks according to EVM).
- Budget spending (in weeks according to EVM).

The details to be entered in the TCM are largely to be obtained from the cluster cards that were developed in the test strategy and further refined in the test design. The budget and planning are also used as input for the TCM.

An important function of the matrix is to display the connections between indicators, e.g. between the phasing of the project, the test activities and the products of a test project. By showing the relevant indicators next to each other and hiding the other indicators, the required overview is obtained. Activities that are interconnected are shown in the same row of the matrix. This method provides insight into the connections between the various indicators – a view of which is often absent in other methods of presenting – through the physical spread of the data. The matrix also provides a good overview of the tasks and responsibilities of those involved in the test project.

The matrix is suitable for a wide variety of projects. In smaller projects, the information requirement is often lower and fewer indicators would probably suffice. In larger projects with a lot of interdependencies the need for a wider overview will be greater. Of course, the matrix must be kept updated, so that current information can be provided to the client and stakeholders "on the run".

10.5.2 EVM in TCM

Details of the budget, planning and progress in accordance with EVM are also included in the TCM. In this way the plans, agreements and interdependencies are all established together with progress monitoring in one single overview.

Table 10.10 shows the budget, planning and progress of the system test. These details can be easily presented graphically in a diagram in the spreadsheet. By closing the System Test Progress (wk) column and opening the System Test Budget spending column, the overview is displayed as in Table 10.11. These details, too, can be set out in a diagram.

Table 10.10. The progress (time) in the TCM

Testing Product	TOOLS	RESULT	PT	ST	Gat	_	_	_	_	SYSTEM TEST PLANNING (wk)	_	_	_	_	_	_	_	_	_	SYSTEM TEST PROGRESS (wk)	_	_	_	_	_	BUDGET	SPENDING
						1	2	3	4	5	6	7	8	9	10	1	2	3	4	5	6	7	8	9	10		
Risk analysis report			10	20	10																						
Test strategy report			20	40	20																						
Project test plan			10	20	10																						
Detailed test plan			50 hrs	100 hrs	50 hrs	20	20	60	80	80	100	100	100	100	100	20	20	60	80	80	80	100	100	100	100	100	100
Test cluster			10	20	10																						
Test cluster			20	40	20																						
Test cluster			100 hrs	200 hrs	100 hrs					20	20	60	60	200	200					20	20	60	60	200	200	200	200
Technical test report			50	100	50																						
Navigation structure			20	40	20																						
Navigation script			50	100	50																						
Engine			100 hrs	200 hrs	100 hrs					20	20	60	60	200	200					20	20	20	160	200	200	200	200
Tab sheet "General"			10	20	10																						
Test findings report			20	40	20																						
Transfer report			10	20	10																						
Final test report			50	100	50	0	0	0	0	20	20	20	20	60	100	0	0	0	0	20	20	20	60	60	100	100	100
Total						**20**	**20**	**60**	**80**	**140**	**160**	**240**	**240**	**560**	**600**	**20**	**20**	**60**	**80**	**140**	**140**	**200**	**380**	**560**	**600**	**600**	**600**

Table 10.11. The budget spending record (money) in the TCM

Testing Product	Test estimate			SYSTEM TEST PLANNING (wk)										SYSTEM TEST BUDGET SPENDING (wk)										
	PT	ST	Gat	1	2	3	4	5	6	7	8	9	10	PR	1	2	3	4	5	6	7	8	9	10
Risk analysis report	10	20	10	20											10	15	7	12						
Test strategy report	20	40	20												5	5		23			5	5		
Project test plan	10	20	10				20																	
Detailed test plan	10	20	10	20	20	60	80	80	100	100	100	100	100		20	20	27	62	78	83	88	88	88	8
	50	100	50																					
(hrs)																								
Test cluster	10	20	10					20		40									8	10	1		10	
Test cluster	20	40	20																12	5			10	
Test cluster	50	100	50																25	6	40			
Test cluster	20	40	20	0	0	0	0	20	20	60	60	200	200			12	16	37	20					
	100	200	100																102				163	
(hrs)																								
Technical test report	20	40	10					20									10	10						
Navigation structure	20	40	20															25	5		5	3		
Navigation script	50	100	50						40	40		100				24		12		25			40	
Engine	20	40	20	0	0	0	0	20	20	60	60	200	200			24	34	81	86	111	119	159	159	
	100	200	100																					
(hrs)																								
Tab sheet "General"	10	20	10					20									9	10	1	5				
Test findings report	20	40	20									40							25			10		20
Transfer report	10	20	10																					20
Final test report	10	20	10	20				20	20	20		60									50	60	60	100
	50	100	50																					
Totals				**20**	**20**	**60**	**80**	**140**	**160**	**240**	**240**	**560**	**600**	**0**	**0**	**56**	**86**	**199**	**311**	**321**	**392**	**410**	**470**	**510**

10.6 Progress Reporting

By combining the information that is required for monitoring the test process, clear progress reporting is created. The EVM diagrams on progress and budget spending form the basis. The bottlenecks and project risks must also be included in the progress reporting. In this section, however, we will restrict ourselves to the methods and instruments mentioned in this chapter for use in progress reporting. In Chapter 12, we will expand on progress reporting and other reporting forms.

10.6.1 Progress of Test Preparation and Test Execution

For the report on test project progress, the EVM diagram on progress can be used (see Figure 10.11). The report should contain explanations of discrepancies in the diagram.

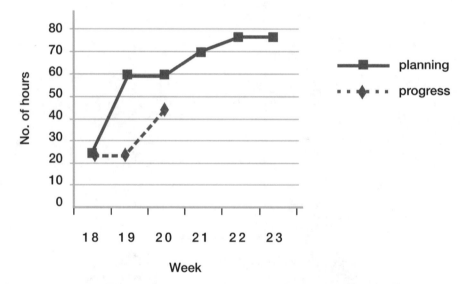

Fig. 10.11. Reporting on progress and planning

The discrepancy in this figure may be owing to, for example, the unexpected absence of one of the testers. Because of this, the tests he had to have prepared were not ready and could not be executed. There have therefore been fewer tasks completed than planned.

10.6.2 Budget Spending

For the report on budget spending, the EVM diagram on budget spending can be used. Explanations of discrepancies should be included in the report.

The absence of the tester has also meant less budget spending than originally planned. Figure 10.12 demonstrates this.

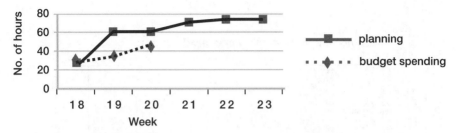

Fig. 10.12. Reporting on budget spending and planning

10.6.3 Quality of the Information System Under Test

In reporting on the status of the quality of the information system to be tested, the most important outstanding issues are included. The diagrams of the test execution results from Section 10.4 can also be included here.

With the aid of these details, a prognosis can be given for the rest of the test project. Across the various test runs, the number of open issues should decrease to an acceptable level. The progress report should contain an explanation of the data in Figure 10.13.

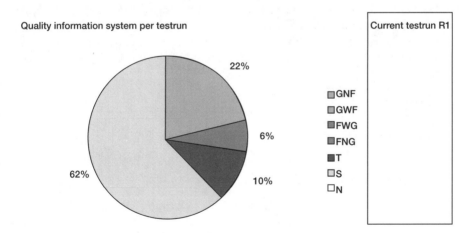

Fig. 10.13. Quality of the information system

Figure 10.14 shows that faults were introduced that were not present in run 1; this is shown by FWG (Fault Was Good). The test manager will report this to the client, who can then decide whether to examine the development process. That appears in this case to be where the problem lies. Fortunately, the percentage of GNF (Good Never Fault) has increased significantly in test run 2.

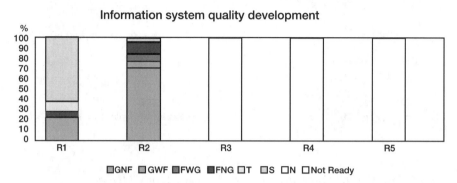

Fig. 10.14. Reporting on the progress of the quality of the information system

10.7 Conclusion

During the execution phase, progress management is a continuous activity on the part of the test manager. A good overview of the status of the test project and the definition, execution and monitoring of measures for solving any bottlenecks is essential to achieving a good result. One of the variables in this is the issues found during the test project. The management of these and coping with them in various situations is the subject of the following chapter.

11

Issue Management

In 1947, a moth got into the hardware of the MARK II "Automatic Sequence Controlled Calculator" and was the cause of various failures. Mrs Grace Hopper discovered the "bug" and logged it in her journal – the first "bug" and bug registration. Nowadays, the registration of bugs (also called defects, or issues) is an important part of test execution, not only because it allows the test team to demonstrate whether the information system is up to the required quality, but also because it enables the developers to reproduce and solve failures.

The testers establish the expected results of specific actions in test cases. When they execute a test case, they compare the expected result with what is actually happening in the information system. These results do not always correspond, leading to what is referred to as an issue.

An issue can have various causes, and is not always necessarily caused by a fault in the information system. A fault in the test environment can also lead to an issue. Or the testers may have made mistakes in the test preparation. It is possible, too, for a fault to find its way into the requirements or a design. The root cause of a fault must always be investigated.

Issues are registered for a number of reasons. In the case of the first real bug, the registration was meant as a simple logging of events. However, issue registration nowadays has the purpose of managing and solving issues. It also forms the basis for reporting on the quality of an information system, establishing whether it complies with the stakeholders' requirements. It provides insight into the extent to which the system satisfies the requirements by establishing a link with the test conditions and the product risks on which these are based.

Good issue reporting and registration is just as important as the setting up of test cases. By reporting on the issues, the test team can demonstrate the (relative) importance of the issue and with that the requirement to solve it.

With issue registration, each team member can at any time check which issues have occurred and how to reproduce them. The test manager can then also check whether the issues marked by the developer as solved have indeed been solved.

In setting up issue management (often also called incident management), Risk & Requirement Based Testing is used as a basis. The initial priority of the issue is derived from the product risks via the test conditions. The stakeholders may decide during the issue meeting to adjust this priority and determine in which order issues should be solved.

Appropriate registration also contributes to the collection of metrics. These metrics can then serve as a basis for process improvement (see Chapter 13).

11.1 Registering Issues

A fault in the information system is passed to the developers. It is the task of the maintenance department to solve faults in the test environment. The information analyst corrects a fault in a functional design, while the test team itself will of course handle a fault in the testware.

In practice, it sometimes happens that a tester – completely satisfied that he has mastered the information system – goes directly to the developer responsible and says: "You've made a mistake!" The developer of course immediately goes on the defensive, and the relationship between tester and developer will probably be cooler as a result. Issue reports should therefore not point the finger at individuals. "The system is not responding as expected; let's look at what the problem can be," sounds a lot friendlier. The test team and the development team will have to share the same atmosphere for some time to come!

Oral communication alone on issues is not sufficient. It has the following disadvantages:

- An issue is of importance not just to the test team and the development team – the client and stakeholders are also interested.
- It cannot be demonstrated that the issues have disappeared following repair.
- Details may be lost. Remembering what is said may succeed if the developer tackles the issue immediately, but it is much more difficult, if not impossible, an hour later.
- Retesting issues is very difficult if it is no longer known what the original issue was and which steps led to it.
- Metrics for evaluation and potential process improvement are absent. By, for example, noting in the issue registration the phase in which an issue is found and in which phase it should have arisen; a process improvement proposal can be made in an evaluation.
- Issues are solved in the order in which they arrive, not on the basis of priority.

- Issues may be completely forgotten and will arise in a subsequent release, or, even worse, only when the information system has gone into production.
- On transfer to a maintenance department, it is not clear which "known errors" remain in the information system.

The test manager must therefore ensure that the issues are denoted in a structured manner.

11.2 The Issue Procedure

Written communication is the best option. The test manager describes in the issue procedure who undertakes which actions and which data the testers should save concerning an issue. Such a procedure is all the more important if parties outside the test project have to work on the issues, as in an organisation with branches in various countries, with the developers based for example in India, while the testers carry out their work in Europe.

The test manager can decide to support the issue procedure with an automated tool. This may vary from a simple, user-friendly tool to a very comprehensive tool containing other functionalities such as a registration facility for all the various test cases and progress monitoring. It is also possible that the development department already has a tool at its disposal linked, for example, to a configuration management system.

The process of registering and following issues may be divided into four main steps (IEEE 1044, 1993):

1. *Recognition*: An issue emerges and the following steps are carried out:
   - Recording of the basic details (environment, tester, date and time).
   - Classification of the issue (test phase, type of issue, reproducibility, version of the information system).
   - Allocation of an initial priority; this is the priority of the product risk with which the test is connected. It is ascertained from the table in which the product risk, the relevant requirement(s) and the test condition are noted (see Appendix C).
2. *Investigation*: Each issue is investigated to determine whether the issue is clear, valid and whether it entails other factors. A proposal will follow as to further handling of the issue. The following steps are taken within the investigation:
   - Recording of the investigation details (start of the investigation, duration, by whom, etc.).
   - Classification of the results of the investigation (actual cause, source, type of issue).
   - Review of priority setting in the issue meeting.

3. *Action*: On the basis of the results of the investigation, the test team determines in consultation with the client and the stakeholders which actions are now required. This can mean that the development team will solve the issue, or that it will not be handled until a later phase. The following steps are taken:
   - Laying down the required actions.
   - Classification of the actions (solve, postpone, next release).
   - Review of the priority setting from the previous phase.
4. *Disposition*: The following steps are carried out here:
   - Recording how the issue was handled.
   - Classification of the handling of the issue (closed, postponed, invalid).
   - Review of the priority setting from the previous phase.

These steps involve the following roles:

- The tester is always responsible for setting up and executing the test. He is also often the person who first registers the issues.
- The test manager ensures that the issues are reviewed and given the correct priority. During an issue meeting, he discusses the issues with the client, stakeholders and developers, and has them adjust, if necessary, the priorities assigned to them based on the priorities of the product risks. Thereafter, the development department goes to work on those issues, the solution of which has been agreed. Following the result of the issue meeting, the test manager will adjust the status of the issues. He is also responsible for monitoring the issues, and will therefore manage them.
- The developer indicates how much time is required to solve an issue. In the event of questions or ambiguities, he will contact the test team. When the issues are solved, he will agree with the test manager when he will deliver a new version. If new releases or test runs are planned, he will indicate in which release particular issues will be solved.
- The client and the stakeholders are responsible for determining the final priority of an issue. They will indicate to the developers with which issues they should begin.

In order to be able to monitor the issues, the issue procedure should contain an indication of the status of an issue. It should be set out who undertakes which action in respect of each status level. In this way, the test manager can hold people to their responsibilities and where necessary enquire why certain actions have not been carried out.

Table 11.1 contains an example of possible status values.

Each status level needs to be dealt with by the appropriate responsible individuals. Figure 11.1 shows the course of the various status levels and the relevant persons responsible for them.

The course of the status levels can be linked with the four main steps within the issue procedure: recognition, investigation, action and disposition. This linkage is shown in Figure 11.2.

Table 11.1. Possible status values of issues

Status code	Status	Description
1	New	The issue is entered into the issue administration
2	Not approved	The issue has been tested again and has not been approved
3	Assigned for analysis	The test team will carry out a further analysis of the issue; for example, when it is unclear whether the issue arises through problems with the system or with the testware
4	Assigned for business decision	It is unclear whether the problem must be solved. The business representative decides whether the problem must be solved or the issue cancelled
5	Assigned for retest	The test manager has assigned the issue to a tester, who will carry out a retest
6	Transferred to development	The issue will be sent to the development team for investigation and solution
7	Additional information requested	The issue is not quite clear to the development team, and it asks the test team for additional information
8	Assigned for development	The project manager has assigned the issue to a developer, who will solve the problem
9	Fixed	The developer has solved the problem and released the software for transfer to the testers
10	Build delivered	The IT project leader has checked the solution and has made a "build" that contains associated solutions. The build is delivered to the test team
11	Postponed	The handling of the issue has been postponed
12	Approved	A retest has been executed in respect of the issue and the result of the retest meets expectations
13	Duplicate	This issue has already been reported; no action will be taken
14	Not reproducible	Issue is not reproducible in retest; no action will be taken
15	No action taken	The issue has been acknowledged, but it is decided that the impact is not relevant and therefore no follow-up will be made
16	Cancelled	Following investigation, it has been decided not to correct the problem (for diverse reasons) and the issue is closed

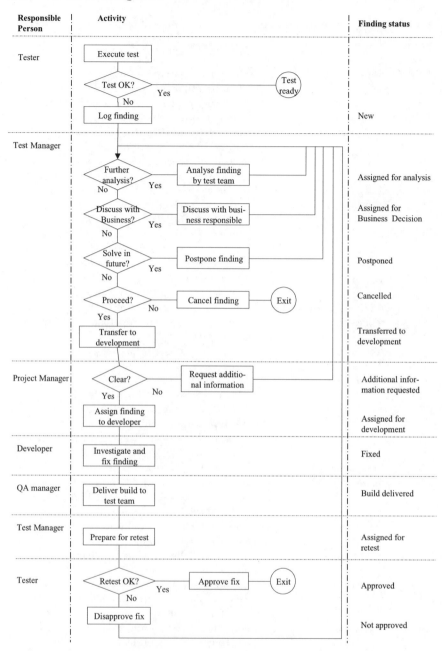

Fig. 11.1. Status levels of issues

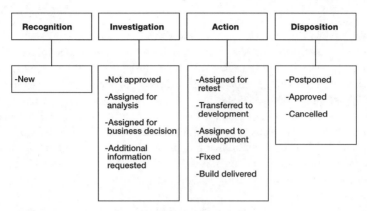

Fig. 11.2. Relations between the status and the main steps within the issue procedure

11.3 Issue Administration

The test analyst registers an issue in accordance with the issue procedure immediately upon discovery – no later. He does not collect issues only to report them at the end of the day (or even the week), for then there is a likelihood that he will forget important details. This often reduces the potential for repair, particularly in the final phase of a test project. The pressure to go "live" is very great at that stage, with the possibility of unclear issues perhaps not being solved. It is also possible that an unclear picture emerges concerning the quality of (parts of) the information system owing to the fact that not all of the issues have been reported. A tester must never automatically assume that a fellow tester has already reported an issue.

To be able to communicate as clearly as possible on an issue, the following details should be retained in respect of every issue:

- A unique number (preferably automatically generated).
- A brief summary of the issue, a "one-liner". This summary must be concise, but provide sufficient information. A summary such as "The system is acting strangely" is too brief. It is better to say something along the lines of "When putting in a long name (31 positions) error message YXZ instead of ABC appears".
- The name of the person reporting the issue, so that the development team can consult this person in the event of questions or ambiguities.
- First impression of the type of issue (fault in testware, test environment or information system).
- The status; if a tool is used, this is usually generated initially by the tool, e.g. the status "new" or "open".
- Date of registration.
- The information system and the version the issue applies to.

- The system part.
- Reference to the test cluster/test condition/test case.
- A clear description of the situation, including the steps to be taken to reproduce the issue. This also means a description of the starting point of the test environment for the test and the procedures that were carried out in sequence before the issue occurred. The most frustrating issues are those that occur intermittently. But these can be of essential importance. Even if an issue cannot be reproduced, it is advisable to pass this on with as much background information as possible. This may provide the developer with sufficient information to allow him, together with his technical knowledge of the information system, to discover the cause and to correct the problem.
- Appendices (screen print, table content). Notes from the test execution or a record of the procedures with a tool or video can help in tracing the steps.
- The project phase in which the issue was found and the phase in which it should have been found (specification set-up, unit test, system test, integration test, etc.). These details are necessary for an evaluation and potential process improvement.

The testers must write down these details as clearly as possible. Surplus information is distracting, while too little information may mean that it is not clear to the developers what is meant. Also, each notification should concern one issue only. Where there are several issues referred to in a single notification, it is difficult to link them to an unambiguous priority and it is also difficult to follow the progress of the issue, for how can the test manager indicate that one of the three issues referred to in the notification is solved and retested, while the other two remain open? Apart from that, the issue will appear longwinded, and it is likely that one or more issues will be forgotten.

In the example shown in Table 11.2, the tester has described which steps he has taken: that is, which screen he started with and which fields he wanted to change. The tester can also include here a reference to the relevant test case, or even add the test case as an attachment. At "Remarks", the tester has indicated what happened. This information is sure to be of use to the developer in solving this issue.

In principle, the testers include all of the issues in the issue administration. It makes no difference here who will eventually tackle and solve the issue. That will be decided during the issue meeting.

11.4 The Issue Meeting

In the course of the test project, the test manager will plan regular meetings during which the issues are discussed. These discussions should be attended at least by the test manager, the IT project leader, a developer (team leader)

Table 11.2. Example of good issue registration

Project XYZ	Issue no.: 2		
Issue description:	Status: New		Latest status change
Data field changed after screen size adjustment			10 Feb. 2003 11:33:58
STEPS			
1. Open "change products" screen			
2. Change "colour code" field or "supplier code"			
3. Maximise the screen			
4. Colour code and supplier code are now placed in wrong fields			
5. Exit the screen and save details			
6. Open the "products" overview			
7. This shows that the colour code and supplier code are now also stored in the wrong fields			
Tester:	Bob	Owner:	Iris
Function:	Change products	Version/date:	1.01 beta
Test case:	XYZ3C02T04	Continued from:	
Business impact:	Must test	Keyword:	
Test impact:	Test obstructing	Amend documentation:	
Cause of fault:	Programming	No. of appendices:	0
Remarks:	If Step 5 is exited without saving the details, the system reverts to the values that were displayed after Step 1.		

and the stakeholders in respect of the clusters being handled. A user may also be involved, who can assess the issue from a functional viewpoint. They all discuss not only the content of the issues, but also the sequence in which the developers should solve them. The frequency of the meeting depends on the phase the test project has reached, but will increase the closer it gets to the finishing date. With business critical information systems, daily meetings in the last weeks are not unusual. It then becomes increasingly important to estimate the feasibility of solving an issue and with what urgency possible measures should be taken to manage product risks before the information system goes into production.

During the issue meeting, the participants go through the outstanding issues, and examine the causes of new issues. The relevant party is then instructed to work on the particular issue. The meeting will examine whether issues discussed in an earlier meeting have been solved. If an issue has not been solved according to plan, the test manager should try to discover the reason for this. If it concerns an issue with a high priority, the client and stakeholders will also be keen to have it solved as quickly as possible.

The participants in the issue meeting will pay particular attention to the priority of every new issue. In order to indicate the priority, the testers use a table showing the product risk, the importance and the relevant requirement that is translated into a test condition (for this table, see Appendix C). Figure 11.3 shows the relation between the product risks and the issues.

Three factors determine the final priority of the issue:

- the business impact;
- the test impact;
- the solution term.

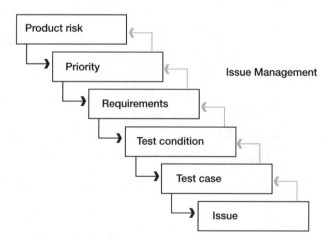

Fig. 11.3. Establishing the initial importance of an issue

11.4.1 The Business Impact

The consequences for normal operations are expressed in the "business impact". The stakeholders assign priority during the product risk analysis phase, at an early stage of the test project. However, the initially ascribed importance of the product risk is not always correct in every case.

> During the product risk analysis in an organisation that ships goods, the following product risk was identified: if perishable goods are shipped a day late, considerable loss results. This risk has been given a "Must Test" priority. To cover this product risk, various test conditions are set up. In the test execution, the test team finds two issues.
>
> *Issue 1.* Seasonal products such as strawberries have not been identified as perishable within the definition of perishable goods. If three or more different products of 1,000 kg (including apples, pears and strawberries) are listed on the plan for shipping, the apples and pears are shipped first according to the plan. The strawberries will not appear in the planning until the following day.
>
> *Issue 2.* During the execution of the test cases set up for this product risk, the tester notices that in the overview screen showing the shipments, "shipping date" is spelled wrongly, and it appears as "shipping dat".
>
> During the issue meeting, it is decided that the first issue has been given the correct initial priority. The business impact remains the same. However, for the second issue, it is decided that the classification "Must Test" is too heavy. This issue appeared during the test execution without being directly related to the underlying product risks. The testers include these issues in the issue administration. No issue must be overlooked. To assess them as objectively as possible, the testers therefore initially copy the priority of the relevant product risk. During the meeting, the stakeholders decide that the priority of this issue may be changed to "Could Test".

11.4.2 The Test Impact

The test impact indicates the consequence of an issue for the execution of the test. The tester's perspective decides this, and he determines the extent to which the issue will obstruct or block the test, or part of it.

In determining the test impact, the test team can employ the following categorisation:

1. *Test stopper.* The testers are unable to execute the remainder of a cluster until the issue has been solved.

2. *Test obstructing.* The testers are unable to continue with a part of a cluster until the issue is solved.

3. *Non-obstructive.* All the test cases in the cluster can be executed despite the issue.

At the start of the test execution, the test impact has the most weight, since the test must proceed as smoothly as possible. An issue with the test impact "test stopper" or "test obstructing" means that not all of the tests can be executed. The test manager is therefore unable to cover all the product risks. During the issue meeting, the developers are therefore asked to solve the issues with this test impact first of all.

As the test project progresses, the test impact and business impact will weigh more or less equally. At the end of the project, the emphasis will be placed on the business impact. The important factor then is how well the information system will operate in practice. The client and stakeholders will want to run as few product risks as possible. This shift in emphasis between the test impact and the business impact is shown in Figure 11.4.

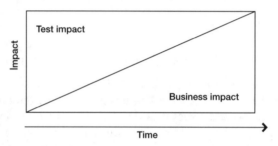

Fig. 11.4. Relations between test impact and business impact over time

11.4.3 The Solution Term

Besides the business impact and the test impact, the solution term also plays a part. Some issues take considerable time to solve owing to the complexity of the function and the problem found in it. If no allowance is made for this, it can happen that solutions are not available in time. This cannot be what is meant in the case of issues with a "Must Test" priority!

As the completion date of the test project approaches, the issue meeting may decide that for the issues with equal priority, those with the shortest solution term will be solved first. After a successful retest, it is then clear that the relevant product risks are no longer present in production. Perhaps, instead of solving a single issue with a long solution term, several issues with shorter solution terms can be handled. This benefits the quality of the information system. Of course, this solution only applies to issues with equal priority.

Following the issue meeting, the test manager will enter information concerning (solved) issues into the administration:

1. An estimate of the solution term.
2. Who solved the issue.
3. When it was solved (date and version number).
4. A general description of the solution.
5. Retest executed (by whom, when and remarks).
6. Any adjustment to the priorities of the issues.

If there is not sufficient time to solve all of the issues, it may be decided during the issue meeting to move these issues to a subsequent release. With this, the issues are cancelled in the administration of the current test project and enter the regular change process. The issue then becomes a Request For Change (RFC). In a subsequent release, the shifted issues can be solved and any expanded functionality added (see Figure 11.5).

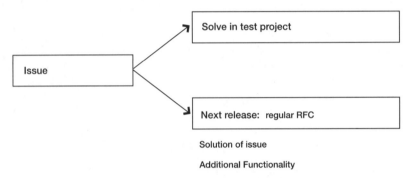

Fig. 11.5. Issues during and after the test project

11.5 Conclusion

The test manager is responsible for keeping the issue administration continually updated. This is of importance not only to the issue meeting, but also to the various reports in the course of the test project. This enables him to provide in his reporting an indication of the quality of the information system. He does this, not by way of numbers of outstanding and solved issues, but by indicating the recognised product risks that have or have not been covered. This will provide a continuous reflection of the system quality in progress reporting. The reports created by the test manager are the subject of the next chapter.

12

Reporting and Advice

"How's testing going? Is the information system ready to go into production?" As soon as the system is delivered to the test project, all the parties involved are interested in the first test results. The test manager will provide regular insight into the progress, the quality of the information system and any problems surrounding the test project. Through regular reporting, the test project holds the attention of the client and stakeholders. They know then which product risks and related requirements are covered and which risks still have to be tested. With this information they can make a decision on whether to go on to a subsequent test level or to put the information system into production.

It is established in the test strategy what the test team will test and what not, and therefore which product risks will be covered in the test project. The test plan (or plans) describes how the test manager has set up the test project. During the course of the test project, the test manager will have to keep the client and all the stakeholders informed of progress of the project. They were, after all, involved in setting up the test strategy and the test plan, and they will want to be kept informed about the quality of the information system under test.

The test manager has various types of reports at his disposal for this purpose. During the execution of a test level, he will use a *progress report*. In the event of a situation requiring immediate action, he will create an *exception report*. When a test level is completed, he creates a *phase report*. A *final report* forms the end of the test project.

12.1 Drawing up Reports

In drawing up reports, the test manager must bear in mind for whom the report is intended and what purpose it serves.

The test manager will create a progress report, for example, a number of times during the execution of a test level, but the project manager will not be prepared to read a bulky report each time. These reports should therefore be short and concise, and only contain relevant information concerning the latest period.

This is in contrast to the final report. The project manager and the stakeholders use this report to decide whether or not the information system can go into production. The test manager will have to provide as complete an overview as possible of the result of the executed test levels.

Various reporting styles are open to the test manager (Perry & Rice, 1997):

- *The informal approach.* The test team communicates informally on the test results (this might be verbally or by e-mail). This style is efficient, but offers little concrete information to either the test team or the recipient. In the event of a dispute, it is difficult in retrospect to demonstrate what exactly happened and whether the appropriate persons were informed in time. Moreover, there is an absence of documentation on the advice issued and on the result of the test.
- *The negative approach.* The test team only passes on the bad news. This often results simply in a list of faults found. The positive, correctly operating parts of the information system are left aside. The disadvantage here is that one loses insight of the total quality.
- *The euphemistic approach.* With this, the test team presents the negative results in such a way that the report suggests a positive scenario. This can result in unjustified faith in the information system.
- *The objective approach.* The results are reflected in actual figures of issues found and solved. The test team presents the information accurately and objectively, but has not yet set up a process for this and often reports on an irregular basis.
- *The structured approach.* The test manager reports the test results on the basis of previously defined standards and with agreed regularity, depending on the phase of the test project.

Clearly, the preference is for a structured approach in which the test manager reports objectively. Where Risk & Requirement Based Testing is used, the test manager reports on the product risks that are covered and those still outstanding. During test execution, the testers record the result of the various test cases. This can be traced back to the product risks via the table in Appendix C.

Whichever form of reporting the test manager selects, in all of the reports he must restrict himself to the facts and not pronounce value judgements on individuals or groups. If there are negative discrepancies between the planned status and progress, it is advisable not only to indicate the problem, but also to provide an approach to a possible solution. For example:

All the planned 620 test cases have been executed. The issue management system currently shows 235 outstanding issues. Of these, 153 have the priority "Should test" and 82 "Could test"; 30 issues are solved per week, starting with the issues with the highest priority. This means that, normally, in 3 weeks' time, there will still be 63 "Should test" issues outstanding. If these are to be actually solved and tested again, the planned finishing date of the project in 3 weeks' time is under threat. The test team proposes to organise an extra issue meeting to coordinate the product risks that are still really crucial. Thereafter, agreement must be reached concerning the planning.

The input of the test team thus provides considerable added value, and this conclusion will have a positive effect on the involvement of the stakeholders and the organisation.

12.2 Types of Reports

During the execution of the quick scan, the test manager examines which reporting structure the organisation employs and whether templates of reports are present. The test manager may adopt these.

In opting for RRBT, the test manager will at any rate want to communicate on the product risks. This may require adjustment to the existing standards.

In any case the test manager will want to use the following types of reports:

- The progress report;
- The exception report;
- The phase report;
- The final report.

These reports have already been mentioned in Chapter 8, Section 8.2. In this chapter, we will discuss the content of the reports.

12.2.1 The Progress Report

In the progress report, the test manager provides the client and stakeholders with information on the progress and status of the test project within one test level.

The frequency with which these progress reports are made depends on the agreements the test manager made at the start of the test project. At the start, it may be sufficient to provide these every 2 weeks. However, during test execution, a weekly report, or even twice a week, may be necessary.

In Chapter 10, it was indicated how the test manager can monitor progress with regards to time, money and quality. He includes this information in the progress report. Since, by using the Earned Value Method (EVM) and the Test Control Matrix (TCM), there is continuous insight into the status of the test project, the test manager can supply reports not only actively with the agreed regularity, but also pro-actively, at any given moment.

If an information system is developed according to an iterative development method, the test manager must be alert to the fact that various test levels can be executed in parallel. While the developers are busy with the development of a new version of a prototype, an acceptance test is carried out on the current prototype. The test manager must therefore ensure that the progress reports on these two test levels are not confused.

It is also possible for a particular test level to cover a large number of extensive clusters. In order to monitor the progress, the test manager appoints a separate test coordinator per cluster. At the end of a period, the test manager receives a progress report from each test coordinator. He collates these for his reporting to the client and stakeholders.

In the progress report, the test manager will include at least the following information:

- Activities, milestones and products of the recent period: on the basis of details supplied by EVM, it is indicated which products are completed. If there have been digressions from the planning, the cause of these should also be indicated.
- Activities, milestones and products that are planned for the coming period.
- The quality of the information system. On the basis of the tests executed and the problems found, it is indicated which of the product risks and requirements recognised in the test strategy have been covered.
- Progress and budget consumption, issuing from information obtained within progress management.
- An overview of the 5 to 10 most important project risks. With this, the test manager shows the problems that exist around the test project.
- Points of focus and problems. The test manager includes a summary from the test logbook with the points of focus and problems that have arisen in the recent period. The exception reports created by him should be included here.

Appendix J provides a template for a progress report.

The focus of the progress report will shift somewhat in the course of the test project. In the first phase of strategy and planning and during the setting up of the test design, the focus is more on the quality of the testware and minimising the project risks. During test execution, the focus shifts increasingly onto the product risks and the associated quality of the information system.

12.2.2 The Exception Report

Some situations demand short-term action. This might be, for example, a project risk for which a warning was issued and which is now materialising. An unforeseen situation may also arise for which no risk countermeasures have been designed. In these situations, the test manager creates an exception report. This may be an official document with a prescribed template, but it may also take the form of an e-mail to the client and stakeholders.

In all situations, an exception report must include the following details:

- A description of the situation or the problem.
- A description of the cause of the situation.
- A description of the consequences this has for the test project in terms of time, money or quality.
- A listing of the alternatives available for dealing with the situation and the influence per alternative on time, money, quality, and whether any additional project risks arise as a consequence.
- A recommendation for an alternative, with supporting information.
- The decision taken; if no decision has been taken, this point obviously cannot yet be answered, but reference should be made to the following progress report, which will contain the decision.

12.2.3 The Phase Report

At the end of a phase (test level), the test manager delivers a phase report. This provides a description of all the tests that have been executed during this phase and their results. The test manager uses the progress report for input here. In addition, the test manager refers to the entry and exit criteria in the test plan for this test level and indicates whether they have been met. This information is necessary, as the client and stakeholders must decide at the end of the phase on whether to proceed to a subsequent phase. A template of a phase report is included in Appendix K.

The most important information in a phase report is:

- An overview of the quality of the information system: the product risks and requirements covered and those not covered by the test execution, a brief overview of the issues (at any rate the "known errors") and the exit and entry criteria. For a complete overview of the issues, the test manager includes a reference to the issue administration. He also provides an explanation of any deviations here. If not all of the product risks have been covered as agreed in the test strategy, the test manager should explain this here. The same applies to the entry and exit criteria. It is possible that this phase accepted the information system despite its not meeting all the entry criteria. The test manager can repeat that fact here. This might be the reason why certain product risks have not been covered.

- An overview of planned versus realised activities on the basis of EVM and the TCM:
  - time;
  - budget;
  - deliverables.

  Here, too, the test manager must mention the reasons for deviation.
- An objective recommendation on the transfer of the information system to a subsequent phase. The test manager bases the advice on the foregoing sections of the phase report. In this, he sets out the test goals against the results achieved.

12.2.4 The Final Report

The final report in many ways resembles the phase report. It contains all the parts of the phase report, with the difference that the test manager describes the total test project. He uses the phase reports as input for the final report. If the test project consists of one test level alone, then the phase report and the final report are the same.

At the end of the total test project, the client and the stakeholders take a decision, based on the final report, on whether to put the information system into production. A template of a final report is included in Appendix L.

The information that the test manager includes in the final report consists of:

- The test goals. By setting out the results of the test project against the goals, the client and the stakeholders can determine whether the goals have been sufficiently met.
- Information on the quality of the information system. Here, the test manager indicates which product risks were covered in which test level, which issues remain outstanding and which acceptance criteria have been met. With the outstanding issues, the test manager also indicates what agreements have been made concerning these: whether the next test project will take these up in its issue administration or the issues will be included in the standard maintenance procedure in the form of Requests For Change (RFC).
- The total costs of the whole test project. For this, the test manager uses the overviews from the phase reports. The costs may be shown in terms of time and money. He also includes here those costs not directly linked to test activities - for example, travel expenses or training costs.
- The benefits of the test project. The benefits are often difficult to quantify. The test manager can try to estimate the costs that would have accrued if the product risks materialized. Since coverage of these has shown that they will not materialize, the associated costs have been saved.
- An overview of the deliverables of the test project.

- The final report also contains a recommendation. However, in this case it concerns advice on putting the information system into production. Here again, the test manager provides objective advice by setting the results of the test project against the original goals.

12.2.5 Advice

Both the phase report and the final report contain advice. This is an important part of both reports. The objective advice of the test manager enables the client and stakeholders to make a decision on whether to go on to a subsequent test phase or to put the information system into production: the go/no-go decision.

A no-go decision means that the client and stakeholders do not yet have complete faith in the information system.

At the end of a test phase, they may decide that the quality of the information system is still so unsatisfactory that further adaptation and testing is necessary in that phase. Obviously, this must fit within the total planning of the project. In the worst case, the drastic decision may be taken to abort the whole project: not enough resources may be available to bring the system up to the required level of quality.

At the end of the total test project, they may decide to move the date when the information system will be put into production. Perhaps they will consider that there are too many outstanding issues. The client and the stakeholder must then decide on the issues that have yet to be solved. When the developers and testers have issued a plan, a new date is set for going into production. This new release date is communicated to all the parties involved.

Example Reporting

During the implementation of the test organisation, the test manager should bear in mind the complexity and extent of the test project. In large projects, clear communication and a reporting structure are essential. This case describes a formal reporting structure that can avoid problems in communication.

This case demonstrates how the test manager in a large international financial institution (which has its operations in the insurance market, among others, and in the area of banking services) tries to create clarity for all the interested parties by using a structured manner of reporting. We will call the financial institution BIFIN (BIg FINancial institution). The example concerns not one large project, but a continuous process that takes place in the line organisation. The department concerned here is responsible for the standardisation of all the workstations. It not only develops the architecture, but also is responsible for the realisation. This involves, among other things, the following tasks: scripting new applications, testing the new applications on a variety of platforms, rollout of all the workstations worldwide (more than 70,000) and the certification of all the applications (more than 2,000) that have to run on the system.

As this concerns more than 70,000 workstations, there are also a lot of stakeholders. This therefore presents the biggest risk. They all have separate interests, which may be conflicting. The test project will have to try to allow for all interests.

The scale of the operation means that it is not clear to everyone exactly what the department is doing. This leads to much discussion and long faces. The organisation's interest is considerable, for the workstation is the basis of the successful functioning of every employee. Without a workstation, they cannot sell new products, assist customers, etc.

Some of the questions issuing from various sources are:

- Why a particular application is still not approved (time aspect).
- Why a particular application has been rejected (quality aspect).
- In which release the application will be included and when (planning).

BIFIN favours a formal manner of communication where possible. This is preferred in view of the large group of interested parties. Furthermore, they are located all over the world (different time zones, language barriers, cultural differences, etc.). In order to implement this structured approach as effectively as possible, a number of standard documents (templates) must be designed by BIFIN, such as progress reports, phase reports and final reports. One of the most important reports is the final report that is used in certifying applications, and for this, the final report template in this book has been chosen. If an application has not been certificated, it is not permitted to run it on the BIFIN system. If the final report is created before the certification advice, it is discussed during a meeting. In this meeting, it is then determined whether the certification committee adopts the advice. After the document has been discussed, it is assigned "official" status and placed on the intranet, so that everyone can see the status of a particular application or build. By introducing this step, a large number of questions such as those mentioned above can be answered.

By way of example, in this case a part of such a final report for certification is demonstrated. It concerns the following sections: the management summary, the quality of the information system and the advice.

Management Summary

Introduction. This report concerns the certification test for approval of release 10 for laptop computers. In this release, a blocking issue is also included relating to the virus scanner for the standard desktop. Among other things, it has been examined whether the virus scanner can now be initiated while other applications are active.

Recommendation. The release still contains some minor issues, but the overall quality is good. Therefore the recommendation is to certify release 10.

Additional Information. Prior to the rollout of this release, the users will require additional training. Also, the source from which the virus scanner obtains information will have to be made available by the maintenance department, if the business units are unable to do this themselves.

Costs. By working overtime, we have succeeded in reducing the duration from 3 days to 1.5 days. According to the planning, 12 hours were required for the certification. In reality, 13 hours were spent. The biggest cause of this was the problem with the virus scanner.

Quality of the Information System

Product Risks and Requirements. The product risks that have to be covered and requirements that have to be proven are shown in Table 12.1

Table 12.1. Overview of BIFIN's product risks

Product risk	MoSCoW	Requirement	Status
Laptop	Must test	Laptop must operate stand-alone	Correct
Laptop	Must test	Laptop must operate connected	Correct
Desktop	Must test	Virus scanner must operate on the desktop	Correct

Overview of issues. The test results are shown in Table 12.2. With low-priority issues, the stakeholders may decide to leave them outstanding and pass them on to the following release. With high-priority issues, however, the status should always be "closed" or "workaround", otherwise the release cannot go into production. The last column shows the measure that has been carried out to correct or minimise the issue. It is also stated why a particular solution was selected. The certification committee can decide on the basis of these details whether a release is approved or disapproved.

Exceptions.
- The application PAYMENT has not been included in this test. As agreed, PAYMENT is not a standard application and therefore falls outside the scope of this test.

Table 12.2. Overview of BIFIN issues

Found issues	Importance	Status	Measures
Outlook is not configured for standalone operation on a laptop	Must test	Workaround	A workaround is available. It has no influence on the users' work
The auto-update path for the virus scanner is incorrect	Must test	Closed	The business units themselves are responsible for correcting the locations
The new settings of the anti-virus program are not installed automatically. The user should set these manually	Must test	Closed	The risk that the user would do this incorrectly or even fail to do it was so great that this was adjusted in the rollout
The background colour does not conform to the standard	Could test	Open	To be taken forward to the next release

- The Exchange server used for the execution of this test does not wholly correspond with the production server.
- The user manual did not fall within the scope of this test and has therefore not been included.

Recommendation

The release retains a few minor issues, but the overall quality is good. Therefore, the advice is to approve release 10 for the laptops, including build 9 for the desktops. All the issues marked "Must test" have been corrected and retested successfully.

The experience of BIFIN was that by introducing a clear and structured manner of communication as seen in the above example, various improvements were realised, including:

- All the stakeholders know exactly what the status is.
- The helpdesk received much fewer calls with questions concerning the status of applications, builds, etc.
- By collecting and analysing the documents, even better planning is now possible.

Obviously, there are always points that a subsequent project might pay closer attention to, or that might be carried out more effectively. These include:

- Consider carefully the target group and attune the reporting to this.
- Ensure that the documents which are of importance to everyone are available, by placing them in the test management file.

12.3 Conclusion

A final report also often includes an evaluation of the test process. This has the advantage that all the information pertaining to the test project is available in a single document. The disadvantage, however, is that there is often a lot of time pressure surrounding the delivery on time of a final report, as the organisation has to take a decision on going into production based onx this report. The reader of a final report is therefore often more interested in the quality of the information system than in an evaluation, and may not even read the evaluation at all.

We recommend that the final report is completed first before starting the evaluation. The test manager can carry out the evaluation as part of the transfer to the line organization (e.g. the maintenance department). Whether this is possible depends on the continued role of the test manager after completion of the test project. These are the subjects of the following chapter.

13

Evaluation and Transfer

When the information system has successfully gone into production and the test project has been discharged, the test manager disbands the team, takes his leave of the project and moves on to the next one. His responsibilities seem to end here. But is that right? If he never looks back at what went well and what did not during the test project, and why, there will be no improvement in the following project. Only by making an evaluation can he, as well as the organisation, learn from and improve on the test process. And if he fails to organise the maintenance of the testware for the information system, he does himself or a colleague in a subsequent project a grave disservice. In short, the test manager must never forget evaluation of the test process and transfer of the testware, even though the information system is operating successfully in the production environment.

To be able to continue operating in the current market, an organisation has to be quicker off the mark than the competition when launching new products or services. As a result, the organisation has to develop information systems as quickly as possible and often at the lowest possible cost. Obviously, it may not run too many risks in doing this, therefore the quality of the systems must also be acceptable. To allow the test process to operate as effectively as possible, regular evaluation and improvement is necessary. This might also have positive influences on the system development process. By providing structured feedback, the number of issues will decrease in the future, thus reducing the repair time and effort and also the time it takes to carry out testing.

By carrying out evaluations during and after the various test projects, the test process will be improved. Well-organised maintenance contributes to the potential for reusing the test products, and this considerably improves the quality and speed of testing new versions of the information system. Moreover, the test products can quickly and relatively easily be applied or adapted by the maintenance department to a new version of the system.

If the test manager only comes to consider transfer and maintenance at the point of the information system going into production, it is already too late. He should examine during the quick scan how maintenance is set up in the organisation and who will be responsible for the maintenance of the test products for an information system.

13.1 Evaluation as a Basis for Improvement

The more an organisation and its information systems (and with these the test products) grow, the more need there is for a structured test process with clearly defined procedures. A first step towards improving the test process is to learn from one's own mistakes and successes in past and current projects.

A much used model as a basis of improvement is the Deming cycle (Deming, 2000). Underlying this model is the idea that process improvement is itself a continuous process (see Figure 13.1).

The four steps may be described in the context of this chapter as:

- *Plan*: The test manager plans the test project and formulates the quality requirements which the result must meet.
- *Do*: execute the plan.
- *Check*: During execution, the test team gathers information on the progress, approach and quality, and compares that information with what is set out in the plan. This is the actual evaluation.
- *Act*: On the basis of the evaluation, the test manager, the client and the stakeholders can decide on actions to be taken and also provide direction where necessary. This constitutes improvement proposals. Thereafter, planning starts again, and so the cycle continues.

The first two steps correspond to the parts as described so far in this book. The test manager sets up a test strategy and test plan(s), describing how the test project is organised. The testers are then set to work designing and executing the tests.

The last two steps in the Deming cycle describe the evaluation and the subsequent steps.

The test manager must ensure that the improvement proposals are implemented in procedure as well as process. A process is what you do, while a procedure describes what you are required to do. Employees should therefore work according to the new, improved procedure.

The test manager takes the initiative for an evaluation at the end of the test project. In a project of long duration, it can be useful to carry out interim evaluations as well. The test manager will have to plan these evaluation activities in the estimate and the plan.

For a proper evaluation, the test manager requires input from others, such as the client and the stakeholders: they can provide him with information on the set-up of the test project and the means of project management and

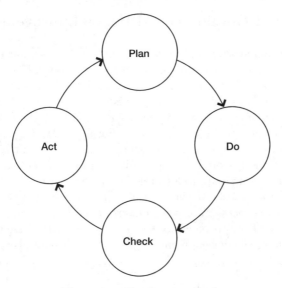

Fig. 13.1. The Deming Cycle

reporting. The testers can also provide him with information on what went well in the test project itself and what went less well: the lessons learned. The test manager also needs people to evaluate the stored metrics. Together they can decide on needed improvements of the test process.

If the test manager wishes to carry out a thorough evaluation, he is best advised to go through the whole of the Test Management Model. He can check for each part whether the selected categories, estimates, assumptions and conditions were correct. Even more important is why deviations occurred. For example, why were the problems with contacts with the external software supplier not foreseen as project risks? What measures could the test manager have taken? Why did some issues not arise during testing, but only in a pilot situation? In other words, what was the DDP[1] (Defect Detection Percentage) (Fewster & Graham, 1999)? DDP can help test managers evaluate how good the testing was and define measures to improve the testing. It can also help predict how many errors will occur during exploitation of the information system, based on the issues found during testing. Answers to these and many other questions can help the test manager, and possibly his successors, with a subsequent release of this information system. Other test projects, too, may benefit from the experiences of this test project.

The evaluation of a test project can lead to improvement proposals in respect of the test process.

---

[1] DDP is the relation between the number of defects found in a particular phase and the number of defects that remain.

13.2 Test and Development Process Improvement

By continually monitoring and adapting the test process, not only does the quality of the test process improve, but also the organisation gets better at preventing defects in the information system. If there is never any feedback provided to the system development process, issues will continue to arise.

An evaluation of the test process may show that both the test process and the development process can be improved. For example, if a record is consistently kept concerning the source of issues, the development team can then ensure that these issues do not arise in future. Improvements in the development process can contribute to a faster time-to-market and a higher quality-to-market. Figure 13.2 shows the relation between test process improvement and development process improvement. From the evaluation, the test manager gains ideas for improvement of the test process. But these may also lead to improvement of the development process. By the same token, the development project can also come up with improvement proposals regarding testing.

From the start of test execution, the test team has kept a consistent record of which test conditions were executed in which test runs. On evaluation of these results, it appears that earlier solved issues regularly recur in a later version. The development team indicates that it carries out configuration and version management manually. When a developer is busy with a particular part, he is the only person working on it and will also be the only one to make changes to it. He makes a copy of the details from a central computer to his PC and he makes the changes from his own PC. When his own unit test is finished, he sends the amended software from his local PC to the central computer. One day he is ill, and someone else takes over. This person makes a copy from the central location, makes changes

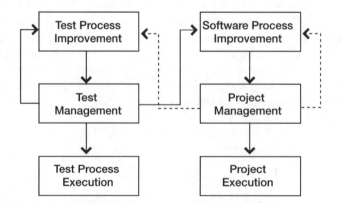

Fig. 13.2. Test process and development process improvement

according to his plan and returns the new version to the central location. After a few days his colleague returns. He completes his most recent tasks and sends the version on his hard disk back to the central location. Unfortunately, the changes that were made while he was ill have disappeared.

There are various ways of avoiding such problems in future. The procedure could be changed: it is prescribed that amended software is copied back to the central location every day. Another solution is to purchase a tool for configuration and version management. This tool would be used not only in software development, but also to include the testware.

13.2.1 Metrics

During the evaluation, the test manager may use metrics to support proposals for improvement of the test and development processes. If the test project is using these, the test manager will have described this in the test plan. In this book, the GQM method is cited as an aid to this (see Appendix F).

For some time, an organisation has been keeping figures on issues. They show that 60% of the issues are caused by incorrect specifications. The organisation wants to reduce this and decides that every project must carry out an inspection following the specification phase. To demonstrate the usefulness of the inspection, a measurement programme has been set up in accordance with the GQM method. It should provide answers to the following questions:

1. What is the total number of issues, grouped according to the phase in which they were found?
2. What is the increase/decrease of the total number of issues?

To answer them, they keep the following metrics:

- Number of issues in the category specification;
- Number of issues in the category environment;
- Number of issues in the category development defects;
- Number of issues in the category testware;
- Total number of issues in the test project;
- Total number of issues in the total project.

Prior to the introduction of inspections, the figures were as follows:

Specification (total project): $329 = 60\%$ of the total number of issues in the total project

Specification (test project): $329 = 60\%$ of the total number of issues in the test project

Environment: $56 = 10\%$ of the total number of issues in the test project

Testware: $26 = 5\%$ of the total number of issues in the test project

In the above situation, the total number of issues in the test project equals that of the total project. This is because there was no inspection carried out and so the issues were found only during testing.

Carrying out inspections in two projects delivered the following statistics:

Specification (total project): 469 = 64% of the total number of issues in the total project

Specification (test project): 176 = 24% of the total number of issues in the test project

Environment: 44 = 6% of the total number of issues in the test project

Development defects: 198 = 27% of the total number of issues in the test project

Testware: 21 = 3% of the total number of issues in the test project

Carrying out inspections has led to a decrease in the "specification (test project)" issues from 60% to 24%. A large number of the "specification issues" was found during the inspection, i.e. 469 − 176 = 293.

On the basis of the metrics, two of the questions are answered:

1. What is the total number of issues, grouped according to the phase in which they were found? By carrying out an inspection, the "specification issues" come to light at an earlier stage of the project and can be linked to the correct phase, namely the specification phase.
2. What is the increase/decrease of the total number of issues? By carrying out an inspection, the total number of issues has increased.

The answers must subsequently be translated into the goal of the measurement programme, i.e. "to demonstrate the usefulness of inspections in numbers and types of issues". The result is twofold. On the one hand the inspections lead to more issues being found that are related to the specification phase. On the other hand, more issues are found.

The fact that more issues are found can be put in a negative light. A lot of time has been spent on inspections, and so too much of everyone's attention has been focused there. However, it can also be explained positively. Since the testers are now finding fewer issues that should actually have been found earlier, they have more time to carry out other tests and so find other issues. These are the issues that they are actually supposed to find with testing. And registering issues takes time.

13.2.2 Test Improvement Methods

In a thorough evaluation and description of improvement proposals, the organisation will have to look critically at its own development and test processes, and not merely at individual projects. Various measuring instruments are available to determine the effectiveness of an organisation's processes. For example, CMM (Capability Maturity Model) or ISO certification.

Many of these measurement instruments for projects and development share the big disadvantage of under-exposure of the test process. Some organisations have therefore developed specific assessments to test improvement processes. Based on a completed questionnaire, a recommendation is issued on the parts of the test process that the organisation might change, and sometimes also how it can do this. Completion of the questionnaire may be done by interviewing representatives of various parties (such as managers, project leaders, testers and users) and by studying project and test documentation. In this way, a picture of the test process emerges. In this chapter, we will discuss two test improvement methods: Test Process Improvement (TPI®) and the testing maturity model (TMM).

13.2.3 Test Process Improvement

The TPI (Koomen & Pol, 1998) model is based on the TMap method. Although the name suggests it, this model bears no direct relation to a model for software process improvement (SPI).

The TPI model is shown in Figure 13.3.

TPI consists of 20 key areas. These areas relate mainly to the black-box test levels (e.g. the system test). Examples of these areas are test strategy, test tools, test environment, specification techniques and issue management.

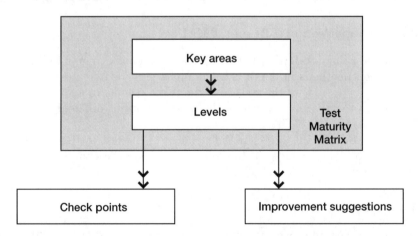

Fig. 13.3. The TPI model

In order to make the method suitable for white-box test levels as well, an extra area of focus is added, entitled "white-box test levels".

TPI has a number of levels, rising from A to D. Each higher level is better than the previous one as regards time, money and/or quality. To determine the level, check points are defined. The check points of each level also contain the requirements of the lower levels. Therefore, a test process at level B covers the requirements of level A as well as those of level B. If a test process does not meet the requirements of level A, the process is said to be at the starting level. No requirements are set for this lowest level.

The levels and key areas are set out in the test maturity matrix. This provides an impression of the current situation and forms a basis for improvement. With this, various improvement suggestions are included in the model.

13.2.4 Testing Maturity Model

The TMM framework was developed in the 1990s by the Illinois Institute of Technology (USA) (Burnstein et al., 1996) as a model to complement the capability maturity model (CMM) (Paulk et al., 1994), aimed at test process improvement.

TMM defines a number of maturity levels that must be gone through during the refinement of a test process. Within TMM, five levels are recognised on the basis of which it may be determined how mature the test process is and which improvements are necessary or should be given priority. At each level of the model a number of key process areas are recognised, and for each key process area a number of maturity goals are defined. An organisation meets the requirements of a particular TMM level when all the defined goals of that level have been achieved.

TMM recognises the levels and key process areas as shown in Figure 13.4.

13.2.5 Comparison of TPI and TMM

It would be going too far beyond the scope of this book to go into both test improvement methods in depth. The summary provided creates as good an impression as possible of the essence of the two methods. In addition to this, Table 13.1 provides an overview of the most important differences between TPI and TMM.

Both TMM and this book are independent of the test method used. TPI is related to TMap, and so in the following section the connection will be made between this book and TMM.

13.2.6 Relation Between this Book and TMM

The various test improvement methods describe what has to be done to improve a test process. They do not explain how. The range of topics in this

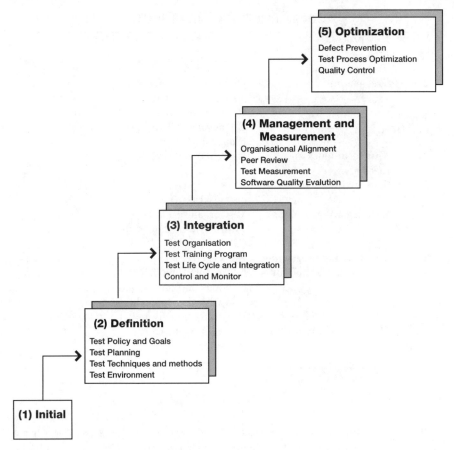

Fig. 13.4. TMM levels and key process areas

Table 13.1. Comparison of TPI and TMM

TPI	TMM
Related to TMap	Related to CMM (I)
Focus on dynamic test types	Focus on all the test types (incl. static tests)
Aimed at testware engineering	Testing seen as evaluating
Test engineering	Strong management involvement
20 key areas	More focused
Very detailed	Detailed
Book	Book, articles and guidelines

book can provide assistance here. Table 13.2 shows an overview of the various key process areas within Levels 2 and 3 of TMM and the associated topics, since these two levels are of most relevance to this book.

Table 13.2. This book and TMM

Level	Key process area	Test management book subject	
2	Test policy and goals	Not covered	
2	Test planning	Quick scan (Chapter 3)	
		Test strategy (Chapter 5)	
		Product risk analysis (Chapter 5)	
		Estimating (Chapter 6)	
		Planning (Chapter 7)	Test management file (Chapter 4)
2	Test techniques and methods	Issue management (Chapter 11)	
2	Test environment	Some coverage in test organisation (Chapter 8)	
	Test organisation	Test organisation (Chapter 8)	
		Transfer and evaluation (Chapter 13)	
3	Test training programme	Not covered	
3	Test life cycle and integration	Not covered explicitly, but regular focus on phasing and integration with development processes Project risk analysis (Chapter 5)	
3	Control and Monitoring	Progress management (Chapter 10)	
		Reporting (Chapter 12)	

13.3 Transfer

When the test manager has completed the evaluation, he is ready to hand over the test project and the accompanying documentation and products, including, therefore, the evaluation report. Or should the test manager also evaluate the transfer? The chicken-and-egg analogy comes to mind.

The test manager will certainly want to know that the transfer has been successful. Whether he has that opportunity depends on his role after completion of the test project. Will he still be involved in the organisation, or does he immediately leave? In the latter case, there is no opportunity to evaluate the transfer, which is a pity. It is important that the transfer is successful, for, after all, this is the starting point for future changes and releases. If the test manager remains involved, he may carry out an evaluation of this aspect together with the parties involved in the transfer. This report will be added to the documentation already handed over, and so a comprehensive overview of a completed test project is retained.

13.3.1 Maintenance of Test Products

Projects are finite. They have clearly defined starting points and finishing points. The project team is only responsible for the information system and all the associated documentation during the course of the project. When a project is completed successfully, the responsibility for the information system no longer lies with the project team, but with the overall (line) organisation. The organisation will normally have one or more departments that are responsible for the maintenance of information systems that operate within the organisation. The test products may be placed under the maintenance of this same department, or perhaps under that of a test centre.[2] The department taking over the maintenance of the test products will be one of the stakeholders involved in setting up the test strategy, and it will also set requirements in relation to the test products. It is important that the test manager starts early on setting up or initiating the maintenance of these. He establishes agreements on this in the test plan.

How formally the maintenance of an information system is set up of course varies from one organisation to another. In a small organisation, often only one person knows which systems are in use, where they are located and how everything is set up. In a larger organisation, a comprehensive maintenance process including all the relevant procedures may be set up in accordance with ITIL (Information Technology Infrastructure Library) (Koppens & Meyberg, 2000), a much used standard. In ITIL, maintenance is described as "the exercise of supervision over and the direction of the IT infrastructure". The IT infrastructure includes all equipment, software, data communication as well as the applicable procedures and documentation required for IT service provision.

In practice, the maintenance of testware is often not as well organised as the maintenance of the information system. For that reason, it is worth examining first of all how the maintenance of information systems is organised and linking this with the test products and test management aspects. The test manager does this during the quick scan.

During the course of the quick scan, the test manager ascertains whether these procedures exist in the organisation, and, if so, to what extent the test products (will) form a part of these processes (see also Chapter 3). He looks at whether test products in general are managed and by which department. He also investigates in detail whether and how the test products should form part of maintenance. Test products do not always necessarily have to be maintained ("throw-away" testware); this often depends on the information system. If an information system is built and implemented for one-time or short-term use, the associated test products will simply be archived, maintenance not strictly being necessary. This is true in the case of, for example, an application set up and issued to shopkeepers for dual pricing of items during the introduction of the euro. This software is no longer required: the testware does not have to be formally maintained. Information systems which are clearly intended to be used in the future, and will be subject to amendment, will require maintenance.

---

[2] In Chapter 8, various organisational forms are described, including a test centre.

If the organisation uses ITIL procedures, the test manager can co-ordinate the maintenance of the test products with this. If the organisation does not use these, he must ensure at the end of the test project that maintenance is set up. This will of course have to form part of the test manager's task description, and that is not always the case.

Table 13.3 shows the test products and test management aspects that have to be delivered and transferred by a test project for the various processes within ITIL.

Any organisation unused to strict procedures and processes will be unable to set up maintenance in accordance with ITIL in one step. The test manager must at least ensure that it is known to whom the test products should be transferred and that this department is also familiar with the products and how to maintain them in the future. This means that the department concerned should also be familiar or should become acquainted with the methods, techniques and standards employed in the test project.

13.3.2 Test Products To Be Maintained

In order to transfer the test products successfully, it must first be clear what exactly is meant by the test products and, what is even more important, which parts of these should be included under the standard maintenance processes.

Test products are products related to an information system that are included in the test management file. The products consist of two parts:

- The *testware*, consisting of the test strategy, cluster cards, test conditions, test cases, automated test scripts, issue administration, test reports and evaluation reports.
- The description of the *test environment*, consisting of the information system to be tested together with the infrastructure required to do this, such as hardware, middleware, database, test tools and test data (including accompanying manuals etc.). The entire test environment cannot form a part of the test management file. But the file must at any rate contain a complete description of the required configuration of the test environment.

This division is necessary, since the maintenance of the two areas is not always performed by the same department. The second part has more of a technical nature than the first part.

Maintenance of the Testware

The test team must be sure to transfer the latest version of all the test products to the organisation. The test manager will therefore have to include in his plan that, following a test run, and particularly following the last test

Table 13.3. Relation between ITIL and test management

ITIL process	Test products and test management aspects
Configuration management: Process aimed at identifying and defining parts of the IT infrastructure including their status and all their correlations	For each version of the information system, an overview must be available of the corresponding testware and which test environment is required to execute the test. The test manager must ensure that the testware is included in the configuration management process
Service desk: Process providing daily contact with the direct users. First point of contact for all users for queries, remarks and complaints on IT use and availability. Questions or problems concerning the information system are received here	If the test team provides aftercare for the information system, the service desk can be a source for expansion of the metrics. Recording issues arising after going into production enable the test team to determine in an evaluation whether the product risks have been correctly estimated and whether the appropriate testing effort has been invested
Problem management: By means of problem management, the highest possible level of stability in IT service provision is aimed for, by tracing and correcting defects in the infrastructure. Problems issuing from this process may lead to a new version of the information system	This new version will of course also require testing. Reusable test products are necessary for this
Release management: Provides procedures for a safe and managed rollout of new releases of parts of the IT infrastructure	This process may be already relevant when transferring the information system to be tested from development to a test environment. The test manager will in that case be the person who approves installing the information system in the environment. On transfer to the production environment, the test manager can check whether the actual version tested by his team is indeed taken into production

run, the test team updates the test products. Products that are not updated are unlikely to be (able to be) maintained by the maintenance department after the transfer.

The quick scan, test plans, issue administration and various reports are so specific to the execution of the test project that they may no longer necessarily be relevant to a subsequent project or the next release of the same information system. These documents could therefore remain outside the maintenance processes; they are project documentation. A test plan that was used for an earlier information system may of course serve as input to a subsequent test plan. It is therefore always advisable to archive documents that do not immediately require to be maintained. The plan and estimate will obviously be different, but the conditions and the approach may still be similar.

If, after completion of the test project, issues remain outstanding, the test manager can transfer these to the department responsible for supporting the end users, such as a helpdesk or the department responsible for functional maintenance, since such a department should be aware of all the known problems and any workarounds. The workarounds enable a helpdesk employee quickly to assist users in the production environment who encounter a known problem. If no workaround is available, it is at least recognised that the problem is a known issue. It may even be reported when the existing problems will be solved. At the start of a new release, the issues concerned are transferred to the project responsible for the new release.

The test strategy, cluster cards, test conditions, test cases and automatic test scripts, on the other hand, will have to be adapted to a new situation for the next release. They therefore must be taken into maintenance. This concerns documentation that is related to the information system and not to the specific project. A large number of the product risks and requirements per cluster card will still be valid. New product risks and requirements may then be added and, where necessary, existing ones may be amended. Product risks or requirements sometimes even disappear.

Maintenance of the Test Environment

As soon as an information system goes into production, the test environment must either remain in operation or be quickly available again by restoring a complete back-up or go through a comprehensive installation description. In the event of production problems, a completely up-to-date test environment is on hand to allow investigation of the problems and a retest and regression test when the problems have been solved. A description of this test environment will most certainly form part of configuration management. This means, therefore, that any changes to this configuration (e.g. a new version of the middleware) also have to be included in the description of the test environment and if necessary must also be physically placed in the test environment.

In an organisation where maintenance of the information systems is well organised, there is often a department that, as in the case of the production environment, is responsible for the test environment. This may be the same department, but it may also be a department that is only responsible for maintaining and managing the test environment. It is also possible, of course, that future projects will themselves be responsible for maintaining the test environment.

The test environment consists of not only the information system and the platform it runs from, but also any test tools and test data that are used as a basis for testing. In particular, with changes to the test data, the maintenance team must determine which changes have to be made to the start database. Test cases with the wrong start database are worthless. It is often difficult to determine which start data still correspond to which test cases, so the organisation then prefers to set up new start data or a completely new test.

13.3.3 When To Set Up Maintenance

The test manager should set up the maintenance and management of the test products at an early stage of the test project. In this, distinction should be made between maintenance of the test products during and after the test project. During the test project, the test manager is responsible for change and version control of the test products. After delivery of the system to production, the responsibility of maintenance of the test products shifts to the maintenance department in the organisation.

Maintenance During the Test Project

Maintenance is already necessary during the test project. Bear in mind the four defined test runs.[3] Figure 13.5 demonstrates how maintenance during a test project may be set up. It shows the versions of the testware keeping pace with the versions of the information system.

In maintaining the test products during the course of the test project, the following agreements are important:

- If stakeholders' requirements change, the test manager must be informed. Unfortunately, this does not always happen in practice.
- The test manager estimates the influence of the changes on the test products and the impact this will have on time and money. If, as a result of the changes, the test effort is changed to the extent of requiring more time and/or budgetary resources for the test preparation and execution, the test manager discusses this with the client. In consultation with the stakeholders, the client must make a decision concerning the product risks to be covered and the final delivery date.
- The test manager delegates to the test team the changes to be made to the testware.

---

[3] Intake test, basic test, complete test and final test. These test runs are described in more detail in Chapter 7.

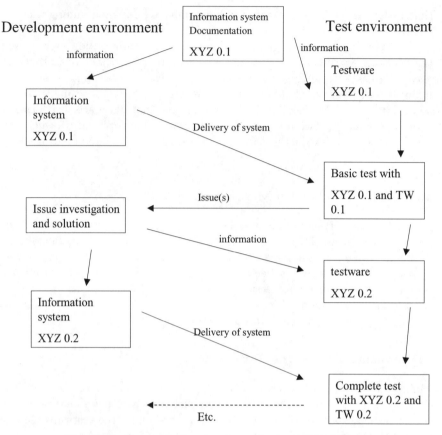

Fig. 13.5. Example of maintenance during a test project

- The development team places a new release of the information system in the test environment only with the approval of the test manager, who is the owner of the test environment.

These are merely examples of agreements that may be made. Each test project and each organisation will have other agreements. It is important that everyone within the organisation knows who is responsible for what when changes take place in the information system. If the procedures are not known to everyone, or, what is worse, no procedures exist, this constitutes a further, almost unacceptable, project risk.

Maintenance After the Test Project

As soon as a new version of the information system is planned, the department that maintains the test products must be in a position to deliver them quickly to whoever is responsible for testing this new release. Figure 13.6

demonstrates how the maintenance of test products after the test project may be carried out. In this, the maintenance operation is shown as though the activities related to changing the information system are always carried out in a project. This does not have to be the case. Except in the case of a (new) test project, a team from the maintenance department could also perform this task. However, this does not change the process of releasing and updating the test products.

The following processes apply to the maintenance of the test products:

- Defining the test goals (test project preparation).
- Reserving and delivering test products and test environment (test project preparation).
- Executing the test goals (test project execution).
- Intake of test products and test environment (test project execution).
- Returning and releasing (test project execution).
- Archiving (test project execution).

Test Maintenance

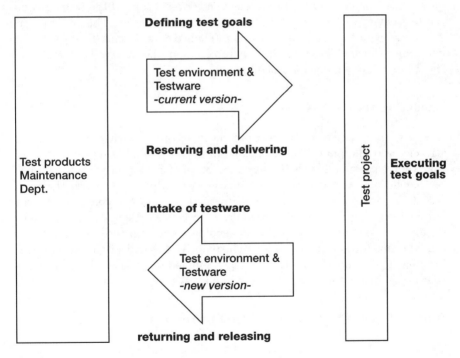

Fig. 13.6. Maintenance process after the test project

Defining the Test Goals

The test manager describes the goals of the test project in the quick scan and the test plan. If this concerns maintenance of an existing information system, it is important to carry out an examination of the existing test products and their reusability. While defining the test goals, he therefore needs to contact the existing maintenance organisation.

Reserving and Delivering Test Products and Test Environment

If a new version of an existing information system is required, the test products delivered by the test team should be included in the testware maintenance. The test manager responsible for the new version should ask the maintenance department whether any test products exist relating to the relevant information system. The maintenance department then informs the test manager about the version of the test products and the version of the information system to which they relate. On the basis of this information, the test manager indicates when he will require these test products. On the date requested, the maintenance department hands over a copy of the testware and the test environment documentation to the test manager. The original version remains in the archives of the maintenance department. The test teams determine which changes to the test products are necessary. They check all the products for significant amendments.

Executing the Test Goals

The test team carries out the test project in accordance with the agreed test strategy and the plan. The team adapts all the available test products so that they correspond with the new version of the information system. The test conditions, test cases and automatic test scripts with which the most recent test was executed are frozen. In the course of carrying out the test goals, changes in the cluster cards may be necessary. Each change is agreed during the test project with the stakeholders and registered with the test case documentation of the various clusters. At the end of the project, the test manager updates the test strategy completely, so that all the changes that arose during the test preparation and test execution are processed.

Intake of Test Products and Test Environment

The test team again delivers the test products to the maintenance department, which checks that all the test products comply with the agreed requirements. It is important here at least that the structure is clear and that it is also clear to which version of the information system these test products belong. The maintenance department will also check that the testware complies with the requirements of maintainability. Each new version of the information system must be accompanied by the new version of the test products. This can be done by saving all the products under new version numbers, but also by using configuration management tools. The version numbers of the test products must correspond to the version numbers of the information system. If the maintenance department considers that the test products do not comply with the set requirements, it should indicate what the test team should change so that it is able to approve the delivered test products. The test manager makes an inventory of these requirements during the quick scan.

Returning and Releasing

Following a positive intake, the test team formally transfers the test environment and the test products to the maintenance department, in whose hands total responsibility for the test products again rests.

Archiving

The maintenance department archives the test products in such a way that in the event of a new release, it can access these products quickly again and reserve them for the team responsible for the next release.

13.4 Role of the Test Manager After Completion of the Test Project

The test manager must not just ensure that the evaluation and its results are communicated. He must also ensure that his recommendations are actually taken on board. If the test manager does not remain involved, it is not certain whether anything really will happen regarding his recommendations. It is therefore not advisable to leave immediately after the information system goes into production. It is likely that the possible improvements will not be carried out, because no one is attending to them. The project is, after all, completed. The test manager can solve this problem by being personally involved in the improvements or by initiating improvements during the project. He may also take upon himself the aftercare at the end of the project (this must be budgeted for, however!). He can then ensure that the test manager and test team of a subsequent project are informed of the recommendations he has provided. Where possible, he assists the following test manager to introduce the improvements. Only when the changes are embedded in the organisation can he turn his attention to other activities with peace of mind, having helped the organisation to progress in the direction of better and faster test execution.

In addition, he can collect further information from the experiences in production. At the end of the test project, he indicates which product risks have been covered, as demonstrated by successful tests. In the executed tests, say, 1,000 issues were found and solved. However, some uncertainty remains: was the testing really carried out well enough? If, in production, it appears that only one issue with a low priority is found, he may consider the test a success. If many issues arise, including those with a high priority, this would suggest that something has been overlooked in the test. These details can then contribute to an improvement in the quality of the test, the quality of a new version of the information system and to an improvement in the test process.

13.5 Conclusion

Whether the test manager remains involved with the information system or not, the test project itself is completed. The test manager has carried out an evaluation and transferred the test products. It is now up to the organisation to ensure that the recommendations in the evaluation report are adopted. The organisation will also have to work on the improvement proposals itself. This will enable the organisation to improve its test process and possibly its development process, all of which will benefit a subsequent test project.

In a subsequent test project, the test manager can start again at the beginning, going through the Test Management Model. As a first step, he carries out a quick scan in which he investigates information that is already present: test strategy, test plan(s), testware and evaluation report. He uses this information to set up the new test project. **The circle is complete!**

A

PRINCE2 and Test Management

PRINCE2 is a project management method that is generally applicable to projects. The name PRINCE stands for PRojects IN Controlled Environments. The PRINCE2 method was developed by the Central Computer and Telecommunications Agency (CCTA) as a process-based method that anyone can use. The CCTA is part of the British government and sets out "best practice" work methods. The method is based on practical experience with various management methods and pays particular attention to changes in environmental factors that might influence the success of a project. PRINCE2 is the standard in many organisations in Europe for managing (ICT) projects.

The test management approach described in this book bears many similarities to the PRINCE2 approach. Test management can therefore function perfectly well in an ICT project driven by PRINCE2. Within the practice of project execution, the two methods can effectively reinforce each other.

A.1 Similarities Between PRINCE2 and Test Management

We describe briefly here how a number of main principles of PRINCE2 compare with the test management approach described in this book. We also discuss how test management fits into a PRINCE2 project.

The PRINCE2 principles are summarised below, followed by a description of the way in which test management corresponds with these.

1. *The instigation of the project is a specified and measurable business case. Evaluation of this business case in the course of the project can lead to suspension of the project.*

   In the test management approach, the test process is set up and controlled by measures based on a risk analysis and on the requirements.

Both of these factors take the business case as the starting point. Test management can therefore offer considerable added value to the evaluation of the business case during the project. The test processes are set up in such a way that they can generate relevant and targeted management information, on progress and quality of the end product, among other things. With the aid of this information, the client (the business case owner) can determine whether the business case of the project is still valid. With an objective and quantified insight into the status of the end product, an estimate can be made, for example, of how much more time and money it will cost to realise an acceptable level of the information system. If the product is delivered too late, or if it appears to be too expensive, this may be reason for the client to halt the project.

2. *The business representation in a project plays a vital role that is not without duties.*

   A fixed part of the test management approach is carrying out a stakeholder analysis at the start of the project. In the analysis, the interests of all the parties involved in the project are surveyed. Subsequently in the test strategy, this is explicitly translated into the tasks, responsibilities and authorities that the parties are to be assigned to in the project execution. The results of this participation are established in as concrete a form as possible. In this way, the input of the business into the testing is secured, just as it is in PRINCE2.

3. *Risk management is one of the core processes within PRINCE2.*

   Risk management also takes a central place in the test management philosophy: as with PRINCE2, a sound risk analysis is carried out at the start of a test project. The risk approach of test management forms the basis of the substantive management of the test project. And it mainly concerns the product risks: which risks are directly related to the information system.

   Besides technical risks, this also concerns business-related risks. With these, the product risk analysis forms the essential input for the test strategy. The test manager monitors these product risks through progress management. He must also monitor the project risks that relate to the project itself.

4. *The planning process is product oriented and uses a product breakdown structure, among other things.*

   The product-oriented planning of the test management approach aligns perfectly with this. Planning on the basis of products is also an important principle of test management, since it allows concrete results to be delivered at an early stage. Testing focuses first on those products that are the most important to the client as regards risk and added value. With these priorities, test management is able to create "benefit-based" reports. These provide the client with an objective picture of the quality of the products.

5. *Plans are iterative in nature.*

The test management approach also develops plans in an iterative way. The specific approach that is used within test management is based on "evolutionary planning" (Gilb, 1988). With this, learning experiences during the test project are used towards the most realistic planning of time possible for the remainder of the course of the test project.

6. *Explicit separation of project initiation (in PRINCE2 the IP phase) and project management (in PRINCE2 the BF phase).*

Test management makes a clear distinction between activities during the preparation of a test project and those during the execution of it. See the Test Management Model.

A.2 Position of a Test Project Within a PRINCE2 Project

PRINCE2 projects have their own structure, based on a client–vendor relationship. An important premise of this is that there is always a client who will specify the required project result, who will use the project result, and who will most probably pay for the project. This makes it clear to the test organisation where the responsibilities lie, who can be called to account on which points, and what the escalation paths are.

Test management in a PRINCE2 project will take the place of what in PRINCE2 terms is called "Team Management". Within that team (or project) the test organisation can be set up in accordance with the structure in the test management approach. The exchange of information with the rest of the project then runs according to the PRINCE2 approach. The team manager (in this case the test manager) will then make concrete agreements with the client or programme manager concerning the results to be delivered.

A.3 More PRINCE2

In various chapters of this book where the phases of the Test Management Model are discussed, references are made here and there to PRINCE2.

If you wish to know more about PRINCE2, you will find information in books (CCTA, 2002) or on the official PRINCE2 website: www.ogc.gov.uk/prince.

B

Checklist of Product Risks

This checklist contains a large collection of questions and answers that can help the test manager in determining the product risks concerning the implementation of an information system.

The questions are divided into the following categories, based on the most usual groups of stakeholders (see Chapter 5, Section 5.2.1):

- end users;
- marketing;
- support department (such as a helpdesk);
- IT department;
- internal security.

An example is provided per product risk together with the quality attribute within ISO 9126 that best applies to the relevant risk.

The last column is meant to indicate the priority per product risk under the MoSCoW rules (i.e. Must test, Should test, Could test or Won't test).

For example:

No.	Product risk indication	Example	Quality attribute (ISO9126)	Importance (MoSCoW)
1.2	Should the correlation between input fields in the information system be checked?	Are we checking whether the prescribed correlations between input fields are correct and complete? (Semantic)	Suitability	

B.1 Checklist of Product Risks – End Users

No.	Product risk indication	Example	Quality attribute (ISO9126)	Importance (MoSCoW)
1.1	Should the input be checked by the information system?	Should it be checked whether all the input fields comply with the prescribed "type" (numeric, alphanumeric, date), length and style (bold, underlined, italics, etc.)? Can correct values be entered, and are incorrect values rejected? (Syntax)	Accuracy	
1.2	Should the correlation between input fields in the information system be checked?	Should it be checked whether the prescribed correlation between input fields is correct and complete? (Semantic)	Suitability	
1.3	Are the users experienced with the user interface of the information system?	How easily can the end users work with a new version of the information system?	Operability	

1.4	Are the error messages and other messages displayed by the information system clear?	Do the error messages and other displayed messages provide the information needed by the users to understand which fault has occurred, or which action has been carried out and/or which action they themselves should take?	Understandability
1.5	Are the help facilities clear?	After starting up a help facility, can the end user operate it easily?	Learnability
1.6	Is the menu structure clear?	Is it clear to the end users how they can navigate through the information system and which functions they can perform with it?	Understandability
1.7	Are the screens clear and legible?	Do the end users quickly understand how and where they should carry out particular actions? Do the screens have a layout that appeals to the end users?	Attractiveness
1.8	Are the generated overviews clear?	Is the layout of the overviews clear to the end users?	Understandability

1.9	Do the overviews contain the required information?	Do the overviews provide the information that the end users require to carry out their tasks?	Suitability
1.10	Is the user manual clear?	Does the user manual provide the users with adequate and useful information?	Learnability
1.11	Are there links with other systems?	When a car insurance policy is concluded, is notification automatically sent to the government department for road transport?	Interoperability
1.12	Are there alternatives for processing data if the information system is not available?	For example, for callback notes. If no alternatives are available, it must be possible to recover the system quickly	Recoverability
1.13	Should the system be available all day?	No down time should occur in a system that is critical to the company's operation 24 hours a day	Maturity
1.14	Should the information system be available in various languages?	If text in the information system has to be translated, mistakes may be created. Different languages can have different address forms, for example	Operability
1.15	Does peak load of the information system occur during the day?	At peak use, the response time of the information system may be longer	Time behaviour

1.16	Should the information system comply with a particular response time?	If a customer is waiting at the counter while the system is being used, it is important that the waiting time is not too long	Time behaviour
1.17	Do many users use the system simultaneously?	With simultaneous use of data, problems may arise concerning consistency of the database	Resource utilisation
1.18	Can the users adapt the system to suit their own preferences?	For example, the users themselves adapt the layout of reports or screens	Adaptability
1.19	Does the information system fit within existing standards and procedures?	Is the system suited to the daily tasks of the end users?	Suitability
1.20	Is the information system intended for processing financial details?	Financial details often require a high degree of accuracy	Accuracy
1.21	Are the details in the information system confidential?	With some information systems, the data must be used in confidence, e.g. bank account details	Security
1.22	Does the information system influence the physical environment?	For example, mission-critical systems, such as heart monitoring equipment	Maturity

1.23	Does the information system concern a primary or a secondary system for the business process?	With a secondary system, an occasional disruption is probably less serious than with a primary system	Maturity
1.24	Are the procedures for the business process stable?	If these often change, there is a risk that the information system is unsuitable for the changed process	Suitability
1.25	Does the information system affect other departments?	For example, a new quotation system may influence the printing channels	Co-existence
1.26	How many people use the system?	With many users, the information system will require more processing capacity	Resource utilisation
1.27	How many different users access the system?	These users will probably use the system in different ways. Have allowances been made for this in the user interface? For example, diverse menu structures and screens	Suitability
1.28	Does the information system have an online or a batch function?	With online systems, higher demands are made on the user interface	Operability
1.29	Is the entire business process covered by the information system?	Does a breakdown in the information system affect the whole of the company process?	Recoverability

1.30	Is the generation of management information the most important function of the information system?	Management uses the information for taking important decisions and will require a high degree of accuracy in this information	Accuracy
1.31	Are the users experienced in the use of information systems?	If the users previously did everything manually, more effort will be required in training and assisting them	Learnability
1.32	How much of the existing functionality from the previous version has been changed?	With many changes, the chances of errors are increased and the degree of end users acceptance may be reduced	Changeability
1.33	Should the information system store historical data?	Companies are obliged to retain transaction details for a certain number of years	Functionality compliance
1.34	Does the information system make complex calculations?	For example, calculation of premiums in an insurance quotation system	Accuracy

1.35	Can other information systems influence the operation of the system?	If another system goes down, can the target system continue operating? Are other systems given priority as regards processing if several systems are active simultaneously?	Co-existence
1.36	Is the processing of input time-critical?	Further processing could be done later if it is not time-critical	Time behaviour
1.37	Is the status of the information system always clear?	Does the information system indicate that it is busy processing? Is a message displayed when a transaction is completed or if a time-out occurs?	Understandability
1.38	Is the information system replacing an existing system?	The new system should be capable of supplying the existing functionality. Regression testing is important in that case	Replaceability
1.39	Should it be possible to operate the functions of the information system in various ways?	Varying the input instrument for repetitive functions can prevent repetitive strain injury (RSI)	Operability

B.2 Checklist of Product Risks – Marketing

No.	Product risk indication	Example	Quality attribute (ISO 9126)	Importance (MoSCoW)
2.1	Is the information system used for selling products?	For example, sales of insurance via the Internet	Operability	
2.2	Should the information system run on various platforms?	Internet applications can run on various operating systems, e.g. Netscape and Internet Explorer	Adaptability	
2.3	Does the information system comply with all the legal privacy regulations?	For example, Personal Data Protection Act	Functionality compliance	
2.4	Should clients be able to install the information system themselves?	When a system is sold to customers, it goes to a variety of end users with varying levels of knowledge and experience	Installability	
2.5	Is there a geographical distribution of the information system?	Is the system used only locally or, for example, worldwide?	Interoperability	

| 2.6 | Is it impor-tant for (a new version of) the infor-mation system to be available for the market by a certain date? | If the time-to-market is short, the system should be easy to adapt | Changeability | |

B.3 Checklist of Product Risks – Support Department

No.	Product risk indication	Example	Quality attribute (ISO9126)	Importance (MoSCoW)
3.1	Can the help-desk provide status informa-tion?	Can the helpdesk supply insight into the status of the in-formation system, and can it indicate how to proceed?	Analysability	
3.2	Is there a pro-duction man-ual?	Does the helpdesk have insight into the information system in production?	Operability	
3.3	Does the infor-mation system have an online or a batch func-tion?	With a batch system, it is more difficult to trace errors	Analysability	
3.4	Do the batches have void lists?	Is it clear which transactions within a batch were unsuccess-ful?	Analysability	

B.4 Checklist of Product Risks – IT Department

No.	Product risk indication	Example	Quality attribute (ISO9126)	Importance (MoSCoW)
4.1	Is a summarised function description available?	This description aids the maintenance department with change implementation	Analysability	
4.2	Are back-ups created?	If the system goes down, can the backup be reinstalled?	Fault tolerance	
4.3	In the event of breakdown, should the information system be restored within a certain time?	Is there a maximum time during which the system is allowed to be unavailable?	Recoverability	
4.4	Is there a contingency plan if the hardware that runs the information system fails?	Is there a shadow system available that can take over the tasks?	Fault tolerance	
4.5	Has the information system been created with new technology?	Using technology that is new to the organisation can be the cause of a lot of errors	Maturity	

4.6	How do we deal with interrupted transactions?	Can the system revert to the situation as it was before the transaction was started?	Recoverability
4.7	Are there contingency plans for when the information system goes down?	Have we considered an emergency scenario?	Recoverability
4.8	Is the information system sensitive to settings on end users' PCs?	Can the users configure the system to their own preferences (e.g. resolution and screen size)?	Adaptability
4.9	Are data from other information systems stored in this system?	Are allowances made for synchronisation of the data between both systems?	Interoperability
4.10	Should the information system operate within the existing infrastructure?	The existing infrastructure may slow down when another system is added on. It is also possible that there is insufficient disk space available in the existing infrastructure	Co-existence

4.11	Are changes to the infrastructure planned?	If changes to the infrastructure will affect the system, they should be accommodated easily within the system	Adaptability
4.12	Are create, read, update and delete (CRUD) functions implemented for the various entities?	If these functions are not present for all the entities, some test cases cannot be carried out	Testability
4.13	Are correlations between entities checked upon the removal of an entity?	If a customer is displayed showing accounts attached, it should not be possible to delete the customer without administering these accounts	Accuracy
4.14	Are system components of third parties used?	Do these system components fit within the information system, or are there, for example, big differences in the layout of data?	Suitability
4.15	Is there a fallback scenario if the implementation of the information system fails?	Is an emergency plan available?	Fault tolerance

4.16	Is there a fixed time for processing batches?	Most companies have to process batches outside office hours. Users may not be logged in during batch processing. If the batch is not ready when an office opens, the employees cannot use the system	Time behaviour
4.17	Do many errors occur in the information system when changes are introduced?	Changes can lead to unexpected errors, particularly with a legacy system where knowledge of the system is lacking	Stability
4.18	Are there any set conditions concerning the time allowed to recover after a fault?	An organisation may set conditions concerning the maximum downtime a system is permitted. (Service level)	Recoverability

B.5 Checklist of Product Risks – Internal Security

No.	Product risk indication	Example	Quality attribute (ISOX9126)	Importance (MoSCoW)
5.1	Are there guidelines for restricting access to the information system?	A procedure stating who may have what level of access to the system	Security	

5.2	Are passwords used?	Are there any rules concerning these passwords: length, change frequency, etc.?	Security
5.3	Are the access attempts monitored?	Is a log kept that registers who is trying to access the system and whether this person is authorised or not?	Security
5.4	Are internal development standards used?	Do the developers maintain these standards?	Maintainability compliance
5.5	Are there links to outside of the organisation?	Many links mean that there are more opportunities for hackers to enter the system	Security
5.6	Are transactions locked?	Locking the information makes it more difficult to use it for illegitimate purposes	Security
5.7	Is an audit trail required for the information system?	With many financial information systems, an audit trail is a legal requirement	Analysability

C

Template for Risk- & Requirement-Based Testing

The template below provides an overview of the information that is important within risk- and requirement-based testing (RRBT).

This table can be used in decision making.

If, for example, a requirement changes, the test manager can see to which product risk it is linked. He can also see the consequences it will have for the test condition(s). Are any adjustments to the test conditions required?

The table can also form the basis of the reports. See Chapter 12.

The testers can link an issue to the relevant product risk during the execution of the test via the test condition. With this, a tester can determine the initial priority of an issue.

The case from Chapter 2 has been used to give an idea of the way in which this table is completed.

No.	Product risk	Quality attribute	MoSCoW	Stake-holder	Requirement	Test condition
1	Customer cannot perform a transaction	Functionality	Must test	End user	Customer able to perform a transaction via own bank	It is possible to perform a transaction at own bank, using an existing pin code
						It is *not* possible to perform a transaction at own bank when using an invalid pin code
					Customer able to perform a transaction via other bank	
					Customer can choose from set amounts	
					Customer can select amount/choice of banknotes	
	...	...	...	...	...	...

D

Quality Attributes According to ISO9126

Quality attribute	Description
Functionality	**The capability of the software product to provide functions which meet stated and implied needs when the software is used under specified conditions**
Suitability	The capability of the software product to provide an appropriate set of functions for specified tasks and user objectives
Accuracy	The capability of the software product to provide the right or agreed results or effects with the needed degree of precision
Interoperability	The capability of the software product to interact with one or more specified systems
Security	The capability of the software product to protect information and data so that unauthorised persons or systems cannot read or modify them and authorised persons or systems are not denied access to them
Functionality compliance	The capability of the software product to adhere to standards, conventions or regulations in laws and similar prescriptions relating to functionality
Reliability	**The capability of the software product to maintain a specified level of performance when used under specified conditions**
Maturity	The capability of the software product to avoid failure as a result of faults in the software
Fault tolerance	The capability of the software product to maintain a specified level of performance in cases of software faults or of infringement of its specified interface
Recoverability	The capability of the software product to re-establish a specified level of performance and recover the data directly affected in the case of a failure
Reliability compliance	The capability of the software product to adhere to standards, conventions or regulations relating to reliability

Usability	**The capability of the software product to be understood, learned, used and attractive to the user, when used under specified conditions**
Understandability	The capability of the software product to enable the user to understand whether the software is suitable, and how it can be used for particular tasks and conditions of use
Learnability	The capability of the software product to enable the user to learn its application
Operability	The capability of the software product to enable the user to operate and control it
Attractiveness	The capability of the software product to be attractive to the user
Usability compliance	The capability of the software product to adhere to standards, conventions, style guides or regulations relating to usability
Efficiency	**The capability of the software product to provide appropriate performance, relative to the amount of resources used, under stated conditions**
Time behaviour	The capability of the software product to provide appropriate response and processing times and throughput rates when performing its function, under stated conditions
Resource utilisation	The capability of the software product to use appropriate amounts and types of resources when the software performs its function under stated conditions
Efficiency compliance	The capability of the software product to adhere to standards or conventions relating to efficiency

Maintainability	**The capability of the software product to be modified. Modifications may include corrections, improvements or adaption of the software to changes in environment, and in requirements and functional specifications**
Analysability	The capability of the software product to be diagnosed for deficiencies or causes of failures in the software, or for the parts to be modified to be identified
Changeability	The capability of the software product to enable a specified modification to be implemented
Stability	The capability of the software product to avoid unexpected effects from modifications of the software
Testability	The capability of the software product to enable modified software to be validated
Maintainability compliance	The capability of the software product to adhere to standards or conventions relating to maintainability
Portability	**The capability of the software product to be transferred from one environment to another**
Adaptability	The capability of the software product to be adapted for different specified environments without applying actions or means other than those provided for this purpose for the software considered
Installability	The capability of the software product to be installed in a specified environment
Co-existence	The capability of the software product to co-exist with other independent software in a common environment sharing common resources
Replaceability	The capability of the software product to be used in place of another specified software product for the same purpose in the same environment
Portability compliance	The capability of the software product to adhere to standards or conventions relating to portability

Reference

ISO/IEC 9126-1, *Software engineering – Software product quality – Part 1: Quality model*, International Organization of Standardization, 2001.

E

Template for Test Plan

This appendix shows the subjects that should be contained within a test plan. This applies equally to a project test plan and a detailed test plan. General aspects such as version management and configuration management are not included in this.

A brief description is provided on the substance of each subject.

E.1 Management Summary

Provide a summary of the test plan here. Usual matters to include are:

- Reason for the project;
- Description of the project;
- Time lines;
- Costs, etc.

E.2 Introduction

What is this test plan about? Reflect the general structure of the document.

E.2.1 Documentation Used

Test Plan Documentation

Provide exhaustive reference to the source documentation used for this test plan, such as:

- Quick scan (inventory of the project using the Test Management Model);
- Planning;
- Test strategy;
- Risk analysis.

Bear in mind general documentation, such as:

- Project plan;
- QA plan;
- Configuration management plan;
- Relevant policies within the company.

The test plan should always refer to a higher level plan. If this template is used for a detailed test plan (e.g. Functional Acceptance Test) refer here to the project test plan.

Documentation for the System to be Tested

Provide a description of the "test basis" here. Think about things such as:

- Requirement specifications;
- Functional design;
- Technical design;
- User manual;
- Installation manual.

E.2.2 Standards and Procedures

Which standards and/or procedures will be used? Think about such standards as ISO 9126, ITIL, etc.

E.3 The Test Assignment

E.3.1 Client

Indicate who the client is.

E.3.2 Supplier

Indicate who, if applicable, the supplier is.

E.3.3 Goal of the Assignment

Provide a clear interpretation of the brief obtained from the client. Highlight the aim of the project and the result to be achieved.

The result to be achieved should be measurable. Establish agreement on how this is to be measured. The project should comply with the SMART principle: the assignment should be Specific, Measurable, Acceptable, Realistic and Timely.

E.3.4 Scope

Which test levels and tests are planned, what is explicitly *not* being tested and why *not*?

System Aspects to be Tested

Provide a description here of (the parts of) the information system, including the interfaces that are to be tested within the scope of the project. Bear in mind also the risks and importance of the system parts. These are defined in the test strategy.

System Aspects not to be Tested

Indicate what explicitly falls outside the scope of the project.

E.3.5 Suspension Criteria and Resumption Requirements

It may be the case that the documentation or software supplied is of poor quality or even incomplete. If so, there is little point in starting with the test analysis or test execution. Specify here, therefore, the criteria for the possible postponement of a part of the testing, or even the entire test. Make a connection to the entry criteria for the various test levels.

Also specify the test activities that should be repeated when testing is resumed following a period of postponement.

E.3.6 Test Project Deliverables

Which products do you intend to produce, and when? Provide a description and not a plan. Also indicate what the clients should do with the deliverables (for information, for approval) and *how* they should do it (they are not test experts).

Deliverables of a test project include:

- Test plan;
- Test specifications/analysis;
- Procedures;
- Test logs;
- Test issue report.

E.3.7 Discharging the Test

When is the testing complete? Who discharges it?

Also indicate the acceptance criteria that have to be met.

E.3.8 Starting Points and Preconditions

Indicate the conditions that must be met to allow the test project to succeed, or that have to be created to allow it to run smoothly. Be as explicit as possible.

E.3.9 Risks and Risk Countermeasures

These can be copied from the project risk analysis. Provide an overview here of the five (plus or minus two) project risks with the highest priority. Be sure to refer to the document with the complete risk analysis.

Plans often outline risks, without including risk countermeasures. Risks are also often mentioned that are really more tasks for the test manager and do not belong in the risk column. It is not necessary in a detailed test plan to describe the risks for which the test manager is responsible. However, in a project test plan, those risks should be described explicitly, in the first place to make the risks clear to the client (as part of prospect management) and secondly because the test manager may be responsible for preventive measures while someone else is responsible for corrective measures. The as-yet-unknown subjects in the cluster cards also form risks to the test project.

E.4 Test Approach

Provide a brief indication of what the quick scan has produced. Below are standard categories within a dynamic test approach. Risk- and requirement-based testing (RRBT) is one approach.

E.4.1 Test Strategy

Provide a brief summary here of the established test strategy. What is your approach; what have you considered, and why; what have you decided against, and why?

E.4.2 Preparation

What will you be doing during preparation of the various tests? Activities such as setting out the test management file, test environments, etc.

E.4.3 Analysis

For which parts of the information system will clusters, test conditions and test cases be made, and which not, and why not? Which testing techniques will be employed for the test specification and analysis? The choice of a particular technique depends on the quality attribute that is being tested, but also on the product risk. With a high risk, a more thorough technique will be employed.

You can refer here to the cluster cards to be set up, in which these subjects are to be covered.

E.4.4 Test Automation

If applicable, for which subjects will test automation scripts be made and for which not, and why not? Preferably refer to a cost–benefit analysis.

E.4.5 Execution and Transfer

What is to be addressed during the various test levels and who will do what? The information on this can be partly obtained from the test strategy.

Provide a brief overview of the various test levels with a description of:

- Where the testing will be done (environment);
- what will be tested;
- when it will be tested;
- who will be doing the testing;
- entry and exit criteria per test level;
- dependencies of other test levels.

Entry criteria may originate from before a test phase *or* elsewhere in the organisation (preconditions!).

Exit criteria may relate to a subsequent test phase or another part of the project (training, implementation).

Acceptance criteria are established in the test strategy. These criteria should be tested within the various test levels. The set with overall acceptance criteria should therefore be translated into entry and exit criteria for the test levels.

Remember, too, to carry out the evaluations, both during and at the end of the test project. When, as test manager, will you carry this out, who will you involve in it, and how will you do it? Will you, for example, use a measurement programme (GQM)? And will your whole project be concerned with this, or only a number of people?

E.5 Planning and Budget

Referring to:

- Test planning;
- resource planning (here or in the test organisation);
- time line planning (starting and finishing dates of the test phases);
- activity planning (Gantt chart in MS Project or EVM);
- milestone planning (brief summary of the test milestones);
- budget.

E.6 Test Organisation

E.6.1 Stakeholders

Who are the stakeholders; which parties play a role in the project (both internally and externally)? Derive an organisation scheme.

E.6.2 Tasks, Authorities and Responsibilities

Indicate per test role who is doing what, who takes which roles, and which tasks, authorities and responsibilities these concern. Possibly also provide information on cost and availability.

When describing the roles pay attention to the desired level of training. Also investigate the training possibilities if the desired level is not available.

When defining the resources, consider not only those in the test team, but also those whom you think you might need outside of the test project; for example, suppliers of the required hardware. It is important to survey all the relationships.

E.6.3 Meetings

When do meetings take place, with whom, about what, and how frequently?

E.6.4 Communication

What are you communicating about, and what agreements do you make with the client/project manager/project leader?

Bear in mind here:

- *Resources.* Who will take on the resources? Who will hold the intake interviews?
- *Reporting* (progress etc.). Who will set up the reporting, to whom will it be sent and with what frequency? If you use the test control matrix (TCM), refer to it.
- *Meetings.* See Section 6.3. To whom are the minutes sent per meeting?
- *Issue management.* Who will carry out the issue administration? Is this reported on, and to whom?
- *Quality plan.* Should a quality plan be written?
- *Training.* Should allowance be made for the training of users (both for the testing and for the implementation of the application)?
- *Escalation.* Who escalates to whom?
- *Reviews* etc. Are reviews to be held? Who will carry them out? Is this to be done in consultation with the client?

E.7 Description of the Test Environment

Hardware, software, tools (including any test tools); what is required to operate (should the environment simulate the production environment)? Much is already described in the test strategy and the various cluster cards, but it is possible to expand on this. Bear the following points in mind!

- Indicate who is responsible for setting up and managing the test environment.
- Indicate who is responsible for making available/ordering the infrastructure.
- Indicate whether you need, for example, production files.
- Describe also the required physical test environment (workstations, telephones, etc.).

E.8 Transfer of Testware to the Organisation

- Which party will transfer what to the recipient party?
- Are there acceptance criteria to be met?

E.9 Appendices

Add here the documents that have added value with the test plan:

- Quick scan;
- Test strategy;
- Planning;
- Risk analysis.

F

The Goal–Question–Metric (GQM) Method applied to testing

A new shoot on the tree of process and product improvement has appeared in the form of the goal–question–metric (GQM) method (Solingen & Berghout, 1999). In this case study we provide a brief description of the method, an explanation of the various steps that an organisation must take in applying it, and an example demonstrating how the application of the GQM method led to a number of clear improvements in an organisation.

Introduction

What exactly is the GQM method? Is it another means of allowing management to control employees from above? *No, not really.* Is it yet another way of documenting more wide-ranging procedures? *No, absolutely not.* Is it the umpteenth method based on the assumption that software testing is a straitjacket for every team and every individual? *No, not that either.* The GQM method is one that assists with the measurement and attainment of the most important goals within a test project. GQM is therefore *the* method for clarifying difficult, obscure situations by a pragmatic but theoretically sound approach. Clear to whom? To the client, to the project team, but especially to the testers themselves.

To demonstrate the kind of "difficult, obscure situations" referred to:

- How do you determine the quality of software components? When are software components suitable for release? What effective measures can you take to improve the quality of software components?
- How do you organise a test team efficiently? How do you determine the quality of test activities? How do you realise efficient reuse of a test?
- Where do software problems come from? What are the underlying causes of faults that are discovered during the test process? What can we do to prevent mistakes being made?

- What is the impact of interrupts in the work of a tester? Are there too many, or indeed too few, interrupts in an organisation? Why are testers disturbed so often, and can these disturbances be reduced?
- How effective are the various test levels? Are mistakes discovered in time?

The GQM method enables an organisation to perform measurements on a continuous basis, or for a fixed period, thus obtaining growing insight into the problems described. A GQM programme succeeds often, thanks to the strong integration, involvement and feedback on the part of development teams and testers. It is an excellent solution to the old problem of a quality organisation spending much time and effort collecting more or less unusable measurement data.

The GQM method has been very successfully applied and further refined by, among others: NASA, Hewlett Packard, Motorola, Schlumberger, Ericsson, Digital, Nokia, Philips, Tokheim, Dräger, Robert Bosch, Daimler Chrysler, Siemens, Allianz and Proctor & Gamble.

The GQM Method

The GQM method is based on the principle of targeted measurement. "To measure is to know" is a well-known Dutch saying, but only holds true if you know what exactly you need to measure. With this method, you start by formulating the Goal of the measurement programme, then you document the relevant Questions to support your goal, and subsequently you determine the Metrics to be set up within the organisation in order to answer the questions. Also, for each question and metric a hypothesis is put to the test team. Comparing real values from the measurement application programme with these hypotheses provides the testers with better insight into their own work. GQM is therefore more than anything else an approach that helps testers to learn from their own work and experiences.

Since GQM specifies the metrics through goals and questions, it is not only an approach for defining metrics, but also for interpreting measurements. The measurements serve to answer the questions, and when all the questions have been answered, it is clear whether the goal has been attained. GQM focuses not only on the specifying of goals, questions and metrics, but above all on providing answers and attaining goals. This goal-oriented aspect of GQM makes the approach suitable for application to (goal-oriented) company environments.

There are four phases of a GQM measurement application programme (see Fig. F.1):

- *Planning.* Selecting the goals of the measurement application programme. The goals are geared towards the specific context of the organisation: what does the organisation want to know, what is the measurement application programme required to achieve?

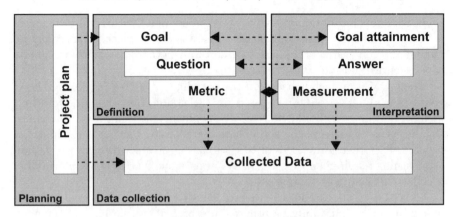

Fig. F.1. The GQM method

- *Definition.* Defining the goals in terms of measurement application, questions and metrics. As with establishing the goals, this is done in close consultation with all the stakeholders in the organisation, the test teams, developers and the testers. Through various interviews, the measurement application programme is defined and documented. In many cases, a process description is also created relating to the relevant test processes being measured (such as the acceptance test process or the performance test process).
- *Data collection.* The collection of data in accordance with the documented measurement application plan. All the testers and developers collect data manually or automatically, and the data are stored centrally.
- *Interpretation.* Presenting the data within the organisation for analysis, for drawing conclusions, taking decisions and proposing measures. The interpretation sessions take place at regular intervals and are the part of the measurement application programme that yields the biggest results. Through intensive feedback with test teams, more and more insight is gained into the problems of the organisation, and improvement proposals are presented which are carried through into the whole of the organisation.

The *interpretation* phase, apart from being the most interesting one, is also the most essential phase of the programme. This is when conclusions are drawn, decisions taken and actions defined. If measurement data are not analysed and interpreted, all the money, time and energy expended represent a waste of precious resources. In feedback sessions, learning is acquired and improvements defined. That feedback sessions are so crucial to the success of a measurement application programme is one of the most important findings of this research in recent years. Absence of the interpretation phase, or carrying it out too late, is the biggest cause of failure of measurement application programmes.

In Solingen and Berghout's GQM book, a list of activities and products is provided for each of these four phases. There is also a checklist that may be used at the conclusion of a phase to ascertain whether any important points have been overlooked.

The GQM approach is based on the paradigm of Victor Basili and David Weiss (see Fig. F.2). GQM is based on the assumption that organisations wishing to improve should first of all document their improvement goals. On the basis of these goals, a course is set whereby metrics are applied in support. It is therefore essential to establish in advance which information and learning requirements exist in the organisation. Quantitative information is collected to support this process.

Since the questions and metrics are defined with an explicit goal in mind, this information must only be used to interpret along the lines of the goal. We should be careful not to yield to the temptation of drawing conclusions beyond the measurement goals. The reason for this is that the collected data are very probably insufficient to draw such conclusions; there is a good chance that important aspects have been left out, and the conclusions might be entirely mistaken. The end result of the application of GQM is a measurement application environment focused on a set of specific improvement goals within an organisation.

Distinction should be made between "improvement goals" and "measurement goals". Improvement goals indicate the degree and direction required in improving performance. For example, a productivity increase of 30%, or a timetable reduction of 50%. Measurement goals, on the other hand, only specify an information requirement with a reason and a focus. As such, measurement goals do not deliver improvements, but they do deliver better insight. With the aid of this insight, of course, measures can be taken to achieve

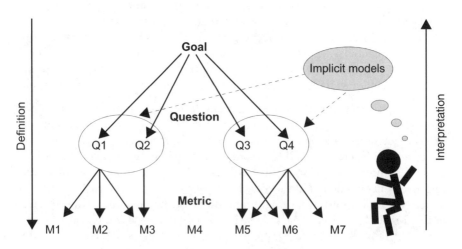

Fig. F.2. The GQM paradigm of Basili and Weiss

the improvement goals. However, the difference between the goals is essential. GQM assists organisations to acquire specific information and explicitly demands interpretation of this information. GQM thus provides an operational learning process. In interpreting the data, questions relating to the "how" and "why" of significant phenomena are analysed and argued. To support this learning process, it is important that an expected answer to each question is documented in advance. Such hypotheses demonstrate explicitly what people expect on the basis of their current thought processes and experiences. Final results can be compared against these expected answers and differences analysed. In this way, GQM stimulates focused learning and links it to people's current knowledge, a process that fits in very well with the way in which adults appear to learn.

Measuring in Practice

If we now look at how measuring is done in practice, we quickly become disillusioned. Only a very few organisations apply structured measurement to test and development activities. Many reasons are given, the most usual of which is that it takes a lot of time. However, research has shown that the input of the testers need be only very limited, provided they are supported appropriately. Calculations of the return on investment (ROI) of measurement application programmes are always positive, and there are situations where ROIs have been measured at 35 or higher. This is logical, when we look at the costs of a problem that is discovered after release. Only a small number of extra problems need be found through a measurement programme for it to end in a positive result. If we look in particular at the market for embedded systems, the ROI is much higher, since changes to embedded systems can often take place only when the manufacturer takes a series of products back to the factory. The direct costs of this (apart from the damage done to the company's image) are so great that such companies very quickly recoup the extra resources spent on finding or preventing problems.

The right way to implement measurement application programmes in practice is with the help of a GQM team. This team supports the testers within a measurement application programme by taking over all those activities that do not necessarily have to be carried out by testers. For example, the writing of a GQM plan, designing data collection forms, preparing a feedback session, collecting measurement data and setting up graphics and tables. Someone outside of the test team can carry out such things perfectly well, so that the normal test activities are put under as little pressure as possible. It is important that this GQM team does not interpret the data – this is a task for the testers themselves!

The analysing of measurement data takes place during feedback sessions. In these sessions, all the parties involved come together and take a collective look at the collective data. During interpretation sessions, conclusions are drawn, decisions taken and actions defined. Analysis is done with the help of the GQM questions. For each question, a number of overviews of the relevant measurement data are indicated and it is examined whether the question can be answered. It often turns out that parties have completely different ideas on correlations and causes. The discussions that ensue stimulate the learning processes of everyone concerned. That is why interpretation sessions represent one of the critical success factors for measurement application programmes in practice.

Example of a Measurement Application Programme Within a Test Department

In the following case, a measurement application programme is described, which was carried out in an industrial organisation. The measurement application goal of the programme was:

Analyse:	The system testing process
With the aim of:	Understanding
In relation to:	Effectiveness and efficiency
From the point of view of:	The system testers

Based on the input of the testers, this measurement application goal was represented as the following list of questions:

1. What is the degree to which conditions for satisfactory testing are met in the current projects?
2. Which factors influence the costs and duration of the system-testing process?
3. What is the contribution of system testing to product quality?
4. What determines the duration of the system-testing process?
5. What are possible indicators and standards on which decisions on halting system testing can be based?

Based on these questions, a list of metrics was set up and data collected over a period of 2 years. In Figs. F.3 and F.4, two examples are provided of measurements that help to answer the questions above. These measurements can also help with decision making during testing, or aid in planning and estimating tests.

Figure F.3 shows the status within project A of the found, open and closed issues. With the help of this overview, developers can plan time for correcting faults. This diagram also shows that it is not so much the number of found issues that indicate quality, but more the number of open issues remaining. This is the number of issues that may confront the client (apart, of course, from the issues not yet found).

Apart from these metrics, the average duration of an issue was also documented, as well as the average time it took to solve an issue. In this way, test

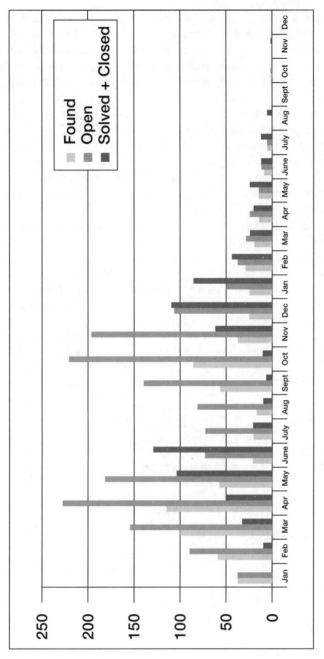

Fig. F.3. Project A: Fault status overview

activities and problem solving can be better coordinated and planned. This is an essential product of measurement application programmes: organisations obtain data on their own performance. It is therefore possible not only to see where improvement is required, but also to see the "personal records". This makes it possible to estimate directly how realistic the set plans and budgets are.

Besides an overview of faults, Fig. F.3 also provides insight into the effectiveness of test techniques. The manner of testing is related to the result. With the help of this figure, it can also be indicated during which period the most success was achieved in finding issues and which techniques were used there. It is notable that the summer period (July–August) shows a decline. This is of course a result not of the techniques used, but the reduced effort owing to holidays.

It is essential that the testers themselves interpret such statistics as shown in Fig. F.3. They know exactly what has been happening in a particular period. There are always influencing factors for which no metrics are collected, and conclusions concerning what exactly the data demonstrate and what action is required can only be taken by the testers themselves. These conclusions are discussed during interpretation sessions, where the most important learning effects take place.

Figure F.4 shows an overview of the subsystems within the project and the conditions required for appropriate testing. The testers have indicated

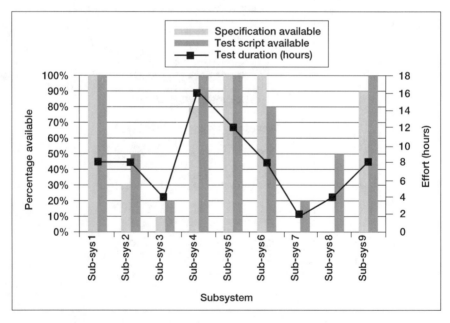

Fig. F.4. Status overview of test conditions per subsystem

for each subsystem to what percentage the required input (specification of the subsystem and test script for the subsystem) is available. Using this, they were able to show that the testing could be carried out much more effectively if such conditions were well organised.

As can be seen from this diagram, for a number of subsystems there is only a limited amount of documentation available and also a limited amount of test scripts. In this way the possible effectiveness of the test process can be estimated, as well as what needs to be done to improve it. The right-hand side of the diagram shows the test effort per subsystem. This shows that for the subsystems with limited compliance with sub-conditions, less time is also required for testing, which is an indicator of effectiveness (note that this relates to system testing!). If we were to show the test coverage in this diagram, the exact opposite would be seen. Subsystems for which test scripts and specifications are available are more thoroughly tested. Furthermore, system tests can be planned and estimated more effectively with these figures.

The above examples demonstrate that metrics can help us to learn about average performances and what can be done to improve them. To measure is to know, and without measuring it is difficult to obtain such exact figures. In test projects especially, it is essential to take measurements. First, because test projects are usually subject to pressures of time and there is a need to work effectively and efficiently. To do so, precise coordination is required and statistics are therefore necessary. Secondly, testing is a discipline in itself and testers should have the opportunity of learning from their own experience. Finally, it is the case that the costs of testing have increased dramatically over recent years in many organisations. More focused testing is necessary to stem these costs. Applying measurements helps in mapping costs and determining which test activities are more or less effective than others.

G

Checklist of Project Risks

This checklist contains a questionnaire regarding possible project risks.
It is subdivided into the following categories:

- Organisation;
- test project;
- test team;
- the selected test method;
- the information system;
- test environment(s);
- automated testing.

Each question is followed by a selection. The bold answer results in the highest project risk.

For example:

No.	Project risk	Selection	Importance (H/M/L)
3.1	Has a project leader been assigned to the test project?	• Yes, full time • Yes, part-time • **No**	

This example shows that the highest project risk occurs when no project leader is assigned to the test project.

G.1 Organisation

No.	Project risk	Selection	Importance (H/M/L)
1.1	Is a clear test organisation defined?	• Yes • **No**	
1.2	Is the project control from the client clearly covered and high enough in the organisation?	• Yes • **No**	
1.3	Are there many changes in the organisation structure? Many changes in the structure of the customer organisation can delay the project	• Stable, remains stable • Unstable, becomes stable • **Unstable, remains unstable during the project**	
1.4	The culture of the customer organisation can be characterized as:	• Open culture, healthy degree of ambition • Average • **Closed, uncooperative, conservative**	

1.5	How can the organisation be characterised (e.g. standards/ procedures)?	• Flexible, quick and strong drive for results. • Pretty formal, many consultation meetings • **Strong hierarchy, long communication lines, decision making highly political**
1.6	Are the (future) users able to cope with changes, or is there resistance?	• High • Medium • **Low**
1.7	Is tooling available for version control of the testware?	• Yes and known • Yes but no experience with the tooling in the test team • **No**
1.8	Are standards and procedures stable and sufficient (document templates, user interfaces etc.)?	• Yes • Yes, not sufficient • **No**
1.9	Are the organisation's expectations regarding the test project realistic?	• Yes • **No**

G.2 Test Project

No.	Project risk	Selection	Importance (H/M/L)
2.1	Have all the test project's conditions been defined and approved, regarding, for example, test environment and tools?	• Yes • Not yet, but this action is part of the starting points of the test project • **No, and this action is *not* part of the starting points of the test project**	
2.2	The scope of the test project can be the extension of an existing test set or the creation of a new test set. The projects scope is:	• Maintenance • Extension of testware • **Development of new testware**	
2.3	What is the estimated size of the test project in working days (size only refers here to test employees)? A working day is based on the amount of work one person with 6 months' test experience can do per day	• Less than 125 days • Between 125 and 350 days • **More than 350 days**	
2.4	The estimated size of the test project expressed in working days is:	• Less than 30 days • Between 30 and 90 days • **More than 90 days**	

2.5	On how many other projects does the test project depend? It can become complex when the test project is dependent on deliveries of other projects.	• No dependencies with other projects • 1 or 2 • **More than 3**
2.6	Can the test project be divided in time boxes (e.g. RAD) where the systems functions are developed in logical coherent and self-containing units? If the project consists of exactly one time box: No	• Yes • Most are • **No**
2.7	Are time boxes that are executed in parallel autonomous? If the project consists of exactly one time box: yes	• Yes • Most are • **No**
2.8	The project consists of how many time boxes? The number of independent time boxes gives the same number of independent components. This implies a consistent development process (for users and developers), integrating components, etc.	• 1 to 5 • 6 to 10 • **More than 10**

2.9	Is technical support included in the project budget? The development team can give input to the test team about technical details of the development environment and other technical details necessary for the test preparation and execution	• 20% or more budget (human resources) available for support • 5 to 20% budget (human resources) available for support • **No budget for technical support**
2.10	Domain experts are essential on the test project, especially when the requirements of the application under evaluation are complex and are poorly or not documented. How do analysts relate to domain experts?	• Average 3 analysts to 5 domain experts • Average 1 analyst to 4 domain experts • **No domain experts available**
2.11	How high is the work pressure for domain experts in their own organisation? This can affect participation of the business experts in the project	• Low • **High**

2.12	Do the domain experts have a mandate to make decisions about the scope of the test? Quick-wittedness, independence, and authority are critical success factors. The mandate must have sufficient support by the management and employees of the committed departments	• Yes • **No**
2.13	When the end user organisation consists of several departments/stakeholders, does this mean that possible opposite interests must be overcome? The end user organisation consists of:	• 1 department • 2 departments • **More than 2 departments**
2.14	Is a procedure defined for approving the testware? Is it clear how the test will be approved with analysts, users and management?	• Yes • **No**
2.15	Are acceptance criteria defined?	• Yes • **No**

2.16	Is it clear how to deal with changes in starting points, functional specifications, requirements, standards, etc.? Is a change control procedure defined and is this procedure connected to the change control procedure of the system under evaluation?	• Yes, connected to the systems change control procedure • No, independent of system • **No**
2.17	Is enough testware review capacity available? Only applicable when this capacity is not in the projects scope	• Yes • **No**
2.18	Is it clear to the client that part of he test effort can only start after delivery of the test object?	• Yes, and clearly part of planning • Sufficient time has been planned for this • Little time has been planned between delivery and start of test execution • **No, fixed planning without dependencies between moment of delivery and start of test execution**
2.19	How many geographical locations does the project have?	• 1 location • 2 to 3 locations • **more than 3 locations**

2.20	Is sufficient support available from, for example, a support department?	• Yes • **No**	

G.3 Test Team

No.	Project risk	Selection	Importance (H/M/L)
3.1	Does the test project have a test manager (TM)?	• Yes, full time • Yes, part-time • **No**	
3.2	Does the TM have experience with test projects?	• TM has been TM before in other test projects • TM has test analysis or test team leading experience • **TM has no test experience**	
3.3	Are the analysts and navigators (test team) capable of working in an independent and structured way?	• All test team members can work independently • Most test team members can work independently • **No, or only a few test team members can work independently**	
3.4	What is the size of the test team?	• 1 or 2 • 3 to 5 • **More than 5**	

3.5	Do the members of the test team have experience with testing?	• All members were previously involved in test projects • Most of the members were previously involved in test projects • **None or some members were previously involved in test projects**
3.6	Are the test team members motivated to participate on the project?	• Yes • Yes, but not their main task • **No**
3.7	To what extent do the project members know the clients organisation?	• All required knowledge • Sufficient knowledge • **Insufficient**
3.8	What will the turnover of staff be during the project?	• Nil • Limited • **Large**
3.9	To what extent can domain experts work together with testers, in terms of open communication, frequency, intensity and physical location?	• Good • Reasonable, if certain conditions are met • **Bad**
3.10	Are enough employees available for test preparation, design and execution?	• Yes • **No**

G.4 The Selected Test Method

No.	Project risk	Selection	Importance (H/M/L)
4.1	If the test method is new to the organisation, does the TM have organisational skills to embed new methods and technologies and to manage the projects environment?	• Yes • **No**	
4.2	Do all testers have knowledge of the chosen test method?	• All testers were previously involved in test projects with the chosen method • Most of the testers were previously involved in test projects with the chosen method • **None or some testers were previously involved in test projects with the chosen method**	
4.3	The choice for adopting the test method is ...	• Explicitly made by the client • Made in consultation with the client • **Implicitly made**	
4.4	The customer organisation is willing and ready to accept the chosen test method	• Yes • **No**	

| 4.5 | Is the customer organisation capable of implementing the new test method? | • Yes in a mature way
• **Hardly: too much innovative enthusiasm or ungrounded conservativeness** | |

G.5 The Information System

No.	Project risk	Selection	Importance (H/M/L)
5.1	The impact of defects in the system increases with the number of concurrent users of the system. The system must support:	• 0 to 5 concurrent users • 6 to 30 concurrent users • **More than 30 concurrent users**	
5.2	How many types of users have to work with the system under test? Also keep in mind supporting users like system administrators, maintenance personnel, etc.	• 0 to 3 types of users • 4 to 6 types of users • **Over 6 types of users**	
5.3	Are domain experts capable of separating essentials from side issues? Is the user capable in weighting the requirements in terms of being required, desirable or optional?	• Yes • **No**	

5.4	The development and test activities of a system that supports the core processes of an organisation will get more priority and a greater budget than a secondary system. The system is a ...	• Primary system • Subsystem of a primary system • **Secondary system**
5.5	Systems that support the core processes of an organisation are often more complex and therefore more effort is required for test activities. The system is a ...	• Secondary system • Subsystem of a primary system • **Primary system**
5.6	In some cases, the repair of defects in or downtime of the system in the production environment is very expensive. Other systems are replaced relatively easy by, for example, manual procedures. The system not functioning under test is ...	• Relatively easy to cope with • Very expensive • **Not possible**
5.7	When the changes that are implemented in the system under test are fewer with respect to the previous release, the effort of the test activities can be reduced. The effort of the test activities can also be reduced when a working version of the system is available during the development of the test set. The system is ...	• Stable and available • Unstable and available • **New, under construction**

5.8	Is it easy to use and control the system s functionality or is extra tooling required?	<ul><li>Data input and validation during testing is easy</li><li>Data input and validation is difficult (e.g. several screens and files must be processed)</li><li>**Additional tools are required for data input and/or validation**</li></ul>
5.9	Are the systems functions clearly documented and is this documentation available?	<ul><li>Yes</li><li>Partially</li><li>**No**</li></ul>
5.10	Is there sufficient documentation about the system available?	<ul><li>Yes</li><li>**No**</li></ul>
5.11	Is the system to be executed on 1 or several platforms?	<ul><li>1</li><li>2</li><li>**3 of more**</li></ul>

G.6 Test Environment(s)

No.	Project risk	Selection	Importance (H/M/L)
6.1	Is a separate, dedicated environment available for testing?	• Yes • **No**	
6.2	In what way is the test environment independent of the development environment?	• Independent, stand-alone • Is partly using the system • **Totally integrated**	
6.3	Is the test environment always available for each test?	• Yes • **No**	
6.4	Are test runs influencing the production environment?	• No • Limited • **Yes**	

6.5	How many technical environments are in the test scope? Number of hardware/software platforms, e.g. DOS/Windows with Power Builder and C++ (= 2 environments), a Sybase Database server and an AS/400 system (= 2 environments), usage of a Sybase database server and an IBM mainframe	• 1 • 2 • **3 or more**
6.6	Number of interfaces with other systems? How many other systems (not in the project scope) must be communicated with?	• 0 • 1 to 2 • **3 or more**
6.7	Is the test environment in line with the production environment? Included are hardware and software, e.g. amount of internal memory, type of display, network, middleware, servers	• Completely identical • Almost identical • **Strongly diverse**
6.8	Is a test development environment available and is it solely available for the project?	• Yes, available for the project only • Yes, but must be shared with other projects • **No**

6.9	Is the test environment completely arranged?	• **Completely** • **Partially** • **No**
6.10	To what extent is the test environment well defined? For example: • All subsystems will be tested or not. • Every field will be tested or not on characteristics. • All functionality within a subsystem will be tested, or only the most important	• Determined, well defined • There is no fine distinction • **Variable, but hardly any knowledge about the distinctions**
6.11	Does a department exist that has control of the test environment as core business?	• Yes • **No**

G.7 Automated Testing

No.	Project risk	Selection	Importance (H/M/L)
7.1	Will automated testing be used on the project? If not, the rest of the questions are irrelevant	• No • **Yes**	
7.2	Are the testers experienced with automated testing?	• All testers have experience with automated testing • Not all testers have experience with automated testing, but they have programming experience • **None or some testers have experience with automated testing or programming experience**	
7.3	Do the testers have knowledge of and experience with the environment of the system under test?	• All • Some • **None**	

7.4	Are the testers experienced with the selected test tool?	• All testers are experienced with the tool • **One or some testers are experienced with a tool, but all followed the training course**
7.5	A test project can support several goals, e.g. to measure if the quality of a version of a system is sufficient or to improve the efficiency of the test process (improved speed over lower cost). Is the goal of the test project the improvement of the test process's efficiency?	• Yes • **No**
7.6	Is the goal of the test project the reduction of test personnel?	• Yes • **No**
7.7	Is the client aware that a short-term investment is required and that this investment will only have long-term results?	• Yes • More or less • **No**
7.8	Is the client experiencing external pressure for the development of repeatable regression tests? For example, auditors, accountants	• Yes • **No**

H

Template for Test Strategy

This template is a tool to develop a test strategy. Analogously to Chapter 5, this template describes seven steps to draw up the test strategy. Also, intermediary products are delivered. In the final version of this document one can choose to incorporate only the final products (product risks, acceptance criteria, cluster matrix and cluster cards). However, the intermediary results should be kept as proof of how the final products were put together.

General aspects such as version management and configuration management are not included in this template.

A brief description is provided on the substance of each subject.

H.1 Management Summary

This paragraph must contain a summary of the test strategy, which describes the most important issues of the tests. Additionally it must describe what is tested and what is not tested in the test project.

This summary must include the cluster matrix.

H.2 Introduction

The test strategy is a way of communication between client, stakeholders and the test team. This document indicates what will and what will not be part of the test project. For this the input of the stakeholders is necessary.

H.2.1 Seven Steps

To draw up a test strategy the following steps must be undertaken:

- *Step 1: Identify the stakeholders* – Who are the parties concerned with the test project, and who is responsible for accepting the various tests and should therefore be involved in the test project?

- *Step 2: Carry out the test product risk analysis* – What are the risks that are directly related to the information system to be tested? What should be tested in order to meet the requirements and wishes of the stakeholders?
- *Step 3: Link the relevant product risks to the quality attributes* – Which product risks can be linked to which quality attributes?
- *Step 4: Determine the test levels* – What are the best ways of testing the various product risks and quality attributes?
- *Step 5: Determine the acceptance criteria* – At which point do the client and stakeholders find the quality of an information system acceptable? What acceptance criteria do they apply?
- *Step 6: Set up the cluster matrix* – Group the tests so that logical clusters are created within which exactly one stakeholder is taking responsibility.
- *Step 7: Set up the cluster cards* – A cluster card contains all the information that is of importance to the testers in setting up the tests for a specific cluster. The test strategy is clearly set out in the cards, showing all the parties involved. The cluster cards form the end of the test strategy and the beginning of the test analysis.

Further, a short description of the test project should be given in this introduction. This description must at least contain the following issues:

- The test object;
- stakeholders identified within the quick scan;
- whether the stakeholders will be assigned to the test level, test environment, department or parts of the information system, including the arguments on which these decisions are based;
- the way in which the risks in the cluster cards are derived.

H.2.2 Documentation Used

Give a full reference to the source documentation used for this test strategy, such as:

- The quick scan;
- the project risk analysis.

H.3 Stakeholders and Organisational Structure

Stakeholders are functionaries or departments that have a direct interest in a properly working information system.

During the quick scan most stakeholders were identified. These stakeholders can be described in this paragraph. To identify the missing stakeholders the following question can be asked: "Who (which department) is responsible for (parts of) the information system?"

H.3.1 Stakeholders of the System

Give in this paragraph an overview of the stakeholders. In general the stake-holders can be categorised in the following way:

- End users;
- marketing department;
- supporting departments, such as the helpdesk;
- IT department;
- internal control/audit.

H.3.2 Organisational structure

Describe here the organisational structure in an organisation chart.

If the organisation chart is also used in the quick scan, it can be reused here. Make sure the stakeholders can be identified in this chart so their place in the organisation is clear.

H.4 Link product risks and quality attributes

In this paragraph, the results of Steps 2 and 3 will be described.

H.4.1 Product risk analysis

Define together with the stakeholders the most important product risks.

The product risk checklist can be used to identify these risks. The risks that where distinguished in the quick scan can also be used here.

The identified product risks should be transferred to a table like that shown below:

Product risk	Priority (MoSCoW)	Stakeholder
...	...	...

H.4.2 Link product risks and quality attributes

In this paragraph the product risks will be grouped into the ISO 9126 quality attributes.

This link will facilitate communication with the client and the stakehold-ers. It will also offer an opportunity to check if the product risks are complete. When there is no link between the risks and a quality attribute, this could mean that some risks are missing. These should be added. It could also mean that the quality attribute in question does not have to be tested. Make an explicit remark for this!

Product risk	Quality attribute	Priority (MoSCoW)	Stakeholder
...	...	...	...

H.5 Test levels and acceptance criteria

H.5.1 Test levels

In this paragraph, the different test levels in the test project will be described. Also give a definition and a description of the test levels to avoid any misunderstandings at a later stage.

Possible test levels are:

- Unit test;
- integration test;
- system test;
- user acceptance test;
- production acceptance test.

H.5.2 Acceptance criteria

The stakeholders will define acceptance criteria for the information system. If the information system meets these predefined criteria, the test team is finished with testing and the product risks are reduced to an acceptable level to the stakeholders.

Acceptance criteria can be defined in many different ways. It is important that an acceptance criterion is specific and measurable. Think of the SMART rules: Specific, Measurable, Acceptable, Realistic and Time driven. The acceptance criteria will be translated in the test plan to entry and exit criteria for the different test levels.

H.6 Cluster matrix

A cluster matrix is an overview in which the test manager will clearly group the stakeholders, the quality attributes and the different test levels. It is then easy to see who is responsible for what quality attributes and at which level they will be tested.

To define the best test levels for the quality attributes, the following questions can be asked:

- Which quality attribute can be tested at what test level?
- Are there quality attributes that can be tested together at one test level?
- Which preconditions apply when performing a test for each specific quality attribute?
- To minimise costs (the earlier a bug is found, the cheaper these are) what is the earliest stage to test a quality attribute?

The above steps result in the cluster matrix. See the table below for an example where the quality attributes are linked to product risks, stakeholders and test levels.

Stake-holder/ test level	End user	Mar-ke-ting	De-part-ment	IT department	Internal control
Unit test					
Integration test					
System test				• Recoverability • Analysability • Changeability	• Accuracy
User accep-tance test	• Suitability • Under-standability • Learnability			• Interoperability	
Product accep-tance test				Time behaviour	

H.7 Cluster cards

The first (main) clusters are defined in the cluster matrix. Then the test manager will look at the relative importance of the different quality attributes within this first clustering. The importance of this is derived from the defined product risks. The more and the higher the product risks, the higher the priority. If all the quality attributes in one cell have the same priority, then this one cell can be directly translated into one cluster card. If one priority of a quality attribute is different, then more cluster cards must be defined. This is necessary, because the test conditions and test cases will have the same priority as the cluster.

A cluster card contains information divided into four categories:

- key information;
- assignment;
- execution;
- result.

Key information	
Cluster name	Logical cluster name
Information system	System name and version
Test level	Within which test level will this cluster be included?
Test department	Which department will test this cluster?
Stakeholder	Who has an interest in, and responsibility for, the correct working of this cluster?
Assignment	

Product risk(s)	Which product risks could materialise if this cluster is not processed, or if faults appear in this part during production?
Requirement(s)	Which requirements are linked to the product risks covered in this cluster? Testing should prove that the requirements are met (proven added value to the organisation)
Priority	What is the importance of this cluster? The importance corresponds to the priority of the product risks, and influences the sequence in which the test manager will plan the clusters. Use the MoSCoW classification: "Must test", "Should test", "Could test" and "Won't test". By inferring the cluster importance from the product risks and their importance, we prevent the stakeholders from allocating the highest importance to all the clusters
Quality attribute	Which quality attributes underlie this cluster?
Source material	A reference should be included here to the requirements, the documentation and interview reports upon which the design of the test will be based

Execution	
Test approach	How will the test be executed? The test manager's choice depends on, among other things, the test level, the quality attribute to be tested, the available source material, the organisation and the circumstances
	A further breakdown is created into:
	• Static testing: auditing and reviewing
	• Dynamic testing: testing the application itself
	Which test techniques will be used: decision tables, entity life cycle, data flow analysis, etc.?
	A choice is also made here between manual or automated test execution
Test environment	What test environment is required to be able to carry out the tests described? Both the technical environment and the necessary resources and time-dependent aspects should be mentioned here
	Which test data will be used?

Results

Acceptance criteria	At which point will the stakeholder accept the cluster?
	Ensure that the acceptance criteria are set out explicitly. All the parties involved should know in advance when the test project will be complete

At this stage of the project, it is not a major problem if the test manager is not able to fill in all the fields in a cluster card. Many of the fields will be filled in while the test team is starting with the design of the tests. Until these empty spots are filled, they are project risks or actions for the test manager. He must guard against the risks.

The cluster card is the first tab in an Excel cluster for analysis. To avoid doing things twice it is best to use and fill this Excel workbook. The test manager can refer to this in the test strategy.

I

Testing Roles

Within organisations it is important to have formally described test functions. By developing a career path in this way an organisation avoids disintegrated test knowledge and expertise and it gives employees the possibility to specialise in testing. Of course this should include education and coaching. This appendix will describe possible test roles: test manager, test team leader, test analyst, tester, test navigator and test consultant.

TEST MANAGER

Function description	The test manager manages the test team. He is responsible for the budgeting, planning and organisation of all test activities: drawing up test plans, progress reports and final reports, directing and executing the test process. In addition, he is responsible for reporting on the quality of the "test object". The scope of the test manager is broader than the scope of the test coordinator. The test manager leads bigger test teams and the focus is on the entire project or multiple projects

Tasks, responsibilities and authorities

- Reaching agreement with the project manager/client about the test assignment and expectations
- Ensuring a test infrastructure is available on time
- Keeping the issue administration continually updated
- Communication on all test issues within the project team
- Transfer of all testware to the maintaining party after completion of the project
- Allowing use of all agreed test methodologies
- Creation and maintenance of project test plans and detailed test plans
- Overseeing the planning, budget and execution of the test process
- Reporting on progress of the test process
- Reporting on the quality of the test object

General knowledge	
	• Higher vocational education or academic work and thought level, study related to ICT

	• ICT - knowledge
	  – familiar with development methods (SDM, DSDM, RAD, CBD)
	  – knowledge of system design techniques (functional design and technical design)
	  – knowledge of ITIL processes
	  – experience with project management methods
	  – experience with test support tools
	  – familiar with quality assurance
	  – familiar with risk management
	  – familiar with prototyping

Technical knowledge	• Detailed knowledge of and experience with test methods, test techniques and test support tools
	• Practical experience in the use of planning and budgeting techniques and support tools
	• Practical experience in providing leadership to the different test roles
	• Knowledge of the application of test process improvement models (TMM, TPI)
	• Knowledge of moderating group inspections (Fagan inspections)
	• Knowledge of the execution of test plan audits
	• Knowledge of the automated test concepts
	• Knowledge of the use of automated test support tools

Skills	• Flexibility
	• Group-directed leadership
	• Individual directed leadership and delegation
	• Persuasive skills
	• Communication skills
	• Planning and organization
	• Problem analysis and judgement forming
	• Performance motivation
	• Drive and self-confidence
	• Ability to listen and be sensitive to circumstances
	• Sensitivity to organisation in which operating
	• Takes initiative
	• Pragmatic approach
Work experience	• Experience as a tester, test analyst and optionally as test navigator
	• At least 1 ear's experience as test coordinator
	• Experience of project-Related leadership (minimum 2 years)

TEST TEAM LEADER

Function description	The test team leader manages the test team. He is responsible for the budgeting, planning and organisation of all test activities: drawing up test plans, progress reports and final reports, directing and executing the test process. In addition, he is responsible for reporting on the quality of the "test object". The scope of the test team leader is narrower than that of the test manager. The test team leader leads smaller test teams and the focus is on one (part of a) project
Tasks, responsibilities and authorities	• Reaching agreement with the project leader/client about the test assignment and expectations • Ensuring a test infrastructure is available in time • Communication about all test matters within the project team • Transfer of testware to the maintaining party after completion of the project • Allowing use of all agreed test methodologies • Creation and maintenance of test plans • Overseeing the planning, budget and execution of the test process • Reporting on the progress of the test process • Reporting on the quality of the test object

General knowledge	• Higher vocational education or academic work and thought level, study related to ICT
	• ICT knowledge:
	  − familiar with development methods (SDM, DSDM, RAD, CBD)
	  − knowledge of system design techniques (functional design and technical design)
	  − knowledge of ITIL processes
	  − experienced with project management methods
	  − experienced with test support tools
	  − familiar with quality assurance
	  − familiar with risk management
	  − familiar with prototyping

Technical knowledge	• Detailed knowledge of and experience with test methods, test techniques and test support tools • Practical experience in the use of planning and budgeting techniques and support tools • Practical experience in providing leadership to the different test roles • Experience with the application of test process improvement models (TMM, TPI) • Experience with moderating group inspections (Fagan inspections)

	• Familiar with the execution of test plan audits
	• Familiar with the automated test concepts
	• Familiar with the use of auto-mated test support tools
Skills	• Flexibility
	• Group-directed leadership
	• Individual directed leadership and delegation
	• Persuasive skills
	• Communication skills
	• Planning and organisation
	• Problem analysis and judgement forming
	• Performance motivation
	• Drive and self-confidence
	• Ability to listen and to be sensi-tive to circumstances
	• Sensitive to the organisation in which he is operating
	• Takes initiative
	• Pragmatic approach
Work experience	• Experienced as a tester, test ana-lyst and optionally as test navigator
	• Experienced with project-related leadership (minimum 2 years)

TEST ANALYST

Function description

The test analyst is responsible for developing the test analysis. In order to determine and define the test conditions and test cases based upon the product risks and requirements, he uses test specification techniques. The test design forms the basis for the test scenario, in which the test analyst defines the execution order of the test cases. In addition, he is charged with the capture of test results and the use of test support methods (as part of the automated test execution). The test analyst uses methods, techniques and support tools to do the job. He also helps with the checking of design documentation. He registers all findings relating to anomalies that arise between the information system and/or the system design and/or the test design

Tasks, responsibilities and authorities

Intake test basis:

- Evaluate delivered design and specifications for testability (in the test basis)
- Report on the established quality of the test basis
- Analysis of the design and specifications
- Design and documentation of test cases with relevant state situations, result expectations and execution instructions

	• Recording the test results and the necessary test support tools (as part of the automated test execution)
	• Maintaining the testware within the project: for both manual and automated testing
	• Transfer of all testware to the maintaining party after project completion
	• Providing support to testers and test automators during test execution
	• Reporting to the test leaders
	• Making use of the prescribed methods, techniques and support tools
General knowledge	• Higher vocational education or academic work and thought level, study related to ICT
	• ICT knowledge:
	– familiar with development methods (SDM, DSDM, RAD, CBD)
	– knowledge of system design techniques (functional design and technical design)
	– knowledge of ITIL processes
	– experience with project management methods;
	– experience with word processors and spreadsheets
	– experience with test support tools

Technical knowledge	<ul><li>Knowledge of the test methods to be used</li><li>Knowledge of basis techniques of structured testing</li><li>Practical experience in the use of test analysis techniques</li><li>Practical experience in the evaluation of test specifications</li><li>Practical experience in the use of checklists</li><li>Practical experience in the use of inspection techniques</li><li>Practical experience in the detection of anomalies in the documentation and systems</li><li>Practical experience in the use of issue administrations</li><li>Knowledge of concepts for automated testing</li><li>Knowledge of the use of automated test tools</li></ul>
Skills	<ul><li>Creative</li><li>Accurate</li><li>Independent</li><li>Planning and organisation</li><li>Problem analysis and judgement</li><li>Team worker</li><li>Can handle stress</li><li>Good communication skills</li></ul>
Work experience	<ul><li>Minimum of 1 year's experience as a tester in the ICT sector is required</li></ul>

TESTEXECUTER

Function description

The test executor is responsible for the execution of the test using the test scenario and test design produced by the test analyst. The test executor also assists with reviewing the design documents. He registers all findings that relate to the deviations found between the information system and/or the system design and/or the test design. Next to that he communicates and reports to the people involved. In his job the provided methods, techniques and tools support the tester

Tasks, responsibilities and authorities

- Intake of the system components to be tested: short inspection concerning the completeness of the system components to be tested
- Intake of the test scenario and test cases: short inspection concerning practicability of the test cases
- Preparation of test execution: fill initial state files in conformity with specifications
- Execution of the tests:
  - dynamic testing based on the test cases
  - static testing, like reviews based on checklists
- Record results
- Review the results

	• Administer the findings
	• Report to test management
	• Manage testware: daily collection, selection and optimising of testware
	• Using prescribed methods, techniques and support tools
General knowledge	• Higher or intermediate vocational education work and intelligence level
	• ICT knowledge:
	– knowledge of development methods (SDM, DSDM, RAD, CBD)
	– knowledge of ITIL processes
	– experienced with project management methods
	– experienced with word processors and spreadsheets
Technical knowledge	• Knowledge of the prescribed test methods
	• Practical experience with reviewing test specification
	• Practical experience with checklists
	• Knowledge of inspection techniques
	• Practical experience with the detection of anomalies in documentation and systems
	• Practical experience with the use of a findings procedure

Other skills	
	• Creative
	• Accurate
	• Independent
	• Planning and organisation
	• Problem analysis and judgement forming
	• Team player
	• Can handle stress
	• Good communication skills
Work experience	• Minimum of 1 year's work experience in ICT desirable

TEST NAVIGATOR

Function description

The test navigator is responsible for navigation through the test scripts that support the automated test execution. With support from the test support tools and the use of macros, manual actions (keystrokes and mouse movements) performed by the test executor are automated. For this, the test navigator records the manual actions in a navigation script that functions as a controlling program

Tasks, responsibilities and authorities

- Intake:
  - test cases
  - test objects
- Test support tools: responsible for the installation of test support tools and other supporting items
- Test scripts:
  - specification of test scripts
  - programming of the test scripts
  - inspection and testing of the test scripts
- Initials state files: making scripts for the creation of test data based on specifications
- Testing:
  - drawing up test sets with test scripts
  - execution and support of automated tests

	• Administration of findings
	• Testware related to automated testing:
	– collation and composition of the testware
	– selection of testware for maintenance
	– transfer of testware to the test analyst
General knowledge	• Higher vocational education or academic work and thought level, study related to ICT
	• ICT - knowledge
	– knowledge of development methods (SDM, DSDM, RAD, CBD)
	– knowledge of structured programming concepts
	– knowledge of programming languages
	– knowledge of ITIL processes
	– experienced with word processors and spreadsheets.
Technical knowledge	• Knowledge of the prescribed test methods
	• Knowledge of the test analysis techniques
	• Knowledge of basic structured testing techniques
	• Practical experience with the use of support tools

	• Practical experience with checklists
	• Practical experience with the detection of anomalies in documentation and systems
	• Practical experience with the use of findings procedures
	• Knowledge of automated testing concepts
	• Proven ability in using automated test support tools
Other skills	• Creative
	• Flexible
	• Accurate
	• Results driven
	• Problem analysis
	• Team player
	• Can handle stress
	• Persistent
	• Good communication skills.
Work experience	• Minimum of 1 year's work experience in ICT desirable

TEST CONSULTANT

| Function description | The test consultant advises and supports the optimal practice of test methods, test techniques and test support tools to project members (in test role or not). In this way he helps set up test projects and outlines the test strategy. He enthuses clients and project members with the goal to improve the test approach within the projects |

Tasks, responsibilities and authorities

- Advise on test phasing
- Advise on test organisation
- Advise on test infrastructure (test environments)
- Advise on and support for applying test methods, test techniques and test support tools
- Advise on applying automated testing
- Advise on reuse of testware
- Advise on various inspection techniques
- Testing of and feedback on the usability of test methods, test techniques and test support tools
- Stimulate collecting, analysing and distributing of data (metrics) in projects
- Support test leaders with setting up the test plan and test (final) report.

General knowledge	<ul><li>Higher vocational education or academic work and thought level, study related to ICT</li><li>ICT - knowledge<ul><li>knowledge of development methods (SDM, DSDM, RAD, CBD)</li><li>knowledge of system design techniques (functional design and technical design)</li><li>knowledge of ITIL processes</li><li>experienced with project management methods</li><li>knowledge of test support tools</li><li>knowledge of quality assurance</li><li>knowledge of risk management</li><li>knowledge of prototyping.</li></ul></li></ul>
Technical knowledge	<ul><li>Thorough knowledge of and experience with test methods, test techniques and test support tools</li><li>Ability to combine (test) theory and pragmatism</li><li>Very thorough knowledge of, experience with and ability to use test methods, test techniques and test support tools</li><li>Practical experience with applying test process improvement models (TMM, TPI)</li><li>Practical experience with moderating group inspections (Fagan inspections)</li></ul>

	• Practical experience with performing audits on test plans
	• Practical experience with applying concepts for automated testing
	• Practical experience with use of test navigation support tools
	• Practical experience with advising on subjects mentioned above
Other skills	• Creative
	• Daring and self-confident
	• Customer focused
	• Listening and sensitivity
	• Verbal skill of expression and presentation
	• Writing skills
	• Awareness of surroundings (expert knowledge)
	• Organisational sensitivity
	• Force of conviction
	• Independent
	• Pragmatic strain
Work experience	• Significant experience as test analyst (minimum 4 years) or test manager (2 years)
	• Experience in a leading role is desirable

J

Template for Progress Report

This template describes the subjects that a test manager should include in progress reporting. He writes the report on a regular basis during the execution of a test level.

A progress report should be brief and the subjects covered should be immediately clear to the client and stakeholders. These documents do not have a formal layout with version and configuration management and contents list.

General Progress

Provide a brief general summary of progress here. Remember also to provide a brief summary on the outstanding issues, connected to product risks.

Activities/Milestones/Products in This Period

Provide an overview here of activities carried out and products delivered. Information on completed activities can be obtained from, for example, the overview from the earned value method. Base this on the latest version of the planning. The following categories could be used:

Planned/Completed
Provide a brief summary of delivered, planned products and executed, planned activities. For example:

- test analysis of cluster XYZ functionality completed;
- preparation of cluster ABC efficiency completed;
- test environment set up by support department.

Planned/Not Completed

Provide a brief summary of planned, but not delivered, products and planned, but not executed, activities *including reasons why not*. For example:

- Preparation of test cluster KLM reliability not started owing to illness of test analyst.

Not Planned/Completed

It could happen that within a test project unplanned activities have to be carried out to "start up" the test project or to keep it going. This could well be activities that are outside the scope of the test project but are necessary for the progress of the project. Mention these activities and how much time they take. Also mention the consequences for the planning.

Activities/Milestones/Products of the Coming Period

Provide an overview of the products to be delivered and activities to be carried out according to planning. If it is already known that certain parts of the plan cannot be realised, it should be reported here. For example:

- Review of cluster XYZ functionality;
- test cluster of KLM reliability, to be delivered, may be delayed owing to illness of test analyst;
- intake test of test environment.

Quality of the Information System

An overview should be given here of the status of the quality of the information system. This may be done by including a separate table as shown in the example below (note that only those product risks are included in the table for which the requirements are to be tested at this test level).

The status may also be recorded in a separate document, or a link may be made between the test case documentation and the product risks, and the status documented here with reference made to this supplementary documentation. At any rate, provide a brief summary here. For example, none of the product risks have been covered as yet as the actual test execution has not yet started. The quality of the information system does not meet the agreed acceptance criteria.

Product risk	MoSCoW	Requirement	Test conditions	Status
Customer cannot perform a transaction	Must test	Customer can perform transaction via own bank	XYZC1, 2	Open
		Customer can perform transaction via host bank	XYZC3, 4	Closed
		Customer can select from standard amounts	XYZ5–8	Reopen
		Customer can select amount/denomination of notes	XYZ 9–14	Open
...	...	...	...	...

The stakeholder wishes to know when an important part of the functionality or goals of the new system will be available. If you have insight into this, report on it!

How do you obtain the insight? As soon as product risks 1, 2 and 3 have tested successfully, functionality A is available for release. This link between product risks and the stakeholder's required functionality or goals can be seen from the cluster cards if the cluster has been arranged by system parts. The product risks are therefore noted in the cluster card for the particular system part (note that this can only apply to some of the quality attributes).

This insight also provides the project manager with a management tool: if another product risk has to be tested to realise a stakeholder's goal, priority can be given to it here during execution.

If you have met the entry or exit criteria set for the test level during this period, you can report that here.

Budget and Progress

Provide a brief summary here of the budget already spent and still to be spent. Also use the forecasting capacity of the earned value method (EVM) to indicate whether the budget is still adequate. Add the graphic overview of progress and budget spending from EVM (this can be found in the test control matrix).

Risk Management (Project Risks)

Provide an overview here of the project risks documented in the test plan and their status (as in the test plan, report here only the 5 to 10 most important project risks). When a project risk has been dealt with, it remains in one progress report with status closed. Thereafter, it will disappear from the list. New risks that arise in the course of the project will of course be added to this list.

Project risk	Impor-tance	Measures	Responsibility	Date	Status
Tester Jack will leave the project in 2 weeks. Replacement still to be found who fits the profile	High	Tester Gary will take over tasks a and d. Recruit new tester with slightly adjusted profile who will take over the remaining tasks and who can support Gary	Resource management	A new employee with adjusted profile must at any rate be present for transfer in 1 week's time (31 Jan. 03)	Open
Connection between Unix and mainframe platform in test environment not present. Management confronted with production faults, which took priority	High	Free up an employee in consultation with management, so that he may provide full-time support to all the test projects and cannot be claimed for production	Head of Management	29 Jan. 03	Closed

Points of Focus and Problems

Situations sometimes require action at short notice. They have then to be put before the parties concerned (this is done in a separate exception report). A summary for the client can then be included in the progress report. This may be a project risk that has been foreseen and has now occurred. A situation may also arise that has not been foreseen and for which no risk countermeasures have been devised. Reflect the following points:

- description of the situation or the problem;
- description of the cause of the situation;
- the consequences for the test project as regards time, money or quality;
- a summing up of the alternatives for dealing with the situation and for each alternative the influence it will have on time, money, quality and any extra project risks that will arise as a result;
- a recommendation for an alternative, with supporting information;
- decision: if no decision has yet been taken, this will of course not yet be completed, but reference should be made to the following report which will contain the decision.

K

Template for Phase Report

This template describes the subjects that a test manager should include in a phase report. The test manager draws up a phase report following conclusion of a test level. If a test project consists of only one test level, the phase report and final report are one and the same.

This template does not cover general topics such as version management and configuration management.

A brief description is provided of the content of each subject.

K.1 Management Summary

Provide a brief summary of the report. Be sure to report on:

- Whether the goals of this test level as stated in the test plan have been achieved.
- The quality of the information system based on risk- and requirement-based testing.
- An overview and analysis of the differences between planned and realised in relation to the following aspects:
  - Time
  - Budget
- Recommendation for proceeding to the following test level.

K.2 Test Assignment Test Level

Describe here the original assignment for this test level. This will be set against the actual realisation in the recommendations.

K.3 Quality of the Information System

This section provides an overview of the quality of the information system. Based on this overview, a recommendation is made in Sect. 5 concerning proceeding to a subsequent test level.

K.3.1 Product Risks and Requirements

Below is an overview of the product risks and requirements that have been covered and those that have not been covered by the test execution. This information is obtained from the progress report of the test level. With the product risks that do not have the status "correct", indicate why this is so. If it is due to an outstanding issue, this will be explained in the next section. It is also possible that a product risk cannot be tested owing to the materialisation of a project risk.

Product risk	MoSCoW	Requirement	Test conditions	Status
Customer cannot perform a transaction	Must test	Customer can perform transaction via own bank	XYZC1, 2	Correct
		Customer can perform transaction via host bank	XYZC3, 4	Correct
		Customer can select from standard amounts	XYZ5-8	Correct
		Customer can select amount/denomination	XYZ 9-14	Correct
...	...	...	...	...

K.3.2 Brief Overview of Issues

Provide a brief summary of the issues still outstanding, including the related product risks and the importance of these (issues are linked to test conditions; product risk and importance can be seen from the table in Section K.3.1). Refer to the issue administration for a complete overview of the issues, or include these as an appendix.

K.3.3 Entry and Exit Criteria

Provide here an overview of all the entry and exit criteria for the test level and indicate to what extent these have been met.

Mention the entry criteria for the test level explicitly, since failure to (fully) meet an entry criterion (e.g. the delivery by the support department of a test environment according to specifications) may delay the project or result in an inability to test a product risk during the test level.

An exit criterion of this test level is often an entry criterion for the following test level. Therefore, provide an explanation when exit criteria have not been met and state what the consequences of this are.

K.4 Planned Versus Realised

K.4.1 Time

Indicate (based on the data from the earned value method (EVM) and the test control matrix (TCM) or the time registration of the project) which discrepancies exist between planned and realised time per part activity. If there is familiarity within the organisation with the TCM method, this can be included here. For convenience it is often necessary to arrange these details in a table (as shown below). The part activities may, for example, be obtained from MS Project.

Activities	Planned hours	Actual	Over/under	Remarks
Test strategy				
Test plan				
Test environment				
Test design				
Test execution				
Test management				
Test automation				
Total				

K.4.2 Money

Provide an overview of the budget and actual spending. For this use an overview of the planned activities and the budgets planned for these. The level of detail in this table depends of course on the level of detail to which the budget is divided across the various activities. Information on these figures can be gleaned from EVM and TCM (or from the above table by calculating hours × cost).

Activities	Budget	Actual	Over/under	Remarks
Test strategy				
Test plan				
Test environment				
Test design				
Test execution				
Test management				
Test automation				
Total				

K.4.3 Deliverables

Provide a summary here of the products that were delivered by this test type. The following test type will use a number of the products again. Other products will be transferred to maintenance after completion of the total test project (the deliverables of the total test project are noted in the test plan).

An overview of the delivered products can be obtained from the progress reports.

K.5 Recommendations

In this section provide a recommendation on proceeding to a subsequent test level. It is of course necessary to support your recommendation (base your recommendation on Section K.3).

Compare the original test assignment to what has actually been realised in the test level. Describe and support the discrepancies (if everything has not been completed in this test level, it does not mean by definition that it is not possible to proceed to the following test level).

Particular actions that still have to be completed before going on to a subsequent phase can also be mentioned here. A recommendation on the current outstanding issues and project risks, and the treatment of these in the following phase, also belong in this section.

L

Template for Final Report

This template describes the subjects that a test manager should include in a final report, which is written up after the conclusion of a test project.

This template does not cover general topics such a version management and configuration management.

A brief description is provided of the content of each subject.

L.1 Management summary

Provide a brief summary here of the report. Outline the following points:

- Whether the goals of the test projects as a whole, as stated in the project test plan, have been met (refer here to the test assignment).
- The quality of the information system on the basis of Risk & Reqirement Based Testing.
- Overview and analysis of the discrepancies between what was planned and what was realised, in relation to the following aspects:
  - time;
  - budget.
- The most important realized benefits of the project.
- Recommendation for transferring the information system into production (Go/NoGo decision).

L.2 Test assignment

Describe the original test assignment here from the project test plan. These will be compared against the actual realisation in the recommendations.

L.3 Quality of the information system

This section provides an overview of the quality of the information system. Based on this overview, a recommendation can be given in Section L.5 on putting the information system into production.

L.3.1 Product risks and requirements

An overview is provided below of the product risks and requirements that have been covered and those that have not been covered by the test execution. This information is obtained from the progress report or phase reports on the various test levels. Provide an explanation next to the product risks that do not have the status "correct" for why this is so. If it is due to an outstanding issue, this is explained in the following section. It is also possible that a product risk could not be tested because of the materialisation (and apparently delayed solution) of a project risk. More so than in a phase report, it is important to explain here why certain product risks do not have the status "correct", and what the possible consequences of this are.

Product risk	MoSCoW	Requirement	Test condi- tions	Status
Customer can- not perform transaction	Must test	Customer can perform transaction via own bank	XYZC1, 2	correct
		Customer can perform transaction via host bank	XYZC3, 4	correct
		Customer can select from standard amounts	XYZ5-8	correct
		Customer can select amount/denomination of notes	XYZ 9- 14	correct
...	...	...	...	...

L.3.2 Overview of issues

Provide a brief summary of the outstanding issues, including the related product risks and their importance (issues are linked to test conditions, and product risk and importance can be seen from the table above).

Also indicate what is being done with the outstanding issues. Solving them within a planned subsequent test level is not an option.

Are solving and testing these being moved to a subsequent release of the system, or will they be covered in regular maintenance? Who will be responsible for monitoring this? Organising the transfer of these issues is mandatory!

Will the issues be closed?

Required actions issuing from this that fall outside the scope of the current test project should be reported in the section on recommendations.

Optionally, provide an overview of the number of issues according to test level (this can be used in an evaluation report for analysis, e.g. to compare the number of issues against the costs of the test level).

Refer to the issue administration for a complete overview of the issues, or include them as an appendix.

L.3.3 Acceptance criteria

The acceptance criteria are documented in the test strategy (and subsequently translated in the test plan into entry and exit criteria for the various test levels). Provide an overview here of all the acceptance criteria. Indicate in this whether or not they have been met, with an explanation of reasons and consequences. If possible, link them to the product risks.

L.4 Costs and benefits of the test project

L.4.1 Costs in time

In the phase reports on the test levels, an overview is given of the costs in time and money relating to the test level. In this document, provide an overview of the costs of the whole test project. Include these data and add them up below.

Another method, similar to the phase reports, is as follows: indicate (based on information from the earned value method (EVM) and the test control matrix (TCM) or the time registration of the project) what discrepancies there are between planned and realised time per activity. If the organisation is familiar with the TCM method, this can be included here. For convenience, it is often necessary to arrange these details in a table (as shown below). The activities, for example, can also be obtained from MS Project.

Activities	Planned hours	Actual	Over/under	Remarks
Test strategy				
Test plan				
Test environment				
Test design				
Test execution				
Test management				
Test automation				
Total				

L.4.2 Costs in money

Provide an overview of the budget and actual spending. For this use an overview of the planned activities and the budgets planned for these. The level of detail in this table will of course depend on the level of detail at which the budget is divided across the various activities. Information for these figures can be obtained from EVM and the TCM (or from the above table by calculating hours × cost).

Do not forget the overall costs, such as the setting up of communal test environments, project audits, travel costs, meeting costs, costs for tooling and consultancy, etc.

Activities	Budget	Actual	Over/under	Remarks
Test strategy				
Test plan				
Test environment				
Test design				
Test execution				
Test management				
Test automation				
Total				
Other costs				
Travel expenses				
Tool for issue manage-ment				
...				
Total				

L.4.3 Benefits of the test project

It is difficult to reflect the benefits of a test project, to say nothing of quantifying them.

One possibility is to make a link between an issue and a product risk, via a test condition. If the fault in the information system had not been found and solved, would the product risk have occurred in the production environment? What would it have cost the organisation to solve this in production? How much time and effort went into solving the issue? What are the costs of (part of) the system being out of use? Would the fault in the system damage the company's image? Would the customers go elsewhere?

Deliverables

Provide an overview of the deliverables of the test project. Discrepancies in relation to the test plan should be explained: why has a deliverable that is stated in the test plan not been delivered, and vice versa?

Costs and benefits of test automation

The costs of test automation are shown in Sects. L.4.1 and L.4.2 above.

In order to determine the benefits of the test automation, compare it with the costs of manual test execution. This can be determined by looking at how much the manual execution of comparable clusters/test conditions has cost (also look at how often a particular test has been carried out: with repeat testing, test automation often pays).

L.5 Recommendations

In this section, provide a recommendation on whether or not to transfer the information system to production (Go/NoGo Decision).

Compare the original test assignment as described in Section L.2 with what has been realised (in the various test levels collectively).

Describe and support the discrepancies.

Formulate the recommendations. It is of course necessary to support them (base the recommendations on Section L.3). Remember, too, to provide a recommendation on the treatment of the outstanding issues and project risks.

Glossary of Terms

Acceptance criteria | Criteria that stakeholders define at the start of a test project. They use these criteria at the end of a test project to accept the information system.

Basic test | The first step in test execution. The testers try to execute every test. But a test might cause a (blocking) issue. If issues occur, multiple retests are necessary.

Black-box test | A test based on the analysis of the specifications of an information system, without having knowledge of the internal structure of this system.

Business controls | The variables the test manager possesses to control the test project. These are: time, money and quality. The project manager possesses an extra control, namely the size of an information system.

Business impact | The consequences of an issue for daily practice.

Chain test | A test in which a whole chain of systems from the first input to the last output is regarded. Synonym: end-to-end test.

Cluster | Logical test unit.

Cluster card

A card containing essential information (i.e. stakeholder, product risks and acceptance criteria) necessary for designing and executing tests related to a cluster. Together with creating the cluster matrix, creating the cluster cards is the last step in describing a test strategy. It is the basis for test analysis.

Cluster matrix

First assignment of quality attributes to be tested to stakeholder and test level. This division indicates which cluster cards will be made.

Complete test

Within the complete test the testers can execute all tests. No issues with test impact remain.

Detailed test plan

A test plan per test level. This test plan is an elaboration of the project test plan when a test project consists of more than one test level.

Dynamic testing

Testing by processing actions on the information system to be tested.

Earned Value Method (EVM)

Method for measuring the progress of a (test) project. The starting point is that progress is measured not only on the basis of hours spent compared with hours estimated (money), but also in terms of actual progress: the timely delivery of products (time). Therefore, budget spend and progress are separated. One characteristic is that a product is only booked as realised when 100% complete.

Entry criteria

Criteria that a test manager defines to start a specific test level. Every test level can have several entry criteria. These entry criteria are described in the project test plan or the detailed test plans.

Error guessing

A test technique (usually unstructured) with which faults in the information system are looked for, based on experience with the system.

Estimation

The definition of the boundaries in time and money within which the testing is allowed to operate.

Evolutionary planning

In this method the total project is divided into smaller parts. Only the part in the near future is planned for in detail; the other parts are only globally planned. After completing a part, the next part is planned in detail.

Exception report

A formal report from the test manager to the client stating a situation that needs to be solved at short notice. For example, a project risk that materialised. Also a situation might occur that was not foreseen and for which no countermeasures were defined.

Exit critera

Criteria the test manager defines to end a specific test level. Every test level can have several exit criteria. These exit criteria are described in the project test plan or the detailed test plans.

Final report

The report the test manager makes after completion of all test levels. The final report contains advice to the stakeholders. In this report the test manager gives an overview of the results of the different test levels. In addition, the extent to which the acceptance criteria are met is an important part of this final report.

Final test

Last in the series of retest runs. In this last retest run the testers check whether all issues that should be solved are solved.

Functional acceptance test

Testing the documented and implied functions (does the system do what it should do?). This test level is based on the functional specifications.

Goal–question–metric (GQM) method

A founded metrics program.

Incident management

See issue management.

Intake test

A test that is performed before the actual test execution. The test team checks whether the information system meets the stated quality (*see* entry criteria). Successfully completing the intake test means that the actual testings can start. If the test is not completed successfully, the system is sent back to the developers.

Integration test

Testing the communication between programs (integration test "in the small") or complete information systems (integration test "in the large").

Issue

Deviation between expected and actual outcome of a test.

Issue management

Managing the issues that occur during test execution via procedures and tooling. It is also known as incident management.

ITIL (Information Technology Infrastructure Library)

A widely used standard in practice for setting up a maintenance process for information systems.

Joint Testware Development (JTD)

A method the test manager and testers can use to develop testware in case good documentation is missing. This information is collected during a brainstorm session following specific rules.

Logical Unit of Test (LUT)

A uniform collection of interrelated activities from test design to test execution.

Metrics

A metric is a quantified measure of a process or product attribute that is characteristic of the product or process object to be measured.

MoSCoW priority

Classification of test priorities based on product risks: Must test, Should test, Could test and Won't test.

Phase report

A formal report from the test manager to the client after completion of a predefined phase of the test project. This might be the completion of a test level.

PRINCE2

PRINCE2 is a project management method that is generally applicable to projects. The name PRINCE stands for PRojects IN Controlled Environments.

Production acceptance test

Tests whether the system can be exploited.

Product risk

A risk that is directly related to an information system. This risk can be covered through testing.

Progress report

The report the test manager draws up during the execution of the test project.

Project risk

A risk that relates to the set-up and control of a (test) project.

Project test plan

The overall test plan with a description of all test levels in a test project. The various test levels are elaborated in detailed test plans.

Regression test

A test to check whether all important unchanged parts of the information system still function as before following a change in the information system.

Requirement-based testing

Testing based on the requirements (functional and non-functional) of the information system.

Risk- & Requirement Based Testing (RRBT)

Test approach in which the product risks and requirements are combined in a structured way. This combination is the basis for setting up and controlling a test project.

Quality attribute

Describes the wishes and demands for an information system. Six attributes with various subattributes are described in ISO9126.

Quick scan

The test manager follows the Test Management Model for the first time in a short period of time. This gives him a first impression of the already existing testware, procedures and tools.

Stakeholder

An employee or department that has a direct interest in the correct operation of an information system. Synonym: interested parties.

Static testing

Executing tests without running the information system. For example, reviews or inspections of specifications or code.

Strategic test slicing method (STSM)

A method to slice tests according to predefined criteria in the case of shortage in time/money. This relates to the priority of the product risks.

System test

Test by the system developer in a laboratory environment to demonstrate whether the system (or parts of it) is developed according to the functional and technical specifications.

Test case

All pre- and post-conditions, test data and expected outcomes of a test. A test case is designed to verify a specific test condition.

Test centre

The test centre is a part of the organisation that designs and executes the tests. The test centre can also play a supervising role by assigning the test process a certain approval or certifying it before a system is taken into production. The test centre is a quality department with regard to testing.

Test competence centre (TCC)

The TCC is a staff department. The TCC centralises several test services, e.g. test methodology, resources, test advice, test automation, education and support.

Test condition

A level under clusters. It indicates what will be tested for a cluster. Test conditions are related to requirements with their accompanying product risks.

Test control matrix (TCM)

Helps to keep account of and presents the business controls of time, money and quality and the dependencies between the test project and development.

Test effort estimation model (TEEM)	A model for estimating test projects based on metrics.
TestFrame	LogicaCMG's approach to structured testing.
Test impact	Indicates the consequences of an issue for the execution of the test. The division is: stopper, test obstructing and non-obstructive.
Test level	A division of the total testing necessary at various levels. These levels are related to stages in system development and those executing the tests, e.g. unit test or functional acceptance test.
Test management file	The file in which the test manager stores all information that is important to the test project. During the term of the test project, all project members can consult this file for the latest updates. After closing the test project, the file will be transferred to a maintenance department.
Test Management Model	LogicaCMG's test management model used as a basis for this test management book. It describes the activities of the test manager from preparation to execution and closure of the test project.
Test run	The period in which a related group of test clusters is executed for a version or build of the information system.
Test strategy	Describes the scope and depth of the test: which product risks will be covered within the test project and which not.
Test technique	A collection of actions to derive test conditions and/or test cases in a reproducible and objective way.
Test type	Test activities aimed at testing an information system on a specific (combination of) quality attribute(s).

Testware   This term contains all products that are developed within a test project.

User acceptance test   Testing whether the end users can work with the system. This test is based on the end users' procedures.

White-box test   Test based on the internal structure of an information system.

Bibliography

Books

Beizer, Boris: *Black-Box Testing – Techniques for Functional Testing of Software and Systems* (Wiley, New York, 1995)

Bersoff, Edward H.: *Elements of Software Configuration Management* (IEEE Computer Society Press, Silver Spring, MD, 1984)

Black, Rex: *Managing the Testing Process* (Microsoft Press International, Redmond, WA 1999)

Boehm, Barry W.: *Software Engineering Economics* (Prentice Hall, Upper Saddle River, NJ, 1981)

Buwalda, Hans, Dennis Janssen & Iris Pinkster: *Integrated Test Design and Automation Using the TestFrame Method* (Addison-Wesley, Harlow, 2002)

CCTA (Central Computer and Telecommunication Agency): *Best Practice for Service Support – ITIL the Key to Managing IT Service* (The Stationery Office, London, 2000)

CCTA (Central Computer and Telecommunication Agency): *Managing Successful Projects with Prince 2* (The Stationery Office, London, 2002)

CMG: *TestFrame: Een praktische handleiding bij het testen van informatiesystemen* (ten Hagen & Stam, Den Haag, 2001)

Collard, Ross: *Realistically Estimating Software Testing Projects* (Collard, New York, 2003)

Coul, Johan C. op de: *Beheer van de informatievoorziening – Een bedrijfskundige benadering* (Samsom Bedrijfsinformatie, Alphen aan den Rijn, 1996)

Craig, Sue: *Make Your Mark, Influencing Across the Organization* (McGraw-Hill, Maidenhead, 1997)

Daich, G., G. Price, B. Ragland & M. Dawood: *Software Test Technologies Report* (Software Technology Support Center, Utah, August 1994)

DeMarco, Tom & Timothy Lister: *Peopleware – Productive Projects and Teams*, 2nd edn (Dorset House, New York, 1999)

Deming, W. Edwards: *Out of the Crisis* (MIT Press, Cambridge, MA, 2000)

Dustin, Elfriede, Jeff Raska & John Paul: *Automated Software Testing: Introduction, Management, and Performance* (Addison-Wesley, Boston, MA, 1999)

Fewster, Mark & Dorothy Graham: *Software Test Automation: Effective Use of Test Execution Tools* (Addison-Wesley, Boston, MA, 1999)

Gerrard, Paul & Neil Thompson: *Risk-Based E-Business Testing* (Artech House, Norwood, MA, 2002)

Gilb, Tom: *Principles of Software Engineering Management* (Addison-Wesley, Harlow, 1988)

Gilb, Tom & Dorothy Graham: *Software Inspections* (Addison-Wesley, Boston, MA, 1993)

Hatton, Les: *Safer C: Developing Software for High-Integrity and Safety-Critical Systems* (McGraw-Hill, Maidenhead, 1995)

Helmer, O.: *Social Technology* (Basic Books, New York, 1966)

Hetzel, Bill: *The Complete Guide to Software Testing*, 2nd edn (Wiley, New York, 1988)

IFPUG (International Function Point User Group): *Function Point Counting Practices* (release 4.1, January 1999)

ISO/IEC 9126-1: *Software engineering – Software product quality – Part 1: Quality Model* (International Organization for Standardization, Geneva, 2001)

Institute of Electrical and Electronics Engineers: *IEEE Standard Classification for Software Anomalies* (IEEE Std 1044 1993)

Institute of Electrical and Electronics Engineers: *IEEE Standard for Software Test Documentation* (IEEE Std 829 1998)

Kaner, Cem, James Bach & Bret Pettichord: *Lessons Learned in Software Testing: A Context-Driven Approach* (Wiley, New York, 2002)

Kaner, Cem, Jack Falk & Hung Quoc Hguyen: *Testing Computer Software*, 2nd edn (Wiley, New York, 1999)

Kit, Edward: *Software Testing in the Real World: Improving the Process* (ACM Press, New York, 1995)

Koomen, Tim & Martin Pol: *Test Process Improvement, leidraad voor stapsgewijs beter testen* (Kluwer Bedrijfsinformatie, Deventer, 1998)

Koppens, Sander & Bas Meyberg: *Operationeel beheer van informatiesystemen* (Kluwer Bedrijfsinformatie, Deventer, 2000)

Kor, Rudy: *Werken aan projecten – Een handreiking*, 3rd edn (Kluwer Bedrijfsinformatie, Deventer, 1999)

Marik, Brian: *The Craft of Software Testing – Subsystem Testing, Including Object-Based and Object-Oriented Testing* (Prentice Hall, Englewood Cliffs, NJ, 1995)

Martens, Marlies, Kees-Jan Groen & Bertram van der Wal: *Publiek Management: 65 modellen* (FC Klap, Utrecht, 2002)

Mors, N.P.M.: *Kwaliteitszorg door acceptatietesten* (Lansa, Leidschendam, 1994)

Myers, J. Glenford: *The Art of Software Testing* (Wiley, New York, 1979)

Onna, M. van, B. Hendriks & G. Schraven: *De kleine PRINCE 2, projectmanagement methodiek voor kleine en middelgrote projecten*, 2nd edn (ten Hagen Stam, Den Haag, 2000)

Patton, Ron: *Software Testing* (Sams Publishing, Indianapolis, 2000)

Perry, William E. & Randall W. Rice: *Surviving the Top Ten Challenges of Software Testing: A People Oriented Approach* (Dorset House, New York, 1997)

Paulk, Mark C., Charles V. Weber, Bill Curtis & Mary Beth Chrissis: *The Capability MAturity Model – Guidelines for Improving the Software Process* (Addison-Wesley Longman Inc., 1994)

Pol, Martin, Ruud Teunissen & Erik van Veenendaal: *Testen volgens Tmap*, 2nd edn (Uitgeverij Tutein Nolthenius, Den Bosch, 2000)

Solingen, Rini van & Egon Berghout: *The Goal/Question/Metric Method* (McGraw-Hill, Maidenhead, 1999)

Stapleton, Jennifer: *DSDM: The Method in Practice* (Addison-Wesley, London, 1997)

Veenendaal, Erik van: *The Testing Practitioner* (Uitgeverij Tutein Nolthenius, Den Bosch, 2002)

Watkins, John: *Testing IT: An Off-the-Shelf Software Testing Process Handbook* (Cambridge University Press, Cambridge, 2001)

Wijnen, Gert & Rudy Kor: *Het managen van unieke opgaven – samen werken aan projecten en programma's* (Kluwer Bedrijfsinformatie, Deventer, 1997)

Articles

Amland, Stale: *Risk Based Testing and Metrics* (5th International Conference EuroSTAR '99, 8–12 November 1999, Barcelona, Spain)

Bach, James: *Heuristic Risk-Based Testing* (Software Testing & Quality Engineering, November 1999)

Black, Rex: *Effective Test Status Reporting – The Upward and Outward Management of Communicating Test Progress and Results* (Software Testing & Quality Engineering, March/April 2000, Vol. 2, Issue 2)

Burnstein, Ilene, Taratip Suwannasart & C.R. Carlson: *Developing a Testing Maturity Model: Part I* (Crosstalk, STSC, Hill Air Force Base, Utah, August 1996, pp. 21–24)

Burnstein, Ilene, Taratip Suwannasart & C.R. Carlson: *Developing a Testing Maturity Model, Part II* (Illinois Institute of Technology)

Chavali, Sreeram Kishore: *Approach to Implementing Risk Based Testing* (19 March 2001)

Collard, Ross: *Speeding the Software Delivery Process, Part 1, Manage and Strengthen Testing* (stickyminds.com)

Collard, Ross: *Speeding the Software Delivery Process, Part 2, Conduct Early and Streamlined Testing* (stickyminds.com)

Collard, Ross: *Speeding the Software Delivery Process, Part 3, Manage the Risks and the Process* (stickyminds.com)

Derby, Esther: *Risky Beginnings* (Software Testing & Quality Engineering, November/December 2000)

Gerrard, Paul: *Risk-Based E-Business Testing, Part 1: Risks and Test Strategy* (2000)

Gerrard, Paul: *Risk: The New Language of E-Business Testing* (Systeme Evolutif Ltd., version 1.0, STAREAST 2001)

Gerrard, Paul: *Risk-Based Test Reporting* (14 February 2002)

Gilb, Tom: *Risk Management: A Practical Toolkit for Identifying, Analyzing and Coping with Project Risks*, version 3.1 (Quality Week, San Jose CA, 1999)

Goodwin, Steve: *Software Risk Management Makes Good Business Sense* (Software Release Magazine, Q4, 2000)

Horne, Geoff (Integrity Software Testing & Quality (NZ) Ltd.): *Testing in a Squeezed, Squeezed World* (February 2002)

Janssen, Dennis: *Developing Software Together, Using the JTD Method*, (Test2000 Conference, 2000)

Janssen, Dennis: *Kwaliteit van testen: onbeheersbaar of ongecontroleerd* (Software Release Magazine, No. 8, December 2002, pp. 32–37)

Kandler, Jim: *Product Risk Analysis Clarifies Requirements* (STAREAST 1999)

Kroll, Per & Philippe Kruchten: *From Waterfall to Iterative Development – A Challenging Transition for Project Managers* (SM/ASM 2002)

Potter, Neil & Mary Sakry (The Process Group): *Planning for Project Surprises – Coping with Risk* (Pacific Northwest Software Quality Conference, 1999)

Rothman, Johanna: *Successful Test Management: 9 Lessons Learned*, (STARWEST 2000)

Rothman, Johanna (Rothman Consulting Group, Inc.): *What to Do When the Right Person Doesn't Come Along* (Conference, SM/ASM 2000)

Slade, Randy (Kaiser Permanente Information Technology): *How To Break out of the Same Old Routine of Bad Quality* (STARWEST 2001)

Statz, Joyce & Susan Tennison: *Getting Started with Software Risk Management* (American Programmer, Vol. 8, No. 3, March 1995)

Veenendaal, Erik van: *Testing Maturity Model: Van detectie naar preventie* (Software Release Magazine, Vol. 6, No. 8, December 2001)

Others

Bach, James: *How Much Testing Is Enough?* (stickyminds.com, 17 September 2002)

Graham, Dorothy: *Test Is a Four-Letter Word* (TestNet presentation, 1999)

Managing Successful Projects Prince 2 Electronic Manual (Central Computers and Telecom Agency & Key Skills Ltd., 1999)

Smith-Brock, Jennifer: *Using Risk Analysis to Prioritize Your Testing* (EuroSTAR 2001)

Test Strategy Questionnaire (ISEB Practitioner, Improve Quality Services)

US Air Force Systems Command: *Cost-Schedule Management of Non-major Contracts* (AFSCP 17303, Andrews AFB, Maryland, November 1987)

Index

Printing: Krips bv, Meppel
Binding: Litges & Dopf, Heppenheim